FISH HABITAT AND AQUACULTURE

ENV BOOKS SERIES

FISH HABITAT AND AQUACULTURE

Editors

Dr. Sanjay Kumar Gupta

Scientist

Directorate of Cold Water Fisheries Research (DCFR), ICAR
Champawat Centre (Uttarakhand), India

Dr. Pawan Kumar 'Bharti'

Vice President (Executive)

Society for Environment, Health, Awareness of Nutrition & Toxicology (SEHAT)
1775, Sohanganj, Near Clock Tower, Delhi-7, India

DPH

DISCOVERY PUBLISHING HOUSE PVT. LTD.
NEW DELHI-110 002

Published by:
Tilak Wasan
DISCOVERY PUBLISHING HOUSE PVT. LTD.
4383/4B, Ansari Road, Darya Ganj
New Delhi-110 002 (India)
Phone : +91-11-23279245, 43596064-65
Fax : +91-11-23253475
E-mail : discoverypublishinghouse@gmail.com
sales@discoverypublishinggroup.com
web : www.discoverypublishinggroup.com

First Edition: **2015**

ISBN: 978-93-5056-744-9

Fish Habitat and Aquaculture

Printed at:
Infinity Imaging Systems
Delhi

ENV Books Series, India

Calls lengthy and error free chapters for further volumes of books on various environmental issues. (Send your manuscripts to envbooks@gmail.com)

Founding Editor (Editor-in-Chief)

Dr. Pawan Kumar 'Bharti'

Society for Environment, Health, Awareness of Nutrition & Toxicology (SEHAT-India)
1775, Sohanganj, Near Clock Tower, Delhi-7, India
E-mail:*gurupawanbharti@rediffmail.com*

Other Titles by Editor-in-Chief:

1. **Advances in Biotechnology and Ecological Sciences (2013)**
   Bharti, P.K., Chauhan, A. and Ray, J. (eds.)
   (ISBN: 978-93-5056-358-8).
2. **Advances in Agriculture and Ecology (2013)**
   Bharti, P.K.; Chauhan, A. and Ezeaku Peter Ikemefuna (eds.)
   (ISBN: 978-93-5056-362-5).
3. **Agriculture and Environmental Biotechnology (2014)**
   Bharti, P.K. and Chauhan, A. (eds.)
   (ISBN: 978-93-5056-479-0).
4. **Agriculture Ecology and Environment (2014)**
   Bharti, P.K. and Olubukola O. Babalola (eds.)
   (ISBN: 978-93-5056-480-6).
5. **Agro-forestry and Climate Change (2014)**
   Bharti, Pawan K. and Singh, Narayan (eds.)
   (ISBN: 978-93-5056-514-8).
6. **Aquaculture and Fisheries Environment (2014)**
   Gupta, S.K. and Pawan K. Bharti (eds.)
   (ISBN: 978-93-5056-408-0).
7. **Aquatic Biodiversity and Pollution (2013)**
   Bharti, P.K.; Chauhan, A. and Kaoud, H.A.H. (eds.)
   (ISBN: 978-93-5056-359-5).

8. **Aquatic Ecology and Biotechnology (2014)**
Bharti, P.K. and Zaki, M.S.A. (eds.)
(ISBN: 978-93-5056-451-6).

9. **Aquatic Environment and Toxicology (2013)**
Bharti, Pawan K. (ed.)
(ISBN: 978-93-5056-236-9).

10. **Biodiversity of Aquatic Ecosystem:** ***Significance, Threat and Conservation*** **(2013)**
Bharti, P.K. and Kaoud, H.A.H. (eds.)
(ISBN: 978-93-5056-297-0).

11. **Clean Technologies and Environmental Protection (2015)**
Chauhan, A.; Sharma, S. and Bharti, P.K. (eds.)
(ISBN: 978-93-5056-731-9).

12. **Climate Change and Agriculture (2012)**
Bharti, P.K. and Chauhan, Avnish (eds.)
(ISBN: 978-93-5056-148-5).

13. **Climate Change and Biodiversity (2013)**
Bharti, P.K. and Chauhan, Avnish (eds.)
(ISBN: 978-93-5056-360-1).

14. **Conservation and Cultivation of Medicinal Plants (2015)**
Bharti, P.K. and Singh Narayan (eds.)
(ISBN: 978-93-5056-740-1).

15. **Eco-toxicology and Eco-technology (2013)**
Bharti, P.K. and Zaki, M. (eds.)
(ISBN: 978-93-5056-313-7).

16. **Environmental Biotechnology and Application (2013)**
Bharti, P.K. and Chauhan, Avnish (eds.)
(ISBN: 978-93-5056-262-8).

17. **Environmental Conservation and Biotechnology (2014)**
Chauhan, A. and P.K. Bharti (eds.)
(ISBN: 978-93-5056-512-4).

18. **Environmental Health and Problems (2013)**
Bharti, P.K. and Gajananda, Kh. (eds.)
(ISBN: 978-93-5056-263-5).

19. **Environmental Pollution and Biodiversity (2012)**
Bharti, P.K.; Chauhan, Avnish and Kumar, P. (eds.)
(ISBN: 978-93-5056-149-2).

20. **Fisheries and Toxicology (2014)**
Zaki, M.S.A.; Bharti, P.K. and Chauhan, A. (eds.)
(ISBN: 978-93-5056-452-3).

21. **Freshwater Ecosystem and Xenobiotics (2013)**
Bharti, P.K.; Zaki, M. and Chauhan, A. (eds.)
(ISBN: 978-93-5056-299-4).

22. **Limnology and Aquatic Science (2015)**
Sharma, S. and Bharti, P.K. (eds.)
(ISBN: 978-93-5056-735-7).

23. **Medicinal Plants: *Distribution, Utilization and Significance* (2015)**
Sharma, P.; Bharti, P.K. and Narayan Singh (eds.)
(ISBN: 978-93-5056-734-0).

24. **Microbial Applications and Environment (2014)**
Bharti, Pawan K. (ed.)
(ISBN: 978-93-5056-515-5).

25. **Microbial Ecology and Habitat (2014)**
Bharti, Pawan K. (ed.)
(ISBN: 978-93-5056-514-8).

26. **Natural Ecosystem and Climate Change (2015)**
Bharti, Pawan K., Gajananda Khwairakpam (ed.)
(ISBN: 978-93-5056-745-6).

27. **Prakriti me Aushadhi (*in Hindi*) (2012)**
Singh, J.R.; Bharti, P.K. and Bharti, B.
(ISBN: 978-93-5056-200-0).

28. **Seed Technology, Plant Growth and Cropping System (2015)**
Tyagi, P.K. and Bharti, P.K. (eds.)
(ISBN: 978-93-5056-738-8).

29. **Soil Contamination and Conservation (2015)**
Ezeaku, P.I. and Bharti, P.K. (eds.)
(ISBN: 978-93-5056-737-1).

30. **Soil Quality and contamination (2013)**
Bharti, P.K. and Chauhan, Avnish (eds.)
(ISBN: 978-93-5056-361-8).

31. **Waste Disposal and Management (2015)**
Bharti, P.K.; Tabassum, B. and Bajaj, P. (eds.)
(ISBN: 978-93-5056-729-6).

32. **Water Resources and Agriculture (2014)**
Bharti, P.K. and Ezeaku Peter Ikemefuna (eds.)
(ISBN: 978-93-5056-481-3).

Preface

Globally, over one billion rural populations in many developing countries rely on fish to enhance nutritional food security, national income, foreign exchange earnings and employment generation. In the last three decades, animal protein consumption per capita in developing countries has considerably increased, as a direct result of technological expansion in aquaculture sector. Aquaculture production from developing countries accounts for about 96% of the total global production which comes from extensive to semi-intensive aquaculture systems, integrated farming and stocking of fish into natural or impounded water bodies. The sustainable approach to the development, management and regulation of aquaculture can ensure environment and aquaculture industry with long-term socio-economic benefits and a step ahead towards food security.

In aquaculture practices, fishes are subjected to a wide variety of environmental and anthropogenic stressors. Environmental pollutants, disease, and various factors involved are some of the examples of these stressors experienced by fishes. Technological advancements have led to the development of environmentally relevant biological responses (biomarkers) that can help measure pollutant exposure and provide assessment of the general health status of individual animals and ecosystem as a whole. The first chapter on biomarker emphasize on certain parameters involved in the phase I and II biotransformation of xenobiotic compounds in relation to their potential as biomarkers in environmental risk assessment (ERA).

Mussels cultured in freshwater aquaculture environment, bear ecological, nutritional, medicinal and economical significance. In this chapter, an attempt has been made to discuss the multi-faceted role of mussels, which will not only help the farmers to generate extra income, but also would be utilized judiciously to disseminate the technology of freshwater pearl culture to the fish farming communities, entrepreneurs, researchers and students of the country.

Environmental impact of tiger shrimp farming has become a major concern in many countries with developing shrimp culture industries.

Deterioration of state of effluent receiving natural water bodies in vicinities of shrimp farms, conflicts with agriculturists, heavy loss of production and earnings due to viral diseases has led farmers to realize that it is a non-profit-making venture. In this context, culture of the high-valued freshwater crustacean, *Macrobrachium rosenbergii* has been thought to be environment-friendly, sustainable and prospectful alternative. Present book insights into problems that have been come up in relation to commercial tiger shrimp culture practices, as well as management practices, farming and recent research taken up in regard to *M. rosenbergii* have been highlighted.

Fertilization is an important step in fish farm management practices; proper application of fertilizers increases pond productivity and consequently production of fish under culture. Although inorganic fertilizers are more efficient and quick in functioning, still in present day conditions, organic fertilizers are preferred over inorganic ones and the former is recommended for application for sustainable fish farming. In order to compost and utilize aquatic weeds along with different organic manures in aquaculture, different combination of substrate macrophytes and animal excreta are mixed with moisture and incubated at room temperature for sustainable composting. Sustainable organic aquaculture aims to provide fish and other products that are ecologically, economically and socially sound, safe the soil, water and nature, help property reduction in remote areas, improve health for both producers and consumers. The characteristic features of different kinds of animal manures and steps/process for organic fish farming have been comprehensively reviewed through two chapters.

Bagarius yarrelli is the single most widely distributed catfish, often called as "Giant devil catfish" is the largest member of the sisoridae family. Present Chapter deals with, investigations on the morphometric and meristic variation among the populations specimens, collected from the Brahmaputra River. The threats and the conservation prospects of the species are discussed in the chapter.

New and advanced water treatment technologies have been developed with very specific targets than conventional technology. Reclaimed water or recycled water or wastewater (sewage) is treated to remove solids and certain impurities to recharge groundwater aquifers. Through domestic sewage and addition of organic resources, coliform bacteria including faecal coliforms and *E.coli* get entry into different aquatic systems. The abundance of these microbial indicators can be reduced following different physical, chemical and biological microbial bioaugmentation processes. This book provides in depth knowledge on the various alternatives water treatment technology such as: grey water system, rain water harvesting system, atmospheric water generator and water remediation which may be used in urban areas where climate change has threatened long-term water security and reduced rainfall over catchment areas.

Aquaculture is one of the main reasons for introduction of alien species in to aquatic ecosystems. As much as 17% of the global aquaculture production is contributed by introduced species (Bartley & Casal, 1998). For instance the culture of *Clarias gariepinus* (Thailand magur) and *Piaractus brachypomus* (Pacu) is one such case. In this book a comprehensive coverage on the methodologies of successful breeding and seed production of Pacu, *Piaractus brachypomus* (Rupchanda) in captivity has been discussed by the authors.

The editors have tried hard to make comprehensive coverage of the fundamental principles, current practices and trends in the field of aquaculture and fisheries. This book updates the subject matter, illustrations and problems to incorporate new concepts and issues related to aquaculture and fisheries environment. Editors have made all possible efforts to avoid any omissions and errors but still some may appear after publication. It is hoped that those oversights will not detract the readers from the wealth of information presented by the authors within this volume.

Publication of the document has been possible through enthusiastic support, assistance and cooperation of dedicated scientists/workers from different institutions working in the field and also in other areas of aquaculture and fisheries. The processing and editing of various articles has taken long time, we express our sincere gratitude to all the contributors for bearing with us.

I wish this book would be of immense benefit to researchers, scientists, students, entrepreneurs and fishers working in the field of aquaculture, limnology, freshwater ecology, aquatic ecosystem, environmental pollution and fisheries.

–Editors

(envbooks@gmail.com)

Contents

List of Contributors

Bhaskar J. Saud, Research Scholar, Central Inland Fisheries Research Institute (CIFRI), Regional Centre, HOUSEFED Complex, Dispur, Guwahati - 781 006.

Biswajit Dash, Scientist, Visakhapatnam Regional Centre of Central Marine Fisheries Research Institute, Visakhapatnam, India.

Himadri Chandra, Fishery Field Assistant (Government of West Bengal), Kushmandi Development Block, P.O. Kushmandi, Dist. Dakshin Dinajpur, West Bengal, India.

Hussein Abdel-Hay El-Sayed Kaoud, Professor, Department of Veterinary Hygiene and Management, Faculty of Veterinary Medicine, Cairo University, Egypt.

Madhumita Das, Scientist, Visakhapatnam Regional Centre of Central Marine Fisheries Research Institute, Visakhapatnam, India.

Madhumita Mukherjee, Executive Director (Tech), NFDB, Hyderabad, India.

Mrinal Kanti Datta, Assistant Professor, College of Fisheries, Central Agricultural University, Lembucherra, Tripura (West), Pin - 799 210, India.

Rishikesh S. Dalvi, Assistant professor, Department of Zoology, Maharshi Dayanand College of Arts, Science and Commerce, Shri Mangaldas Verma Chawk, Dr. S.S. Rao Road, Parel, Mumbai - 400 012, India.

S.K. Gupta, Scientist, Directorate of Coldwater Fisheries Research, Chhirapani Fish Farm, Champawat, Uttrakhand - 262 523, India.

Sagar C. Mandal, Assistant Professor, College of Fisheries, Central Agricultural University (Imphal), Lembucherra, West Tripura - 799 210, India.

Shailesh Saurabh, Scientist, Central Institute of Freshwater Aquaculture Kausalyaganga, Bhubaneswar - 751 002, Odisha, India.

Shubhadeep Ghosh, Sr. Scientist, Visakhapatnam Regional Centre of Central Marine Fisheries Research Institute, Visakhapatnam - 530 003, India.

Subrato Ghosh, Fishery Field Assistant (Government of West Bengal), Kushmandi Development Block, P.O. Kushmandi, Dist. Dakshin Dinajpur, West Bengal, India.

U.L. Mohanty, Senior Technical Officer (T-6), Central Institute of Freshwater Aquaculture Kausalyaganga, Bhubaneswar - 751 002, Odisha, India.

Pages: 1-25

FISH HABITAT AND AQUACULTURE
Edited by: Dr. Sanjay Kumar Gupta; Dr. Pawan Kumar 'Bharti'
ISBN: 978-93-5056-744-9
Edition: 2015
Published by: Discovery Publishing House Pvt. Ltd., New Delhi (India)

1

Biomarkers of Environmental Contamination in Fish *Biotransformation* and *Oxidative Stress*

Rishikesh S. Dalvi and **S.K.Gupta**

ABSTRACT

Pesticides have been used for centuries in the agriculture for increasing food production, for eradicating insect pests and for controlling disease vectors. Runoffs of pesticides from agricultural fields continuously contaminate the aquatic environment resulting in serious damage to certain physiological and biochemical processes in non-target species including fish. Once internalised, fish can accumulate these pollutants from the water, sediments and food making them harmful for human consumption. Fishes also have mechanism to biotransform individual pollutants. The biological responses to contaminants are increasingly used as biomarkers for monitoring their effects in the ecosystems. Technological advancements have led to the development of environmentally relevant biological responses (biomarkers) that can help measure pollutant exposure and provide assessment of the general health status of individual animals and ecosystem as a whole. Present review emphasis on certain parameters involved in the phase I and II biotransformation of xenobiotic compounds and those of pollutants caused oxidative stress responses in relation to their potential as biomarkers in environmental risk assessment (ERA).

Key words: Biomarkers, Xenobiotics, Contamination, Biotransformation, Oxidative stress.

INTRODUCTION

Ever increasing urbanization and industrial development has concomitantly loaded the environment with foreign organic chemicals or xenobiotics. Thousands of organic compounds such as polychlorinated biphenyls (PCBs), organochlorine pesticides (OCPs), polycyclic aromatic hydrocarbons (PAHs), polychlorinated dibenzofurans (PCDFs), dibenzop-dioxins (PCDDs) etc. have been produced and are continuously released into the environment. Most of these contaminants ultimately find their way in the aquatic environment, either due to direct release or due to hydrologic and other natural processes. Although most of these chemicals are prepared with a view to cater human needs, increase food production and overall welfare, there are also numerous examples of chemicals that have caused harm to both human and the ecosystem (Preston and Shackelford, 2002). Presence of complex mixtures of these chemicals in the environment may cause metabolic disorders in the aquatic animals through different mechanisms of action and in some cases may even cause mortality at very low concentrations. The toxic effects of different pollutants in aquatic organisms is directly associated with the chemical nature of the xenobiotic compound which determines it's extra and intra bioavailability. Some chemicals can globally affect the cellular metabolism e.g. blocking of ATP production leading to increased mortality, whereas some xenobiotics at sub-lethal levels can elicit a multitude of biological responses including disruption of signal transduction, genetic damage and epigenetic disorders (Amiard-Triquet et al., 2012). However, simply presence of a xenobiotic compound may not indicate damage to the environment or its habitants. It is therefore crucial to understand and establish a link between the external levels of contaminants, the internal levels of contaminant in tissues of the organism and the adverse effects it has on the functions of the organisms. Understanding the basic mechanisms of toxicological processes in an organism is essential for ecological or environmental risk assessment (ERA).

The ERA is defined as the procedure by which the likely or actual adverse effects of pollutants and other anthropogenic activities on ecosystems and their components are estimated with a known degree of certainty using scientific methodologies (Depledge and Fossi, 1994). ERA has gained importance not only among the scientific community but also among the general public due to the realisation that the xenobiotics that are not toxic to humans may have serious effects on the valuable natural resources. ERA is basically performed, to reduce the risk for environmental harm (Suter, 1993). ERA is most often based on simple toxicity tests, both acute and chronic, using small crustaceans, fish, and algae. Such toxicity tests help establish presumed safe concentrations, assuming that the chemical can be used without harming the environment if the such concentrations are not exceeded in the environment following normal use. However, there are substantial difficulties in implementing results from short experiments in the laboratory to long term effects in the environment (Cairns and Mount, 1990). Furthermore, ERA is performed taking in consideration only one chemical at a time, whereas, in the environment they may occur as mixtures with other contaminants and can be influenced by other abiotic factors (Suter, 1993). The ability of various xenobiotics, and their derivatives, to mutually cause toxicity in organisms makes it difficult to assess risk based solely on their concentrations in the environment (Calabrese, 1991). Deleterious effect of such mixtures of pollutants in most organisms is often difficult to detect because many of these effects are manifested only after long time. It may happen that when such effect finally becomes apparent, the destructive process may have gone beyond the point of recovery by remedial actions. This has therefore compelled researchers to increase their efforts for generating information relating to hematology, histology, histochemistry, metabolism, pharmacokinetics, and physiological or biochemical process to establish early-warning signals, or biomarkers, for measuring the effects of toxicity in organisms (Bucheli and Fent, 1995). Changes in biological processes at an earlier stage are generally followed by effects at higher hierarchical levels, which facilitate development of early-warning signals or biomarker of effects at later response levels (Bayne et al., 1985) (Figure 1.1). From an environmental perspective, biomarkers have great potentials as sensitive indicators because they indicate that the pollutants have penetrated in organisms, have been distributed between tissues, and eliciting toxic effects in critical target organs (McCarthy and Shugart, 1990). Biomarkers have been extensively studied are studied in fish and several comprehensive reviews and books on the subject are available (Adams, 1987; NRC, 1987; Schlenk, 1999; Stegeman et al., 1992). Biomarkers are measurements in body fluids, cells, or tissues that can indicate biochemical or cellular modifications resulting from the presence of toxicants or stress, or of host response (NRC, 1987). For several reasons, fish have been considerably used for assessing biological and biochemical responses to environmental contaminants (Powers, 1989). Fish are virtually ubiquitous in the aquatic environment and play a major ecological role in the aquatic food-webs as energy carrier from lower to higher trophic levels (Beyer, 1996). Therefore understanding uptake of toxicants, behaviour and responses in fish may have a high ecological importance.

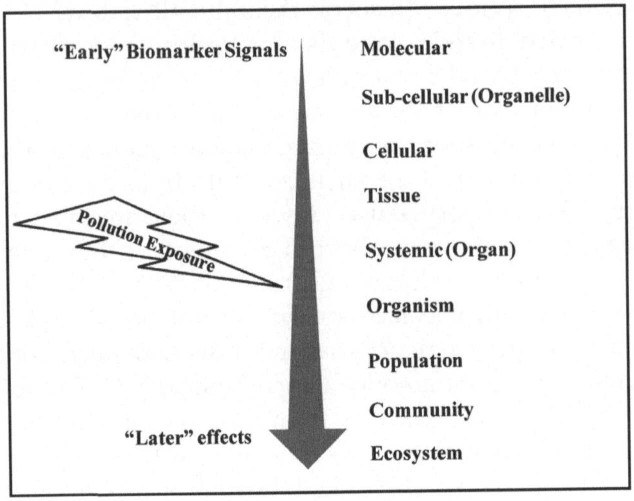

Fig. 1.1: Schematic Representation of Responses of Biological System to Pollution Stress. (Modified from Bayne et al.,1985)

DEFINITIONS OF BIOMARKER

The first consensus definition of biomarker was proposed by the Committee on Biological Markers of the National Research Council (NRC) (1987). The NRC (1987) defined biomarkers as "indicators signaling events in biological systems or samples following chemical exposure" and classified biological markers into three types, those of (1) exposure; (2) effect; and (3) susceptibility, and describes the events in each type as follows:

1. **Biomarkers of exposure:** A biological marker of exposure may be the identification of an exogenous substance within the system, the interactive product between a xenobiotic compound and endogenous components, or other event in the biological system related to the exposure.
2. **Biomarkers of effect:** A biological marker of effect may be an indicator of an endogenous component of the biological system, a measure of the functional capacity of the system, or an altered state of the system that is recognized as impairment or disease.
3. **Biomarkers of susceptibility:** A biological marker of susceptibility is defined as an indicator that the health of the system is especially sensitive to the challenge of exposure to a xenobiotic compound (a compound originating outside the organism).

The original definition and classification by the NRC (1987) emphasises more on human health. Several authors have defined biomarkers in their own way. Shugart et al. (1992) defined biomarkers as a xenobiotically induced variation in cellular or biochemical components or processes, structures, or functions that is measurable in a biological system or samples. Peakall and

Walker (1994) defined biomarkers as a change in a biological response (ranging from molecular through cellular and physiological responses to behavioral changes) which can be related to exposure to or toxic effects of environmental chemicals. Van Gestel and Van Brummelen (1996), defined biomarkers as any biological response to an environmental chemical at the subindividual level, measured inside an organism or in its products (urine, faeces, hair, feathers, etc.), indicating a deviation from the normal status that cannot be detected in the intact organism. McCarthy and Munkittrick (1996) defined biomarkers as functional measures of exposure to stressors expressed at the sub-organismal, physiological or behavioural level. The EPA (2000) defined biomarkers as a contaminant-induced physiological, biochemical, or histological response of an organism. Shugart (2005) defined biomarkers as "molecular-, biochemical-, or cellular-level indicators in either wild populations taken from contaminated habitats or in organisms experimentally exposed to pollutants that indicate that such organisms have been exposed to toxic chemicals and the magnitude of the organism's response to the contaminant" (Rojas-Garciìa et al., 2011). Sedeño-Díaz and López-López (2012) defined biomarkers as "any biological measurable response from an organism, induced by the exposure to a xenobiotic or complex mixture of them". Bonnineau et al. (2012) defined biomarker "as a biological element belonging to a wider system whose observation is expected to give information on the wider system based on the a priori knowledge of the links and interactions existing between the biomarker and this system". All of these definitions have one thing in common i.e. biological responses to contaminants exposure.

The most important reason for using biomarkers is that they provide information on the effects of pollutants on the biological system rather than merely the levels of pollutants in the environmental. Investigating various biomarker responses may provide important information about organism toxicant exposure and stress. Stress caused due to pollutant triggers variety of biological responses, each of which may act as a biomarker (McCarthy et al., 1991). However, improper application or interpretation of biomarker responses may mislead conclusions on pollutant caused stress or environmental quality. The biomarker responses may vary for every species under investigation. Additionally, data obtained from the ecotoxicological studies in laboratory mostly fail to accurate predict the effects in the field (ECETOC, 1993). It is therefore essential to validate the laboratory observations on biomarkers with field. Van der Oost et al. (2003), based on the criteria formulated by Stegeman et al. (1992), proposed six criteria to evaluate the strength and weaknesses of fish biomarkers as follows:

1. The assay to quantify the biomarker should be reliable [with quality assurance (QA)], relatively cheap and easy to perform.

2. The biomarker response should be sensitive to pollutant exposure and/ or effects in order to serve as an early warning parameter.
3. Baseline data of the biomarker should be well defined in order to distinguish between natural variability (noise) and contaminant-induced stress (signal).
4. The impacts of confounding factors to the biomarker response should be well established.
5. The underlying mechanism of the relationships between biomarker response and pollutant exposure (dosage and time) should be established.
6. The toxicological significance of the biomarker, e.g. the relationships between its response and the (longterm) impact to the organism, should be established.

In addition to these criteria the biomarkers should be non-invasive or non-destructive so as to facilitate safe monitoring of pollution effects in protected or endangered species (Fossi and Marsili, 1997).

BIOTRANSFORMATION OF XENOBIOTICS

Organisms eliminate xenobiotics by two main ways: (1) either by excreting them in their original form or (2) by biotransforming them into more hydrophilic compound which can then easily excreted compared the original compound (Vermeulen, 1996). Biotransformation or metabolism can be defined as an "enzyme-catalyzed conversion of a xenobiotic compound into a more water-soluble form, which can be excreted from the body more easily than the parent compound" (Lech and Vodicnik, 1985). One of the determinants of xenobiotic persistence in the body and subsequent toxicity to the organisms is the extent to which they can be metabolised and excreted (Rose and Hodgson, 2004). However, during biotransformation may undergo a detoxication reaction in which the toxicity of the compound is reduced while the excretion is generally elevated or may undergo bioactivation during which the compound is transformed into a reactive metabolite, which is more toxic than the parent compound (Vermeulen, 1996). Schematic representation of biotransformation of xenobiotic compounds is given in figure 1.2. Biomarkers that are investigated most extensively include enzymes involved in the biotransformation of xenobiotics and their metabolites. Several metabolic enzymes with wide arrays of substrate specificity are involved in metabolism of xenobiotic compounds. The liver is most common organ involved in the biotransformation of foreign compounds because it is devoted to synthesis of many important biologically functional proteins and mediates chemical transformations of xenobiotics.

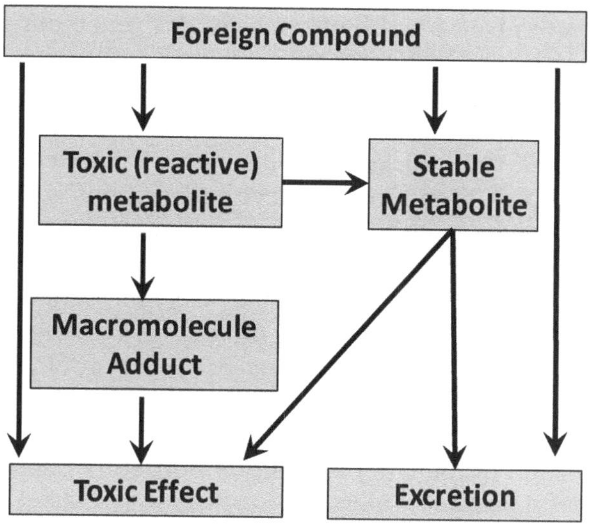

Fig. 1.2: Schematic Representation of Possible Toxication and Detoxification Pathways of Xenobiotic Compounds. (Modified from Timbrell, 1991)

Most xenobiotics that enter the body are lipophilic, which enables them to bind to lipid membranes and be in the blood transported by lipoproteins. After entrance into the liver, xenobiotics may undergo biotransformation, according to the simplified mechanism of route I, which can be subdivided into phases I, II and III (Fig. 1.3, route I) (Commandeur et al, 1995). Phase I is a non-synthetic alteration of the xenobiotic compound, during which a polar reactive group is introduced into the molecule converting it into a suitable substrate for phase II enzymes and catabolism in phase III. Enzymes typically involved in phase I metabolism include the cytochrome P450 monooxygenases, flavin-containing monooxygenases, and hydrolases, which unmask or add reactive functional groups by oxidation, reduction or hydrolysis of the xenobiotic compound (Goeptar et al., 1995). Addition of a polar group, such as sugars, sulfates, or amino acids increases water solubility of the xenobiotic making it easy to excrete. However, in this process reactive intermediates may be formed that are much more toxic than the parent compound. Phase II enzymes and cofactors are involved in the conjugation of the xenobiotic parent compound or its metabolite with an endogenous ligand. The major pathway for electrophilic compounds and metabolites is conjugation with reduced glutathione (GSH) by the glutathione-S-transferases, while for nucleophilic compounds conjugation with glucuronic acid by the UDP- glucuronyl-transferases (George, 1994). The phase III enzymes (e.g. peptidases, hydrolases and b lyase) catabolise conjugated metabolites to form easily excretable products.

Another important aspect of xenobiotic biotransformation is the possible direct induction of phase I and II enzymes by the xenobiotic compounds via the aryl hydrocarbon (Ah) receptor (Fig. 1.3, route II) (Van der Oost et al., 2003). In this pathway enzymes are inducted by the binding of a specific xenobiotic to a protein complex comprising of Ah receptor and the heat-shock protein 90 (HSP 90), the latter is subsequently released. The Ah receptor – xenobiotic complex then binds to aryl hydrocarbon nuclear transferase (ARNT or Ah receptor nuclear translocator) and migrates into the nucleus. In the nucleus, ARNT binds to a DNA recognition sequence upstream of the cytochrome P450 genes resulting in increased messenger RNA (mRNA) synthesis and subsequent elevation in protein levels (Stegeman and Hahn, 1994). The Ah pathway can enhance gene expression of enzymes of both, phase I (Stegeman and Hahn, 1994) and phase II such as NADPH menadione oxidoreductase, ALDH, UDPGT and GST (Nebert et al., 1990; Celander, 1993), but induction of the latter is less pronounced (Andersson et al., 1985; George, 1994).

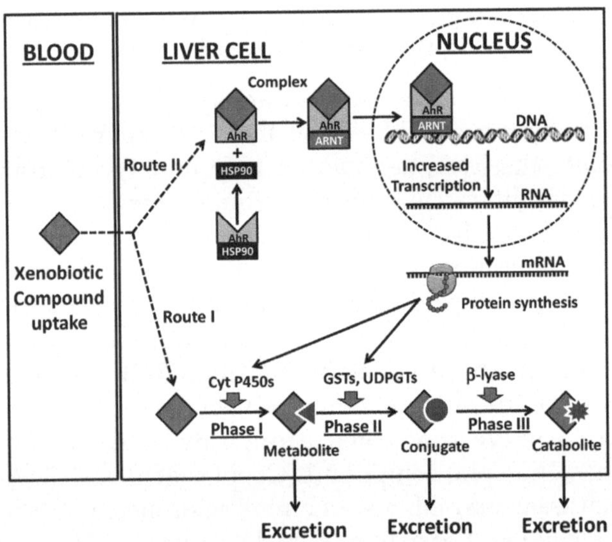

Fig. 1.3: Schematic Representation of Fate of Xenobiotic Compounds in the Liver Cell. (Modified from Van der Oost et al., 2003)

BIOTRANSFORMATION BIOMARKERS IN FISH

Various biochemical responses in fish exposed toxic substances have been examined to evaluate their potential use as biomarkers of exposure or effect. The impact of toxic xenobiotics in fish can be analysed using various types of exposure and effect biomarkers as described below. Alterations in levels and activities of the biotransformation enzymes are most sensitive biomarkers. In fish, these enzymes may be induced or inhibited upon exposure to xenobiotics (Bucheli and Fent, 1995). These biomarkers include both Phase I and Phase enzymes II that are involved in biotransformation xenobiotic. Some of the important enzymes that are used and validated as biomarkers are described below:

(a) Phase-I biomakers

The phase I reactions of are catalyzed by microsomal monooxygenase (MO) enzymes including cytochrome P450 (cyt P450), cytochrome b5 (cyt b5), and NADPH cytochrome P450 reductase (P450 Red).

(i) Total Cytochrome P450 (cyt P450)

In fish biotransformation of xenobiotic is mainly mediated by the Cytochrome P450 (cyt P450) - dependent monooxygenases. The cyt P450 monooxygenases are enzymes belonging to multi-gene family that play a critical role in the biotransformation of pollutants. The cyt P450, are carbon monoxide-binding heme proteins (pigments) of microsomes, which help in xenobiotic biotransformation by catalysing one-electron reductions (Lu, 1969). Monooxygenations, earlier known as mixed-function oxidations, are those oxidation reactions in which one atom of a molecule of oxygen is incorporated into the substrate while the other is reduced to water. Since the reduction of cyt P450 involves electrons derived from NADPH, the overall reaction can be written as follows, (Rose and Hodgson, 2004):

$$\text{substrate (RH)} + O_2 + \text{NADPH} + H^+ \rightarrow \text{NADP+} + \text{ROH} + H_2O$$

In laboratory and field studies, an increase in the total cyt P450 levels was observed in various fish species exposed to organic trace pollutants such as polycyclic aromatic hydrocarbons (PAHs), polychlorinated biphenyls (PCBs) and polychlorinated dibenzofurans (PCDFs), and polychlorinated dibenzop-dioxins (PCDDs) (Van der Oost et al., 2003). However, significant decrease in cyt P450 levels has been reported in bullhead (*Cottus gobio*), eel (*Anguilla anguilla*) and rainbow trout (*Oncorhynchus mykiss*) exposed to Organotins (tributyltin [TBT] and triphenyltin [TPT]) (Fent and Bucheli, 1994). Significant decrease in cyt 450 was also reported in the feral brown bullhead (*Ameiurus nebulosus*) and roach (*Rutilus rutilus*) from polluted environments (Lindström-Seppä and Oikari, 1991).

(ii) Cytochrome P450 1A (CYP1A)

Among the known 18 cyt p450 families of mammalian only three families (families CYP1 to 3) are most responsible for xenobiotic metabolism and are considered to be derived from the "ancestral" cyt p450 families. The CYP1 family consists of three known human members, namely, CYP1A1, CYP1A2, and CYP1B1. Among these the CYP1A1 and CYP1A2 are highly homologous forms and highly conserved among all classes of the animal kingdom. Both these proteins possess distinct but overlapping substrate specificities: with the CYP1A1 preferring neutral PAHs, and the CYP1A2 preferring polyaromatic and heterocyclic amines and amides (Rose and Hodgson, 2004).

The CYP1A subfamily is the most common and highly conserved, and is therefore widely used as a biomarker of effect both in vertebrates and invertebrates including fish (Di Giulio and Hinton, 2008).

In fish, the CYP1A1 and CYP1A2 class of cyt P450 isozymes are responsible for the biotransformation of a variety of xenobiotic compounds including PAHs, PCBs, dioxins, etc. (Goksøyr and Förlin, 1992; Stegeman and Hahn, 1994). Field and laboratory studies in fish species have reported an increase in the levels of hepatic CYP1A protein after exposure to PAHs, PCBs, PCDDs and PCDFs (Van der Oost et al., 2003). Rice and Roszell (1998) reported that in channel catfish (*Ictalurus punctatus*) organotins such as tributyltin (TBT), at environmentally relevant doses increased the PCB-induced CYP1A levels, while a decrease of induction was observed at higher TBT doses. Van Veld et al., (1997) observed a route-specific cellular expression of CYP1A in mummichog (*Fundulus heteroclitus*) following exposure to benzo[a]pyrene (BaP), wherein aqueous BaP exposure increased the CYP1A levels in gills, heart, liver and blood vessels, while dietary BaP exposure increased the CYP1A levels in gut epithelium. Since, exposure to environmental pollutants results in increase in levels of CYP1A mRNA followed by CYP1A protein levels (Stegeman and Hahn, 1994), measurement of CYP1A mRNA by Northern blots has become an integral part of investigations on CYP1A regulation, and is considered as a suitable biomarker in several field trials (Bucheli and Fent, 1995). A relationships between expression of CYP1A and alterations in reproduction following exposure to PCBs or 2, 3, 7, 8-tetrachlorodibenzo-dioxin (TCDD) has been reported in fish (Cook et al., 1997; Teraoka et al., 2003). The levels of CYP1A protein can be immunologically determined using ELISA, Western-blotting or histochemical techniques with mono or polyclonal antibodies (Bucheli and Fent, 1995). The CYP1A activity can also be measured using the substrate ethoxyresorufin, which is o-deethylated by ethoxyresorufin-O-deethylase (EROD) to a fluorescent product 'resorufin', which can be measured easily (Di Giulio and Hinton, 2008; Rojas-Garciìa et al., 2011).

In fish, the hepatic levels of CYP1A protein is suggested to be a sensitive biomarker of PAHs and HAHs exposure, and feasible in ERA procedures (Van der Oost et al., 2003). Levine and Oris (1999) suggested that the expression of CYP1A should be measured in tissues such as the gill and intestine since they are in direct contact with the environment. Stegeman et al. (1992) suggested that the determinations of CYP1A may be used during ERA process, such as quantification of impact and exposure of various organic trace pollutants, environmental monitoring of organism and ecosystem 'health', identifying subtle early toxic effects, triggering of regulatory action, identification of exposure to specific compounds, toxicological screening and the research on toxic mechanisms of xenobiotics.

(iii) Ethoxyresorufin O-deethylase (EROD)

Apart from the estimation of CYP1A protein or mRNA levels, a common method for examining the CYP1A isoenzyme is to determine its catalytic activity. The ethoxyresorufin O-deethylase (EROD) activity is reported to be the most sensitive catalytic probe for determining the induction of the cyt P450 system in fish (Goksøyr and Förlin, 1992). The EROD activity is measured by observing increase in fluorescence of the reaction product resorufin (Burke and Mayer, 1974). Whyte et al. (2000) extensively reviewed the use and limitations of EROD activity as a biomarker of chemical exposure in fish, and ranked chemicals according to the level of EROD activity in exposed fish compared to untreated fish: (1) "weak" inducers included contaminants that induce more than 10 fold EROD above control levels; (2) "moderate" inducers inducing 10- to 100-fold; and (3) "strong" inducers for chemicals that induced more than 100-fold EROD. Dioxins, PCBs and PAHs (benzo[a]pyrene) were categorised as "strong" inducers. Increase in the EROD activities have been reported in many species of fish exposed to organic trace pollutants such as PAHs, PCBs, PCDDs and PCDFs (Van der Oost et al., 2003). Jung et al., (2001) observed that substances such as nitrated polycyclic aromatic hydrocarbons (NPAHs) and Nheterocyclic aromatic hydrocarbons (azarenes) can significantly induce CYP1A in fish from PAH-contaminated environments. Van der Oost et al., (1996) observed a good correlation between levels of CYP1A protein and EROD activity. Similar strong and significant induction of hepatic protein levels and activity of CYP1A are reported in field studies in many species of fish from polluted environments (Van der Oost et al., 2003). Decrease in EROD was observed in bullhead, eel and rainbow trout exposed to organotins Organotins (TBT and TPT) (Fent and Bucheli, 1994). Rice and Roszell, (1998) reported PCB-induced inhibition of EROD in channel catfish by low doses organotins, although the activity was higher compared to control fish. Fent et al. (1998) reported a degenerative effect of organotins in scub microsomal monooxygenase (MO) system exposed to triphenyltin (TPT). Sole et al. (2000) reported reduction in the EROD activity and CYP1A protein in carp after intra-peritoneal administration of 17α-ethynylestradiol. It has been suggested that the EROD activities in fish liver are very sensitive biomarkers and may help in ERA processes. The induction of CYP1A catalytic activities, together with levels of CYP1A protein and mRNA, may serve for assessment of exposure as well as early-warning sign for potentially harmful effects of many organic trace pollutants (Whyte et al., 2000).

(iv) Cytochrome b5 (cyt b5)

The Cyt b5 is involved in the biotransformations through electron donation by NADH, an reaction catalysed cytochrome b5 reductase (Timbrell, 1991). In laboratory studies, elevated levels of cyt b5 have been reported in Mullit (*Chelon labrosus*) exposed to PCB (Phenoclor DP 6) (Narbonne and

Gallis, 1979), Striped mullet (*Mugil cephalus*) exposed to crude oils (Chambers, 1979), and Scup (*Stenotomus chrysops*) exposed to PBB (33□ 44□ -TCB) (White et al., 1997). In field studies, increase in cyt b5 levels have been reported in eel due to PCBs, OCPs and PAHs contamination (Van der Oost et al., 1996), and Nile tilapia from PCBs and HCS contaminated waters (Bainy et al., 1996), while decrease in cyt b5 levels was reported in roach from a site polluted with PCBs, OCPs and PAHs (Van der Oost et al., 1994).

(v) NADPH cytochrome P450 reductase (P450 RED)

The P450 RED is regarded as a MO enzyme in fish liver (Braunbeck and Vö lkl, 1991), because it plays important role in the reduction of the heme iron by electron transfer from the flavoprotein P450 RED, and in some cases from cyt b5 required for Cyt P450 activity (Kloepper-Sams and Stegeman, 1992; Goeptar et al., 1995). Increased in liver P450 RED activity has been reported in Atlantic salmon (*Salmo salar*) exposure to PAHs (Goksøyr and Larsen, 1991; Kloepper-Sams and Stegeman, 1992; Sole et al., 2000) and Striped mullet (*Mugil cephalus*) exposed to crude oil (Chambers, 1979). Similar observations have been reported from field studies in salmon (*Salmo salar*) exposed to halogenated xenobiotics (Pesonen et al., 1999), bream (*Abramis brama*) exposed to BKME (Lindström-Seppä and Oikari, 1991), carp (*Cyprinus carpio*) exposed to PHAHs and PAHs (Curtis et al., 1993), eel (*Anguilla anguilla*) exposed to PCBs, OCPs, PAHs and PCDF/Ds (Van der Oost et al., 1996), sunfish (*Lepomis auritus*) exposed to PCBs and Hg (Adams et al., 1990) and grayling (*Thymallus thymallus*) exposed to PCBs (Monod et al., 1988). Laboratory studies have reported decrease in the P450 RED activities in bullhead (*Cottus gobio*) and eel (*Anguilla anguilla*) (Fent and Bucheli, 1994), scup (*Stenotomus chrysops*) (Fent et al., 1998) and rainbow trout (Fent and Bucheli, 1994) exposed to organotins (TBT and TPT), while field studies have reported decrease in the P450 RED activity in nase (*Chondrostoma nasus*) from waters polluted with PCB (Monod et al., 1988).

(b) Phase-II biomakers

During the phase-II biotransformation of the xenobiotic compound, the parent compound or its metabolites is conjugated which large and often polar chemical groups such as sugars and amino acids (Lech and Vodicnik, 1985). Majority of the enzymes of phase II catalyze conjugation of more polar groups, such as glutathione (GSH) and glucuronic acid (GA), to xenobiotic compounds facilitating their excretion (Commandeur et al., 1995; Mulder et al. 1990). Some of the xenobiotic compounds may possess the required functional groups, such as COOH, OH or NH_2, for direct metabolism by phase II enzymes, while some other chemicals require prior modification of xenobiotic compound by the phase I enzymes (George, 1994; Lech and Vodicnik, 1985; Sijm and Opperhuizen, 1989). The phase II enzymes therefore play critical role in maintaining homeostasis and in detoxification and excretion of many xenobiotic compounds. Major pathway for electrophilic compounds and their metabolites is conjugation with GSH, while that of nucleophilic compounds is conjugation with GA. In fish, the knowledge of phase II systems is restricted to the enzymes that catalyze glucuronidation and GSH conjugation (George, 1994). The phase II enzymes like NADPH menadione oxidoreductase, aldehyde dehydrogenase, UDP-glucuronyl transferases (UDPGT) and Glutathione S-transferases (GST) are suggested to be regulated via the Ah-receptor (Sutter and Greenlee, 1992; Hayes and Pulford, 1995). Additionally, the levels of phase II cofactors may also be affected due to environmental pollutants (Stegeman et al., 1992; Lindström-Seppä and Oikari, 1991; Van der Oost et al., 1996).

(i) Glutathione S-transferases (GSTs)

The GSTs catalyze nucleophilic conjugation of different biologically active and potentially carcinogenic compounds for biotransformation into mercapturic acids (Oude et al., 1998). Based on the amino acid sequence, immunogenic properties and physiological role, the glutathione S-transferases are classified into eight families namely, alpha, kappa, mu, pi, sigma, theta, zeta and omega (George, 1994). These enzymes are present in almost all tissues, but occur in high amount in liver, kidney, intestine, testis and lung, localized in the cytoplasm or the endoplasmic reticulum of cells (Klaassen, 2008). The GSTs plays critical role in defence against oxidative damage and peroxidative products of DNA and lipids (George, 1994). The total GST activity is mostly determine using the artificial substrate 1-chloro-2, 4-dinitrobenzene (CDNB), which is conjugated by all GST isoforms with the exception of the q-class enzymes (George, 1994; Van der Aar et al., 1996). Induction of hepatic GST activity in fish exposed to PAHs, PCBs, OCPs and PCDDs, has been reported in several studies. However the results of GSTs in field study are conflicting, with several studies reporting increasing in activity but most studies no difference between the control and pollutant exposed fishes (Van der Oost et al., 2003). Significant decrease in GST activities has been reported in fishes such as rainbow trout (Hektoen et al., 1994), sea bass (Lemaire et al., 1996), seabream (Pedrajas et al., 1995) and sunfish (Oikari and Jimenez, 1992) exposed to PCDDs, pesticides or PAHs. However, the total GST activity in fish liver does not qualify to be suitable biomarker for ERA due to ambiguity in the results.

(ii) UDP-glucuronyl transferases (UDPGTs)

The major pathway for the inactivation and subsequent excretion of endogenous and xenobiotic organic compounds is the increase synthesis of glucuronides by microsomal UDP glucuronyl transferases (Lech and Vodicnik, 1985; Mulder et al., 1990; George, 1994). The glucuronic acid (GA) is first converted to uridine 5□- diphosphoglucuronic acid (UDPGA), which is then conjugated to a wide variety of acceptor substrates (aglycones) to form O-, N-, S- and C glucuronides by UDPGT (Kasper and Henton, 1980; Mulder et al., 1990), the majority being O-glucuronides (George, 1994). In fish, glucuronidation of xenobiotics has been reported in liver, kidney, gills and intestine (George, 1994). Multiple UDPGT isoforms with differing substrate specificities are reported in fish (Clarke et al., 1992). The isoenzymes are generally named according to the substrates, e.g. bilirubin, steroid and phenol UDPGTs. The UDPGT isoform, which is induced by PAHs, preferentially conjugates planar phenols most probably via an Ah receptordependent mechanism (Nebert et al., 1990; George, 1994). In fish, the UDPGT activity is also reported to be influenced by sex, season, pH and temperature (Stegeman et al., 1992). Increased UDPGT activities in liver have been reported in fish exposed to PAHs, PCBs, OCPs, PCDDs, and bleached kraft mill effluent (BKME) and have been validated by field experiments (Van der Oost et al., 2003). Decreased UDPGT activities in whitefish (*Coregonus muksun*) (Lindström-Seppä and Oikari, 1989) and rainbow trout (*Salmo gairdneri*) (Lindström-Seppä and Oikari, 1990) exposed to BKME. The UDPGT activity is suggested to be suitable parameter for investigating the phase II pathway during xenobiotic exposure, and validated as a biomarker in ERA programmes.

OXIDATIVE STRESS

Many pollutants are known to cause oxidative stress in fishes. Oxygen toxicity is defined as injurious effects due to cytotoxic reactive oxygen species (ROS), or reactive oxygen intermediates (ROIs), oxygen free radicals or oxyradicals (Di Giulio et al., 1989; Halliwell and Gutteridge, 1999). Oxidative stress can be defined "as the disturbance between ROS concentration and the antioxidant defences concentration, favoring the first" (Monserrat et al., 2007). Kisby et al., (2009) proposed that oxidative stress and DNA damage are the mechanisms linking pesticide exposure to health effects such as cancer and neurological disease. The reduction of molecular oxygen (O_2) leads to the formation of superoxide anion radical ($O_2^{-\bullet}$), hydrogen peroxide (H_2O_2) and the hydroxyl radical ($OH^{\bullet}$), which are extremely potent oxidants capable of reacting with critical cellular macromolecules, possibly leading to enzyme inactivation, lipid peroxidation (LPOX), DNA damage and, ultimately, cell death (Winston and Di Giulio, 1991). Oxidative stress trigger adaptive mechanisms in organisms, inhibit oxyradical formation include the antioxidant enzymes such as superoxide dismutase (SOD), catalase (CAT), glutathione-dependent peroxidase (GPOX) and glutathione reductase (GRED) which can be used as biomarkers for ERA (Rojas-Garciìa et al., 2011).

BIOMARKERS OF OXIDATIVE STRESS

(i) Superoxide dismutase (SOD)

The SOD, a group of metalloenzymes, catalyse the conversion of $O_2^{-\bullet}$ to form H_2O_2 (an important ROS itself), which is subsequently detoxified by CAT and GPOXs. Increase in SOD activity has been reported in fish exposed to paraquat (Vig and Nemcsok, 1989), PCFD (2, 3, 7, 8-TCDF) (Palace et al., 1996) or HCB -contaminated food (Roy et al., 1995), but most studies could not demonstrate any significant alterations (Van der Oost et al., 2003). Significant increase of SOD activity in liver was reported in brown bullhead (*Ameiurus nebulosus*) exposed to PCBs, DDE (Otto and Moon, 1996), carp (*Cyprinus carpio*) exposed to PHAHs and PAHs (Van der Oost et al., 1998), dab (*Limanda limanda*) exposed to PAHs (Livingstone et al., 1993), grey mullet (*Mugil* sp.) exposed to OCPs (Rodriguez-Ariza et al., 1993), Nile tilapia (*Oreochromis niloticus*) exposed to PCBs and HCHs (Bainy et al., 1996), red mullet (*Mullus barbatus*) exposed to PAHs (Burgeot et al., 1996), sardine (*Sardina pilchardus*) exposed to PAHs, PCBs and DDE (Peters et al., 1994) and spot (*Leiostomus xanthurus*) exposed to PAHs (Roberts et al., 1987).

(ii) Catalase (CAT)

Catalase, hematin-containing enzymes, metabolizes hydrogen peroxide (H_2O_2) to molecular oxygen (O_2) and water. Few studies have demonstrated increases in hepatic CAT activity in fish exposed to PCBs (Rudneva-Titova and Zherko, 1994), BKME (Mather-Mihaich and Di Giulio, 1991) and PAH-containing sediments (Di Giulio et al., 1989), but most laboratory studies could not demonstrate any significant alterations (Van der Oost et al., 2003). Significant decrease in CAT activity was reported in fish exposed to PAH, DNOC, 3,3□,4,4□- TCB, engine exhaust extracts or cadmium exposure and in a field study with Nile tilapia.

(iii) Glutathione peroxidase (GPOX)

Peroxidases (POXs) are enzymes that reduce a variety of peroxides to their corresponding alcohols. In fish, the principal peroxidase is a selenium-dependent tetrameric cytosolic enzyme that utilizes Glutathione as a cofactor. The GPOX metabolises H_2O_2 to water concomitantly oxidizing the reduced GSH to its oxidized form (GSSG). The GPOX plays important role in protecting membranes from damage due to LPOX indicating that the major detoxification function of GPOX is the termination of radical chain propagation (Lauterburg et al., 1983). Increase in the activity of GPOX has been reported in fish exposed to paraquat (*Cyprinus carpio*, Gabryelak and Klekot, 1985), PCBs (*Scorpoena porcus*, Rudneva-Titova and Zherko, 1994) and HCB-contaminated food (*Oncorhynchus mykiss*, Roy et al., 1995), while decrease was only observed after exposure to PAH (3MC) (*Dicentrarchus labrax*, Lemaire et al., 1996). One one field have shown increase in the GPOX activity in Grey mullet (*Mugil* sp.) exposed to OCPs (Rodriguez-Ariza et al., 1993). Decrease in the activity of GPOX has also been reported in field experiments such as rainbow trout (*Salmo gairdneri*) exposed to PCBs (Otto et al., 1996), red mullet (*Mullus barbatus*) exposed to PAHs (Burgeot et al., 1996) and seabream (*Diplodus annularis*) exposed to Oil and others contaminants (Bagnasco et al., 1991).

(iv) Glutathione reductase (GRED)

Though Glutathione reductase is not involved in antioxidant defence it plays crucial role in maintaining GSH/GSSG equilibrium under oxidative stress conditions (Winston and Di Giulio, 1991). The GRED catalyses conversion of the oxidized disulfide form of glutathione (GSSG) to the reduced form (GSH), simultaneously oxidizing the NADPH to $NADP^+$. This facilitates an easy way for measuring its activity spectrometrically by detecting the decrease in NADPH levels (Worthington and Rosemeyer, 1974). In laboratory experiments, the GRED activity has been reported to increase in Rainbow trout exposed to PCBs (Otto and Moon, 1995), PAHs (Tjärnlund et al., 1996), DDE (Machala et al., 1998) and HCB contaminated food (Roy et al., 1995), while file studies have reported significant increase in hepatic GRED activity in Atlantic salmon (*Salmo salar*) exposed to Halogenated xenobiotics (Pesonen et al., 1999) and shorthorn sculpin (*Myoxocephalus scorpius*) exposed to PAH (Stephensen et al., 2000). Significant decreases in the activity of GRED in laboratory experiment has been reported in red mullet exposed to PCBs (Rudneva-Titova and Zherko, 1994), and in field studies in Nile tilapia (*Oreochromis niloticus*) from contaminated environment (Bainy et al., 1996).

(v) Reduced and oxidized glutathione (GSH and GSSG)

Oxidative stress causes a general disturbance of the cellular ratio of reduced to oxidized glutathione (GSH/GSSG) and the NADH/ NAD^+ ratio (Abele and Puntarulo, 2004). Reduced GSH is a tripeptide consisting of g-glutamine, cysteine and glycine. The GHS plays two critical roles in detoxifications (1) as a key conjugate of electrophilic intermediates, via the GST activities in phase II metabolism, and (2) as an important antioxidant (Stegeman et al., 1992; Commandeur et al., 1995). The GSH is conjugated with electrophilic compounds, catalyzed by one of the various GSTs, and replaces hydrogen, chlorine and nitro-groups. This is followed by the formation of mercapturic acids after catabolism of the GSH conjugate with peptidases and acetylases. The mercapturic acids thus formed can be excreted either in the bile or in the urine (Lech and Vodicnik, 1985; Commandeur et al., 1995). Increase in oxyradical-generating compounds may modulate GSH status and/or metabolism in several ways (Stegeman et al., 1992; Otto and Moon, 1995). Increased fluxes of oxyradicals can increase consumption of GSH due to the direct scavenging of oxyradicals or as a cofactor for glutathione peroxidise (GPOX) activity (Di Giulio et al., 1995). Indirectly, the oxidative stress can further reduce the reductant pool as a due to energetic costs of mounting a defence against an increased flux of oxyradicals (Winston and Di Giulio, 1991). The most direct effect of certain pollutants is a decrease in the ratio of reduced to oxidized glutathione (GSH : GSSG), due to either direct radical scavenging or increased peroxidise activity (Stegeman et al., 1992; Otto and Moon, 1995).

Increase in GSH levels has been reported in laboratory studies in Channel catfish (*Ictalurus punctatus*) exposed to BKME (Mather-Mihaich and Di Giulio, 1991) and PAHs (Di Giulio et al., 1989), Crucian carp (*Carassius auratus*) exposed to PCDDs and metals in sediment (Chen et al., 1998), and Rainbow trout exposed to PCB (3,3□,4,4□-TCB) (Otto and Moon, 1995) and OCP (HCB) (Lindström-Seppä et al., 1996) while increase in the GSH has been reported from firled studies in bream and roach (Lindström-Seppä and Oikari, 1991), perch (Huuskonen and Linström-Seppä, 1995) from BKME polluted environments. A significant decrease in the GSH has been reported in field studies with bullhead (*Ameiurus nebulosus*) from water polluted with PCBs and DDE (Otto and Moon, 1996), and carp from water polluted with PHAHs and PAHs (Van der Oost et al., 1998). Laboratory studies have shown elevated levels of hepatic GSSG channel catfish exposed to PAH-containing sediments (Di Giulio et al., 1989) and rainbow trout exposed to PCBs (Otto and Moon, 1995), while in field studies the elevated levels was observed in eel (*Anguilla anguilla*) from water polluted with PCBs and PAHs (Van der Oost et al., 1996). The hepatic GSH:GSSG ratio has been suggested to be a potential biomarker for oxidative stress in fish (Van der Oost et al., 1996).

(vi) Lipid peroxidation (LPOX)

An important effect of oxidative stress that has been investigated extensively is the oxidation of polyunsaturated fatty acids (Stegeman et al., 1992; Hageman et al., 1992). Lipid peroxidation leads to the formation of degradation products such as aldehydes (malondialdehyde) and hydrocarbons (ethane and ethylene) (Gutteridge and Halliwell, 1990; Freeman and Crapo, 1982). Various chemicals have been reported to have increased LPOX in different fish species such as paraquat exposed carp (Gabryelak and Klekot, 1985), channel catfish and brown bulhead exposed to t-butyl hydroperoxide (Ploch et al., 1999), sea bass exposed to heavy metals (Romeo et al., 2000) and bluegill sunfish exposed to anthracene and UV-light (Choi and Oris, 2000). The LPOX has been suggested as a potential a biomarker for ERA (Stegeman et al., 1992; Hai et al., 1995).

CONCLUSION AND FUTURE DIRECTIONS

In conclusion, it could be suggested that most of the enzymes involved in the biotransformation of xenobiotics and oxidative stress in fish have potentials for use as reliable biomarkers for ERA. However, further investigations needed to validate and interpret these biomarkers in response to other environmental factors and in combinations of different contaminants so as to develop acceptable quality assurance procedures.

REFERENCES

Adams, S.M., (1987): Status and Use of Biological Indicators for Evaluating the Effects of Stress on Fish. In: Adams SM (ed) Biological Indicators of Stress in Fish. Am Fish Soc Symp 8-18.

Adams, S.M., Shugart, L.R., Southworth, G.R., and Hinton, D.E., (1990): Application of Bioindicators in Assessing the Health of Fish Populations Experiencing Contaminant Stress. In: McCarthy, J.F., Shugart, L.R. (Eds.), Biomarkers of Environmental Contamination. Lewis Pub, pp. 333-353.

Amiard-Triquet, C., Amiard, J.C., and Rainbow, P.S. (Eds.) (2012): Ecological Biomarkers: Indicators of Ecotoxicological Effects. CRC Press.

Andersson, T., Pesonen, M., Johansson, C., 1985. Differential Induction of Cytochrome P-450-dependent Monooxygenase, Epoxide Hydrolase, Glutathione Transferase and UDP Glucuronosyl Transferase Activities in the Liver of Rainbow Trout by b-naphthoflavone or Clophen A50. Biochem. Pharmacol. 34, 3309-3314.

Bagnasco, M., Camoirano, A., De Flora, S., Melodia, F., and Arillo, A., (1991): Enhanced Liver Metabolism of Mutagens and Carcinogens in Fish Living in Polluted Seawater. Mutat. Res. 262, 129-137.

Bainy, A.C.D., Saito, E., Carvalho, P.S.M., and Junquieira, V.B.C., (1996): Oxidative Stress in Gill, Erythrocytes, Liver and Kidney of Nile Tilapia (*Oreochromis niloticus*) from a Polluted Site. Aquat. Toxicol. 34, 151-162.

Bayne, B.L., Brown, D.A., Burns, K., Dixon, D.R., Ivanovici, A., Livingstone, D.A., Lowe, D.M., Moore, M.N., Stebbing, A.R.D., and Widdings, J., (1985): The Effects of Stress and Pollution on Marine Animals. Praeger, New York, USA.

Beyer, J., (1996): Fish Biomarkers in Marine Pollution Monitoring; Evaluation and Validation in Laboratory and Field Studies. Academic Thesis, University of Bergen, Norway.

Bonnineau, C., Moeller, A., Barata, C., Bonet, B., Proia, L., Sans-Piché, F., Schmitt-Jansen, M., Guasch, H. and Segner, H. (2012): Advances in the Multibiomarker Approach for Risk Assessment in Aquatic Ecosystems. In: Guasch H., Ginebreda A., and Geiszinger A. (Eds), The Handbook of Environmental Chemistry - Emerging and Priority Pollutants in Rivers: Bringing Science into River Management Plans, Vol. 19. Springer Berlin Heidelberg. pp. 147-179.

Braunbeck, T., and Völkl, A., (1991): Induction of Biotransformation in the Liver of eel (Anguilla anguilla L.) by Sublethal Exposure to dinitro-*o*-cresol: An Ultrastructural and Biochemical Study. Ecotoxicol. Environ. Safe 21, 109-127.

Bucheli, T.D. and Fent, K. (1995): Induction of Cytochrome P450 as a Biomarker for Environmental Contamination in Aquatic Ecosystems. Crit. Rev. Environ. Sci. Technol. 25, 201-268.

Burgeot, T., Bocquéné, G., Porte, C., Dimeet, J., Santella, R.M., Dimeet, J., Santella, R.M., Garcia de la Parra, L.M., Pftol-Leszkowicz, A., Raoux, C., and Galgani, F., (1996): Bioindicators of Pollutant Exposure in the Northwestern Mediterranean Sea. Mar. Ecol. Prog. Ser. 131, 125-141.

Burke, M.D., and Mayer, R.T., (1974): Ethoxyresorufin: Direct Fluorometric Assay of a Microsomal O-dealkylation which is Preferentially Inducible by 3-methylcholanthrene. Drug Metab. Dispos. 2, 583- 588.

Cairns, J, Jr. and Mount D.I., (1990): Aquatic Toxicology. Part 2. Environmental Science and Technology 24(2): 154-161.

Calabrese, E.J., (1991): Multiple Chemical Interactions. Lewis Publishers, Chelsea, MI, USA, p. 704.

Celander, M., (1993): Induction of Cytochrome P450 in Teleost Fish; with Emphasis on the CYP1 Gene Family. Academic Thesis, University of Göteborg, Sweden.

Chambers, J.E., (1979): Induction of Microsomal Mixed-function Oxidase System Components in Striped Mullet by Short-term Exposure to Crude Oil. Toxicol. Lett. 4, 227-230.

Chen, G., Xu, Y., Xu, L., Zheng, Y., Schramm, K.W., and Kettrup, A., (1998): Influence of Dioxin and Metal-contaminated Sediment on Phase I and II Biotransformation Enzymes in Silver Crucian Carp. Ecotoxicol. Environ. Safe 40, 234-238.

Choi, J., and Oris, J.T., (2000): Evidence of Oxidative Stress in Bluegill Sunfish (*Lepomis macrochirus*) Liver Microsomes Simultaneously Exposed to Solar Ultraviolet Radiation and Anthracene. Environ. Toxicol. Chem. 19, 1795-1799.

Clarke, D.J., Burchell, B., and George, S.C., (1992): Differential Expression and Induction of UDP-glucuronosyltransferase Isoforms in Hepatic and Extrahepatic Tissues of a Fish, Pleuronectus Platessa: Immunochemical and Functional Characterisation. Toxicol. Appl. Pharmacol. 115, 130-136.

Commandeur, J.N.M., Stijntjes, G.J., and Vermeulen, N.P.E., (1995): Enzymes and Transport Systems Involved in the Formation and Disposition of Glutathione S-conjugates. Role in Bioactivation and Detoxication Mechanisms of Xenobiotics. Pharmacol. Rev. 47, 271-330.

Cook, P.M., Zabel, E.W. and Peterson, R.E. (1997): The TCDD Toxicity Equivalence Approach for Characterizing Risks for Early Life-stage Mortality in Trout. In Chemically Induced Alterations in Functional Development and Reproduction of Fishes, Rolland, R.M.; Gilbertson, M. and Peterson, R.E. Editors, pp. 9-27, SETAC Press, Pensacola, FL, ISBN 1880611198, Racino, Wisconsin.

Curtis, L.R., Carpenter, H.M., Donohoe, R.M., Williams, D.E., Hedstrom, O.R., Deinzer, M.L., Bellstein, M.A., Foster, E., and Gates, R., (1993): Sensitivity of Cytochrome P450-1A1 Induction in Fish as a Biomarker for Distribution of TCDD and TCDF in the Willamette River, Oregon. Environ. Sci. Technol. 27, 2149-2157.

Depledge, M.H., and Fossi, M.C., (1994): The Role of Biomarkers in Environmental Assessment (2). Ecotoxicology 3, 161-172.

Di Giulio R.T. and Hinton D.E. (2008): The Toxicology of Fishes. Taylor and Francis, London.

Di Giulio, R.T., Benson, W.H., Sanders, B.M., and van Veld, P.A., (1995): Biochemical Mechanisms: Metabolism, Adaptation, and Toxicity. In: Rand, G.M. (Ed.), Fundamentals of Aquatic Toxicology: Effects, Environmental Fate, and Risk Assessment, Second ed.. Taylor and Francis, London, UK, pp. 523-562.

Di Giulio, R.T., Washburn, P.C., Wenning, R.J., Winston, G.W., and Jewell, C.S., (1989): Biochemical Responses in Aquatic Animals: A Review of Determinants of Oxidative Stress. Environ. Toxicol. Chem. 8, 1103-1123.

ECETOC, (1993): Environmental Hazard Assessment of Substances. European Centre for Ecotoxicology and Toxicology of Chemicals: Technical Report No. 51. Brussels, Belgium.

EPA, (2000): Stressor Identification Guidance Document. U.S. Environmental Protection Agency, Washington, DC.

Fent, K., and Bucheli, T.D., (1994): Inhibition of Hepatic Microsomal Monooxygenase System by Organotins *in vitro* in Freshwater Fish. Aquat. Toxicol. 28, 107-126.

Fent, K., Woodin, B.R., and Stegeman, J.J., (1998): Effects of Triphenyltin and Other Organotins on Hepatic Monooxygenase System in Fish. Comp. Biochem. Physiol. C Pharmacol. Toxicol. Endocrinol. 121, 277-288.

Fossi, M.C., and Marsili, L., (1997): The Use of Non-destructive Biomarkers in the Study of Marine Mammals. Biomarkers 2, 205-216.

Freeman B.A., and Crapo J.D., (1982): Biology of Disease, Free Radicals and Tissue Injury. Lab. Invest. 47:412-26.

Gabryelak, T., and Klekot, J., (1985): The Effect of Paraquat on the Peroxide Metabolism Enzymes in Erythrocytes of Freswater Fish Species. Comp. Biochem. Physiol. 81C, 415-418.

George, S.G., (1994): Enzymology and Molecular Biology of Phase II Xenobiotic-conjugating Enzymes in Fish. In: Malins, D.C., Ostrander, G.K. (Eds.), Aquatic Toxicology; Molecular, Biochemical and Cellular Perspectives. Lewis Publishers, CRC press, pp. 37-85.

Goeptar, A.R., Scheerens, H., and Vermeulen, N. P. (1995): Oxygen and Xenobiotic Reductase Activities of Cytochrome P450. CRC Critical Reviews in Toxicology, 25(1), 25-65.

Goksøyr, A., and Förlin, L., (1992): The Cytochrome P450 System in Fish, Aquatic Toxicology and Environmental Monitoring. Aquat. Toxicol. 22, 287-312.

Goksøyr, A., and Larsen, E., (1991): The Cytochrome P450 System of Atlantic Salmon (*Salmo salar*): I. Basal Properties and Induction of P450 1A1 in Liver of Immature and Mature Fish. Fish Physiol. Biochem. 9, 339-349.

Gutteridge J.M.C., and Halliwell B., (1990): The Measurement and the Mechanism of Lipid Peroxidation in Biological Systems. Trends Biochem. Sci. 15: 129-35.

Hageman, J.J., Bast, A., and Vermeulen, N.P.E., (1992): Monitoring of Oxidative Free Radical Damage *in vivo*: Analytical Aspects. Chem.- Biol. Interact. 82, 243-293.

Hai, D.Q., Varga, I.S., and Matkovics, B., (1995): Effects of an Organophosphate on the Antioxidant Systems of Fish Tissues. Acta Biol. Hungar. 46, 39-50.

Halliwell, B., and Gutteridge J.M.C., (1999): Free Radicals in Biology and Medicine, Third ed.. Oxford University Press, Oxford, UK.

Hayes, J.D., and Pulford, D.J., (1995): The Glutathione S-transferase Supergene Family: Regulation of GST and the Contribution of the Isoenzymes to Cancer Chemoprotection and Drug Resistance. Crit. Rev. Biochem. Mol. Biol. 30, 445-600.

Hektoen, H., Bernloft, A., Ingebrigtsen, K., Skaare, J.U., and Goksøyr, A., (1994): Response of Hepatic Xenobiotic Metabolizing Enzymes in Rainbow Trout (*Oncorhynchus mykiss*) and cod (*Gadus morhua*) to 2,3,7,8-tetrachlorodibenzo-p -dioxin (2,3,7,8-TCDD). Aquat. Toxicol. 28, 97-106.

Huuskonen, S., and Lindström-Seppä, P., (1995): Hepatic Cytochrome P4501A and Other Biotransformation Activities in Perch (*Perca fluviatilis*): The Effects of Unbleached Pulp Mill Effluents. Aquat. Toxicol. 31, 27-41.

Jung, D.K.J., Klaus, T., and Fent, K., (2001): Cytochrome P450 Induction by Nitrated Polycyclic Aromatic Hydrocarbons, Azaarenes, and Binary Mixtures in Fish Hepatoma Cell Line PLHC-1. Environ. Toxicol. Chem. 20, 149-159.

Kasper, C.B., and Henton, D., (1980): Glucuronidation. In: Jakoby, W.B. (Ed.), Enzymatic Basis of Detoxication, Vol. II. Academic Press, New York, pp. 3-36.

Klaassen, C.D., (2008): Cazarett and Doull's Toxicology the Basic Science of Poisons, (Seventh Edition), McGraw-Hill, ISBN 0071470514, New York.

Kloepper-Sams, P.J., and Stegeman, J.J., (1992): Effects of Temperature Acclimation on the Expression of Hepatic Cytochrome P4501A mRNA and Protein in the Fish Fundulus Heteroclitus. Arch. Biochem. Biophys. 299, 38-46.

Lauterburg, B.H., Smith, C.V., Hughes, H., and Mitchell, J.R., (1983): Determinants of Hepatic Glutathione Turnover: Toxicological Significance. In: Lamble, J.W. (Ed.), Drug Metabolism and Distribution. Elsevier Biomedical Press, Amsterdam, Netherlands, pp. 166-180.

Lech, J.J., and Vodicnik, M.J., (1985): Biotransformation. In: Rand, G.M., Petrocelli, S.R. (Eds.), Fundamentals of Aquatic Toxicology; Methods and Applications. Hemisphere Publishing Corporation, New York, USA, pp. 526-557.

Lemaire, P., Förlin, L., and Livingstone, D., (1996): Responses of Hepatic Biotransformation and Antioxidant Enzymes to CYP1A-inducers (3-methylcholanthrene, b-naphthoflavone) in sea bass (*Dicentrarchus labrax*), dab (*Limanda limanda*) and rainbow trout (*Oncorhynchus mykiss*). Aquat. Toxicol. 36, 141-160.

Levine, S.L., and Oris, J.T., (1997): Induction of CYP 1A mRNA and Catalytic Activity in Gizzard shad (*Dorosoma cepedianum*) after Waterborne Exposure to benzo[a]pyrene. Comp. Biochem. Physiol. C. Pharmacol. Toxicol. Endocrinol. 118, 397-404.

Lindstriöm-Seppä, P., and Oikari, A., (1989): Biotransformation and Other Physiological Responses in Whitefish Caged in a Lake Receiving Pulp and Paper Mill Effluents. Ecotoxical. Environ. Saf. 18, 191-203.

Lindström-Seppä, P., and Oikari, A., (1990): Biotransformation and Other Toxicological and Physiological Responses in Rainbow Trout (*Salmo gairdneri* Richardson) Caged in a Lake Receiving Effluents of Pulp and Paper Industry. Aquat. Toxicol. 16, 187-204.

Lindström-Seppä, P., and Oikari, A., (1991): Biotransformation Activities of Feral Fish in Waters Receiving Bleached Pulp Mill Effluents. Environ. Toxicol. Chem. 9, 1415-1424.

Lindström-Seppä, P., Roy, S., Huuskonen, S., Tossavainen, K., Ritola, O., and Marin, E., (1996): Biotransformation and Glutathione Homeostasis in Rainbow Trout Exposed to Chemical and Physical Stress. Mar. Environ. Res. 42, 323-327.

Livingstone, D.R., Lemaire, P., Mathews, A., Peters, L., Bucke, D., and Law, R.J., (1993): Pro-oxidant, Antioxidant and 7-ethoxyresorufin O-deethylase (EROD) Activity Responses in Liver of dab (*Limanda limanda*) Exposed to Sediment Contaminated with Hydrocarbons and Other Chemicals. Marine Pollition Bull. 26, 602-606.

Lu, A.Y.H., Junk, K.W., and Coon, M.J., (1969): Resolution of the Cytochrom P450 Containing Hydroxylation System of Liver Microsomes into Three Components. J. Biol. Chem. 244, 3714-3721.

Machala, M., Drabek, P., Neca, J., Kolarova, J., and Svobodova, Z., (1998): Biochemical Markers for Differentiation of Exposures to Nonplanar Polychlorinated Biphenyls, Organochlorine Pesticides, or 2, 3, 7, 8- tetrachlorodibenzo-p -dioxin in Trout Liver. Ecotoxicol. Environ. Safe 41, 107-111.

Mather-Mihaich, E., and Di Giulio, R.T., (1991): Oxidant, Mixed-function Oxidase and Peroxisomal Responses in Channel Catfish Exposed to a Bleached Kraft Mill Effluent. Arch. Environ. Contam. Toxicol. 20, 391-397.

McCarthy, L.S., and Munkittrick, K.R., (1996): Environmental Biomarkers in Aquatic Ecology: Fiction, Fantasy or Functional?. Human and Ecological Risk Assessment. 268-274.

McCarthy, J.F., Halbrook, R.S., and Shugart, L.R. (1991): Conceptual Strategy for Design, Implementation, and Validation of a Biomarkerbased Biomonitoring Capability. Publication No. 3072, ORNL/TM- 11783. Environmental Sciences Division, Oak Ridge National Laboratory, Tennessee, USA.

McCarthy, J.F., and Shugart, L.R., (1990): Biological Markers of Environmental Contamination. In: McCarthy, J.F., Shugart, L.R. (Eds.), Biomarkers of Environmental Contamination. Lewis Publishers, Boca Raton, FL, USA, pp. 3-16.

Monod, G., Devaux, A., and Riviere, J.L., (1988): Effects of Chemical Pollution on the Activities of Hepatic Xenobiotic Metabolizing Enzymes in Fish from the River Rho^ne. Sci. Total Environ. 73, 189-201.

Monserrat, J.M., Martínez P.E., Geracitano L.A., Amado L.L., Gaspar Martins C.M., Leães Pinho G.L., Chaves I.S., Ferreira-Cravo M., Ventura-Lima J., and Bianchini A. (2007): Pollution Biomarkers in Estuarine Animals: Critical Review and New Perspectives. Comparative Biochemistry and Physiology, Part C 146: 221-234.

Mulder, G.J., Coughty, M.W.H., and Burchell, B., (1990): Glucuronidation. In: Mulder, G.J. (Ed.), Conjugation Reactions in Drug Metabolism; An Integrated Approach. Taylor and Francis, London.

Narbonne, J.F., and Gallis, J.L., (1979): In vivo and *in vitro* Effect of Phenoclor DP6 on Drug Metabolizing Activity in Mullet Liver. Bull. Environ. Contam. Toxicol. 23, 338-343.

Nebert, D.W., Peterson, D.D., and Fornace, A.J., (1990): Cellular Responses to Oxidative Stress: the [Ah] gene Battery as a Paradigm. Environ. Health Perspect. 88, 13-25.

NRC: Committee on Biological Markers of the National Research Council, (1987): Biological Markers in Environmental Health Research. Environmental Health Perspectives 74, 3-9.

Oikari, A., and Jimenez, B., (1992): Effects of Hepatotoxicants on the Induction of Microsomal Monooxygenase Activity in Sunfish Liver by b-naphtoflavone and benzo[a]pyrene. Ecotoxicol. Environ. Safe 23, 89-102.

Otto, D.M.E., Buttner, J.K., Arquette, D.M., and Moon, T.W., (1996): Impaired Inducibility of Xenobiotic and Antioxidant Responses in Rainbow Trout Exposed to Polychlorinated biphenyl Contaminated Sediments in the St. Lawrence River. Chemosphere 33, 2021-2032.

Otto, D.M.E., and Moon, T.W., (1995): 3, 3□, 4, 4□-tetrachlorobiphenyl Effects on Antioxidant Enzymes and Glutathione Status in Different Tissues of Rainbow Trout. Pharmacol. Toxicol. 77, 281-287.

Otto, D.M.E., and Moon, T.W., (1996): Phase I and II Enzymes and Antioxidant Responses in Different Tissues of Brown Bullheads from Relatively Polluted and Non-polluted Systems. Arch. Environ. Contam. Toxicol. 31, 141-147.

Oude Ophuis, M.B., van Lieshout, E.M., Roelofs, H.M., Peters, W.H., and Manni, J.J., (1998): Glutathione S-transferase M1 and T1 and cytochrome P4501A1 Polymorphisms in Relation to the Risk for Benign and Malignant Head and Neck Lesions. Cancer. 82: 5, 936-943.

Palace, V.P., Dick, T.A., Brown, S.B., Baron, C.L., and Klaverkamp, J.F., (1996): Oxidative Stress in Lake Sturgeon (*Acipenser fulvescens*) Orally Exposed to 2, 3, 7, 8-tetrachlorodibenzofuran. Aquat. Toxicol. 35, 79-92.

Peakall D.B., and Walker, C.H., (1994): The Role of Biomarkers in Environmental Risk Assessment (3): Vertebrates. Ecotoxicology. 3: 173-179.

Pedrajas, J.R., Peinado, J., and Lopez-Barea, J., (1995): Oxidative Stress in Fish Exposed to Model Xenobiotics. Oxidatively Modified Forms of Cu, Zn-superoxide Dismutase as Potential Biomarkers. Chem. Biol. Interact. 98, 267-282.

Pesonen, M., Andersson, T.B., Sorri, V., and Korkalainen, M., (1999): Biochemical and Ultrastructural Changes in the Liver of Baltic Salmon sac Fry Suffering from High Mortality (M74). Environ. Toxicol. Chem. 18, 1007-1013.

Peters, L.D., Porte, C., Albaige´s, J., and Livingstone, D.R., (1994): 7- Ethoxyresorufin O-deethylase (EROD) and Antioxidant Enzyme Activities in Larvae of Sardine (*Sardina Pilchardus*) from the North Coast of Spain. Mar. Pollut. Bull. 28, 299-304.

Ploch, S.A., Lee, Y.-P., MacLean, E., and Di Giulio, R.T., (1999): Oxidative Stress in Liver of Brown Bullhead and Channel Catfish Following Exposure to Tert -butyl Hydroperoxide. Aquat. Toxicol. 46, 231-240.

Powers, D.A., (1989): Fish as Model Systems. Science 246, 352-358.

Preston, B., and Shackelford, J., (2002): Multiple Stressor Effects on Benthic Biodiversity of Chesapeake Bay: Implications for Ecological Risk Assessment. Ecotoxicology 11: 85-99.

Rice, C.D., and Roszell, L.E., (1998): Tributyltin Modulates 3,3□, 4, 4□, 5- pentachlorobiphenyl (PCB 126)-induced hepatic CYP1A activity in channel catfish, Ictalurus punctatus . J. Toxicol. Environ. Health 55, 197-212.

Roberts, M.H., Sved, D.W., and Felton, S.P., (1987): Temporal Changes in AHH and SOD Activities in Feral Spot from the Elizabeth River, a Polluted Sub-estuary. Mar. Environ. Res. 23, 89-101.

Rodriguez-Ariza, A., Martinez-Lara, E., Pascual, P., Pedrajas, J.R., Abril, N., Dorado, G., Toribio, F., Barcena, J.A., Peinado, J., Pueyo, C., and Lopez-Barea, J., (1993): Biochemical and Genetic Indices of Marine Pollution in Spanish Littoral. Sci. Total Environ. Suppl. 1, 109-116.

Rojas-Garciìa AE, Medina-Diìaz IM, Robledo-Marenco ML, Barroìn-Vivanco BS and Peìrez-Herrera N (2011): Pesticide Biomarkers, Pesticides in the Modern World - Pests Control and Pesticides Exposure and Toxicity Assessment, Dr. Margarita Stoytcheva (Ed.), ISBN: 978-953-307-457-3, InTech, Available from: http://www.intechopen.com/books/pesticides-in-the-modern-world-pests-control-and-pesticides-exposure-andtoxicity-assessment/pesticide-biomarkers

Romeo, M., Bennani, N., Gnassia-Barelli, M., Lafaurie, M., and Girard, J.P., (2000): Cadmium and Copper Display Different Responses Towards Oxidative Stress in the Kidney of the Sea Bass *Dicentrarchus labrax*. Aquat. Toxicol. 48, 185-194.

Rose, R. L., and Hodgson, E. (2004): Metabolism of Toxicants. In: Hodgson, E. (Ed.), A Textbook of Modern Toxicology, Third Edition. John Wiley and Sons, Inc. pp. 111-148.

Roy, S., Lindström-Seppä, P., Huuskonen, S., and Hänninen, O., (1995): Responses on Biotransformation and Antioxidant Enzymes in *Lemna minor* and *Oncorhynchus mykiss* Simultaneously to Hexaclorobenzene. Chemosphere 30, 1489-1498.

Rudneva-Titova, I.I., and Zherko, N.V., (1994): Effects of Polychlorinated Biphenyls on the Activity of Anti-oxidant Enzymes and Lipid Peroxidation in Muscle and Liver of Two Black Sea Fish Species. Biochemistry (Moscow) 59, 25-31.

Schlenk, D., (1999) Necessity of defi ning Biomarkers for Use in Ecological Risk Assessments. Mar Poll Bull 39: 48-53.

Sedeño-Díaz, J. E., and López-López, E. (2012): Freshwater Fish as Sentinel Organisms: From the Molecular to the Population Level, a Review. In: New Advances and Contributions to Fish Biology, Prof. Hakan Turker (Ed.), pp 151-173.

Shugart, L.R., McCarthy, J.F., and Halbrook, R.S., (1992): Biological Markers of Environmental and Ecological Contamination: An Overview. Risk Analysis. 12: 353-360.

Shugart, L.R, (2005): Biomarker Environmental, In: Enciclopedia of Toxicology, Wexler P., (Editor in Chief), pp. 287-290.

Sijm, D.T.H.M., and Opperhuizen, A., (1989): Biotransformation of Organic Chemicals by Fish: Enzyme Activities and Reactions. In: Hutzinger, O. (Ed.), Handbook of Environmental Chemistry Reactions and Processes, Vol. 2E. Springer, Berlin, pp. 163-235.

Sole, M., Porte, C., and Barcelo, D., (2000): Vitellogenin Induction and Other Biochemical Responses in Carp, *Cyprinus carpio*, After Experimental Injection with 17 alpha-ethynylestradiol. Arch. Environ. Toxicol. 38, 494-500.

Stegeman, J.J., Brower M., Di Giulio R.T., Förlin L., Fowler B.A., Sanders B.M., Van Veld P.A., (1992): Molecular Responses to Environmental Contamination: Enzyme and Protein Systems as Indicators of Chemical Exposure and Effect. In: RJ Huggett, Kimerle RA, Mehrle Jr PP, Bergman HL (eds) Biomarkers: Biochemical, Physiological and Histological Markers of Anthropogenic Stress. Lewis, Chelsea, MI, pp. 235-335.

Stephensen, E., Svavarsson, J., Sturve, J., Ericson, G., Adolfsson- Erici, M., and Förlin, L., (2000): Biochemical Indicators of Pollution Exposure in Shorthorn Sculpin (*Myoxocephalus scorpius*), Caught in Four Harbours on the Southwest Coast of Iceland. Aquat. Toxicol. 48, 431-442.

Suter, G., (1993): Ecological Risk Assessment. Boca Raton, FL (USA): Lewis Publishers.

Sutter, T.R., and Greenlee, W.F., (1992): Classification of Members of the Ah Gene Battery. Chemosphere 25, 223-226.

Teraoka, H; Dong, W; Tsujimoto, Y; Iwasa, H; Endoh, D; Ueno, N; Stegeman, J.J; Peterson, R.E. and Hiraga, T., (2003): Induction of Cytochrome P450 1A is Required for Circulation Failure and Edema by 2, 3, 7, 8–tetrachlorodibenzo-p-dioxin in Zebrafish. Biochemical and Biophysical Research Communications, Vol. 304, No. 2, (May 2003), pp. 223-228.

Timbrell, J.A., (1991): Principles of Biochemical Toxicology, Second Edition. Taylor and Francis, London.

Tjärnlund, U., Ericson, G., Lindesjöö , E., Petterson, I., .Åkerman, G., and Balk, L., (1996): Further Studies of the Effects of Exhaust from Two Stroke Outboard Motors on Fish. Mar. Environ. Res. 42, 267-271.

Van der Aar, E.M., Buikema, D., Commandeur, J.N.M., te Koppele, J.M., van Ommen, B., van Bladeren, P.J., and Vermeulen, N.P.E., (1996): Enzyme Kinetics and Substrate Selectivities of rat glutathione S-transferase Isoenzymes Towards a Series of New 2-substituted 1-chloro-4-nitrobenzenes. Xenobiotica 26, 143-155.

Van der Oost, R., Beyer, J., and Vermeulen, N. P. (2003): Fish Bioaccumulation and Biomarkers in Environmental Risk Assessment: A Review. Environmental Toxicology and Pharmacology, 13(2), 57-149.

Van der Oost, R., Goksøyr, A., Celander, M., Heida, H., and Vermeulen, N.P.E., (1996): Biomonitoring Aquatic Pollution with Feral eel (*Anguilla anguilla*): II. Biomarkers: Pollution-induced Biochemical Responses. Aquat. Toxicol. 36, 189-222.

Van der Oost, R., Lopes, S.C.C., Komen, H., Satumalay, K., van den Bos, R., Heida, H., and Vermeulen, N.P.E., (1998): Assessment of Environmental Quality and Inland Water Pollution Using Biomarker Responses in Caged Carp (*Cyprinus carpio*); Use of a Bioactivation:-Detoxication Ratio as Biotransformation Index (BTI). Mar. Environ. Pollut. 46, 315-319.

Van der Oost, R., van Gastel, L., Worst, D., Hanraads, M., Satumalay, K., van Schooten, F.J., Heida, H., and Vermeulen, N.P.E., (1994): Biochemical Markers in Feral Roach (*Rutilus rutilus*) in Relation to the Bioaccumulation of Organic Trace Pollutants. Chemosphere 29, 801-817.

Van Gestel, C.A.M., and Van Brummelen, T.C., (1996): Incorporation of the Biomarker Concept in Ecotoxicology Calls for a Redefinition of Terms. Ecotoxicology. 5: 217-225.

Van Veld, P.A., Vogelbein, W.K., Cochran, M.K., Goksøyr, A., and Stegeman, J.J., (1997): Route-specific Cellular Expression of Cytochrome P4501A (CYP1A) in Fish (*Fundulus heteroclitus*) Following Exposure to Aqueous and Dietary benzo[a]pyrene. Toxicol. Appl. Pharmacol. 142, 348-359.

Vermeulen, N.P.E., (1996): Role of Metabolism in Chemical Toxicity. In: Ioannides, C. (Ed.), Cytochromes P450: Metabolic and Toxicological Aspects. CRC Press, Boca Raton, FL, USA, pp. 29-53.

Vig, E., and Nemcsok, J., (1989): The Effects of Hypoxia and Paraquat on the Superoxide Dismutase Activity in Different Organs of the Carp, *Cyprinus carpio* L. J. Fish Biol. 35, 23-25.

White, R.D., Shea, D., Solow, A.R., and Stegeman, J.J., (1997): Induction and Post-transcriptional Suppression of Hepatic Cytochrome P450 1A1 by 3, 3□, 4, 4□-tetrachlorobiphenyl. Biochem. Pharmacol. 53, 1029-1040.

Whyte, J.J., Jung, R.E., Schmitt, C.J., and Tillitt, D.E., (2000): Ethoxyresorufin- O-deethylase (EROD) Activity in Fish as a Biomarker of Chemical Exposure. Crit. Rev. Toxicol. 30, 347-570.

Winston, G.W., and Di Giulio, R.T., (1991): Prooxidant and Antioxidant Mechanisms in Aquatic Organisms. Aquat. Toxicol. 19, 137-161.

Worthington, D.J., and Rosemeyer, M.A., (1974): Human Glutathione Reductase: Purification of the Crystalline Enzym from Erythrocytes. Eur. J. Biochem. 48, 167-177.

Pages: 26-37

FISH HABITAT AND AQUACULTURE
Edited by: **Dr. Sanjay Kumar Gupta; Dr. Pawan Kumar 'Bharti'**
ISBN: 978-93-5056-744-9
Edition: **2015**
Published by: **Discovery Publishing House Pvt. Ltd., New Delhi (India)**

2

Multi-faceted Role of Mussels

U.L. Mohanty and **Shailesh Saurabh**

ABSTRACT

Freshwater mussels are long-lived, benthic aquatic organisms having more than 840 species globally. These species bear ecological, nutritional, medicinal and economical importance. In this chapter, an attempt has been made to discuss the multi-faceted role of mussels, which will not only help the farmers to generate extra income, but also they will utilize their time judiciously by taking interest in engineering other useful items prepared from shell material. The Central Institute of Freshwater Aquaculture is working on freshwater pearl mussels, *Lamellidens marginalis, L. corrianus* and *Parreysia corrugata* for freshwater pearl production and also taken the lead to disseminate the technology of freshwater pearl culture to the fish farming communities, entrepreneurs, researchers and students of the country. In conclusion, some species of freshwater mussels, especially *L. marginalis* provides a wonderful opportunity for income generation and nutrition, not only by providing pearly gem and cheap protein and dietary factors, but also providing antioxidants effective against many diseases.

Keywords: Mussels, Food, Pearl, industry, biocompatible nucleus, Handicrafts, Biological indicator.

INTRODUCTION

The molluscs or mollusks compose the largest phylum of invertebrate animals known as the Mollusca, second only to arthropods in numbers of living animal species. The word mollusk originated from the Latin word molluscus, which derivedfrom word 'mollis' meaning soft. They live in a wide rangeof habitat viz. terrestrial, marine and freshwater. They are highly diverse, not only in their habitat, but also in size, anatomical structure and in behavior. Freshwater mussels are mollusks which are coming under class Bivalvia which comprises about 14% of total molluscan species. They are similar to marine clam and oyster cousins. They have two shells connected by a hinge-like ligament. Around the world, mussels live in a variety of freshwater habitats ranging from derelict pond water to the flow through streams and rivers.

This primitive animal has shown its versatile uses in many aspects of scientific research. From an economic perspective, mussels have been valued for their beauty, shell material, and natural pearls for centuries. Unfortunately, this has also led to the overharvesting of mussel resources. In addition to its best uses in pearl industries, the shell of mollusks has quantified uses in pharmaceutical, lime, dye and so many. In this chapter, an attempt has been made to discuss the multi-faceted role of mussels, which not only enable the entrepreneurs to utilize this species in a multifold dimension, but also helps to generate extra income by utilizing this species in a various ways which are discussed elsewhere in this chapter.

MUSSEL AS FOOD AND FEED

(A) As human food

Freshwater mussel, *Lamellidens marginalis* earns its importance as a dietary item of rural and tribal populationof India (Subba Rao and Dey, 1989; Chakraborty *et al.*, 2010). It is reported that some Communitiesuse freshwater mussels and other molluscan species as food in their diet (Panda and Misra, 2007). About 250 to 350 kg of molluscan species are sold in daily in Imphal market (Ramakrishna and Dey, 2007). We have also observed that many molluscan species are used as food in Meghalaya and sold at Garo market in Shillong. Details are presented in table 2.1. Recently Jha *et al.* (2014) reported that freshwater bivalves *Lamellidens* and *Parreysia* contain 59-62% and 57-61% protein respectively. They also reported that PUFA is higher in genus *Lamellidens* whereas EPA is higher in genus *Parreysia*. Thus, these species are useful for the extraction of omega 3 oil for the benefit of human health. The freshwater bivalves could thus prove to be the best and cheap source of nutritious food. These study not only helpful for farmers interested in bivalve cultivation, but also useful to small and medium entrepreneurs for exploring the economic advantage of these species.

Table 2.1: Mussels Used as Human Food

Sl. No.	Species	State
1.	*Lamellidens marginalis*	Jharkhand, Odisha, West Bengal, Meghalaya
2.	*L. corrianus*	Manipur, Jharkhand, Odisha, West Bengal
3.	*L. generosus*	Manipur
4.	*L. phenchooganjensis*	Mizoram
5.	*Parreysia burmanus*	Manipur
6.	*P. flavidens*	Jharkhand, Odisha, West Bengal, Manipur, Mizoram
7.	*P. sikkimensis*	Manipur, Mizoram
8.	*P. caerulea*	Jharkhand, Odisha, West Bengal, Mizoram
9.	*P. occata*	Manipur

(B) Food for lower animals

Freshwater mussels maintain a remarkable position in the aquatic food chain. Historically, Native Americans were eating freshwater mussels, but its chewy consistency and unpleasant taste made them lost from present consumption (Parmalee and Klippel, 1974). The flesh of mussel is rich in nutrients and protein. Hence this is used as one of the feed ingredients for poultry, prawn and other carnivorous fish. In Spain mussel shells have been used as an animal feed additive. Even ducks, geese and flatworms have also been known to eat these invertebrates.

MUSSELS USED FOR PEARL PRODUCTION

Pearly mussels are among the most imperiled of all organisms around the world (Strayer *et al.*, 2004). During the mid-1800s, freshwater mussels were commonly collected by people seeking fortune in the form of freshwater pearls. Following a valuable discovery, successive collecting often led to the wholesale destruction of entire mussel beds (Anthony and Downing, 2001). The foundation of natural pearl formation by mussels is calcium carbonate in the form of aragonite crystals, secreted essentially by the epithelial cells of mantle tissue as nacre. Only very few species of freshwater mussels are responsible for pearl production. Naturally, the nacre would surround the nuclei injected into the living mussel and over time add layers upon layers of calcium carbonate making the pearl. In India it has been successfully done with only three species viz. *L. marginalis, L. corrianus* and *P. corrugata*. Only that mussel which carries the pearl mother layer can give birth to a pearl in an immune phagocytic defensive method when a foreign particle invades into the mantle and gets stuck there. In Vietnam and other countries like Japan, China and India etc., the culture of mussels to produce pearl is carried out by combining natural conditions with core and tissue implanting (Janakiram, 2003). This method brings a good result, increasing the pearl yield, reducing time, thus the profit is higher.

To develop human resource on freshwater pearl culture in the country, pearl culture unit of CIFA conducts hands on national training on freshwater pearl culture for the progressive pearl growers and government officials. The schedule of the training programme is advertised every year on CIFA website. Interested participants may also contact the Director, CIFA on this aspect.

MUSSEL SHELL IN PREPARATION OF BIOCOMPATIBLE NUCLEUS

The pearl culture unit of CIFA has developed the technology of nucleus preparation from indigenous raw materials which was found to be at par with the imported shell-made nuclear bead. The indigenous nuclei developed are made from inexpensive and locally available ingredient like stelon material, egg-shell powder or mussel shell powder. The procedure for the preparation of these nuclei is fairly simple and most importantly it is found to be accepted by the mussels resulting best quality pearls comparable with the pearls from imported shell beads.

For the preparation of the designer pearl nucleus, dead shells of freshwater mussels are collected and wash thoroughly in tap water in order to remove mud and sand particles. The dry flesh materials, if present, are scraped out. The shells are then dipped in 5000 ppm of chlorine solution for 5 days. The completely lye-peeled shells are sorted out and are then thoroughly washed in tap water. They are then kept in an oven maintained at 60°C, for more than two hours or can even be sun dried for a longer duration to ensure the complete removal of chlorine from the treated shells. The dried shells are made into small pieces by using a mortar and pestle and are then finely powdered by means of an electric grinder. The powdered shells are then processed through a sieve of 0.01-0.05 mm mesh size. The commercial glue Araldite hardener and resin (acts as a binder) are mixed in a ratio of 1:1 to prepare a paste. To this paste the sieved shell powder is added gradually to prepare dough of thick consistency. The ratio of the shell powder to the paste should be 5:1. Immediately, nuclei of desired shape and size are prepared using designer die and then air dried till they become hard. Prior to implantation, the nuclei are boiled in water and cooled.

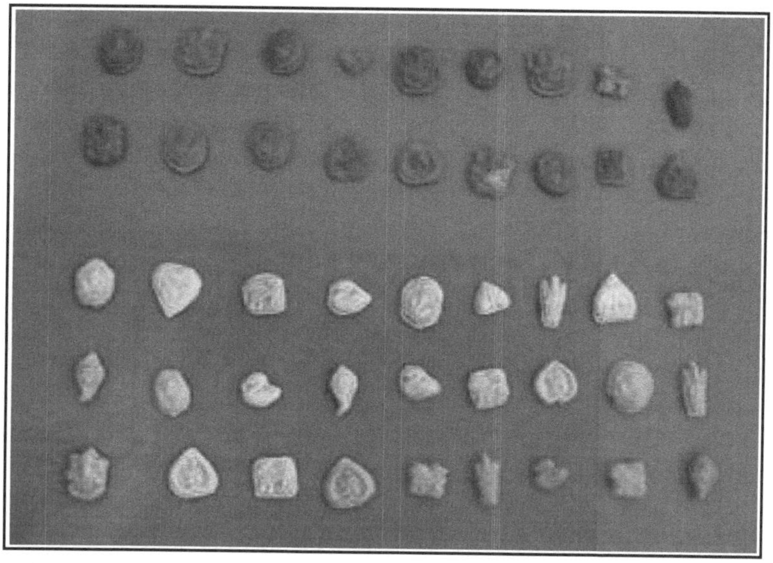

SHELLS USED IN BUTTON INDUSTRY

Before the advent of plastics in the 1800's and early 1900's, most buttons for clothing were made from mussel shells (Coker, 1919). This industry created buttons from the durable hard and shining shells of freshwater mussels. Thousands of tons of shells were harvested in Eastern North America from the late 1800s to the mid-1900s raise the button industry. To make good quality buttons, the nacre or mother-of-pearl should be white, preferably iridescent, and neither brittle nor chalky. The shell should be large enough to furnish several button blanks and the thicker the better. Mainly mussels from rivers like Illinois, Mississippi and streams are harvested and shipped to the Button industries for further processing. Some of the preferred kinds for buttons are the Mucket, Pocketbook, Three-ridge, Pimpleback, Heelsplitter and Buckhorn.

USE OF SHELL IN PHARMACEUTICAL AND COSMETIC COMPANIES

The substances/molecules isolated from bivalves are used in the treatment of antithrombotic, extravasations agent, arthritis, ischemic heart disease and hyperlipidemia. Chondroitin is a low molecular compound, a medicine for arthritis, is naturally occurring substance in the body of mussels and is responsible for the elasticity of cartilage. Along with glucosamine, chondroitin sulfate has become a widely used dietary supplement for treatment of osteoarthritis. The ground and processed oyster shells are used as calcium supplements both for human and animals. In Vietnam a wide variety of shells are used as traditional medicine.

Powdered oyster shell is taken to treat acid indigestion, fatigue and to stop hemorrhage. It is also sprinkled over open wounds and boils. Powdered pearls from oysters are used as a tropical eye medicine and it has been scientifically proven to have some anti-inflammatory effects on a painful condition called conjunctivitis, where the surface of the eyes becomes red and sore (Kim and Pallela, 2012). Powdered pearl also has a long history of use in face and body powders. It is composed of aragonite (a form of calcium carbonate) held together by the protein conchiolin which forms a soft, fine, white powder with a fine lustre when ground. The practice of powdering pearls for use in cosmetics may have started in China where it continues to this day.

Prabhakar and Roy (2009) showed that the foot portion of mollusk is eaten for its ethnomedicinal benefits in North-Bihar, India. It is reported that polyphenols protein secreted from the specialized phenol glands of the mussel foot (Padro *et al.,* 1990), act as the main antioxidants of mussels in pollution defence (Moncheva *et al.,* 2004). Chakraborty *et al.* (2012) showed that the edible portion of Indian freshwater mussel, *L. marginalis* contains antioxidants, particularly the unique phenolic proteins that are effective in the prevention of arthritis, a chronic inflammatory disease. Hence this makes this mussel a suitable candidate in the design of integrated nutritional approach.

USE OF SHELLS AS TOOLS

Prehistoric American Indians used shells to make a variety of tools. They were using shells to scrape maize kernel from cobs during harvest. It is found in Odisha too,the tribal people use sharpened mussel shells to peel off mangoes. Moreover, the Archaeological excavations show the evidences that the people of North America were using the mussel shells to temper pottery, utensils and for the making of tools like Shovels, plow blades and hoes for tilling the soil, fishing gear.In prawn hatcheries, it has been an indigenous practice to suspend the strings of shells for shelter of post larvae, as well as their harvest from the rearing tanks.

USE OF SHELL IN LIME INDUSTRY

The shell is a composite biomaterial, of which the mineral portion, calcium carbonate, accounts for 95-99% by weight and the remaining 1-5% is the organic matrix (Marin and Luquet, 2004), and small amounts of other elements viz., nitrogen, sulfur, phosphorus, potassium and magnesium. Hence, this CaCO3 can be best utilized for liming (Álvarez-Rodríguez *et al.*, 2009). Different communities inhabiting in the coastal area of the Ganjam district, Orissa have traditionally been engaged in the mussel shell collection. These shells are used for various purposes in very indigenous ways. Other than making decorative, they use them in preparation of lime. This lime is being used for white washing and in preparation of various types of tobacco products, cement, bleaching powder, in making Unani medicines, jagerry industries and in country liquor distillation units (Naidu and Misra, 1998; Pattanayak and Misra, 2004; Panda and Misra, 2007).

USE OF SHELLS AS DECORATIVE (HANDICRAFTS)

Shell crafts remain a distinctive form of decoration. Many of the art forms of today started in the early eighteenth century. The chief credit for making shell work so popular and fashionable goes to England, but culture of France and many countries also use shell decorative for their home. Oil lamps made from shells are found throughout the Middle East. India is not behind it in these days. This easy to handle trade can be taken up by women self-help groups (WSHGs) in both rural and urban sectors for making small decorative and handicrafts for income generation. The items may be like paper weights, pen/ mobile phone stand, ashtray, oil lamp, key stand etc. The same can be done easily from the shells of Indian pearl mussel, *L. marginalis.*Very recently the polished shells are too used for decorating the fish aquaria. The mother pearl layer is also directly crafted into ornaments. One can generate good profit out of these handicraft products.

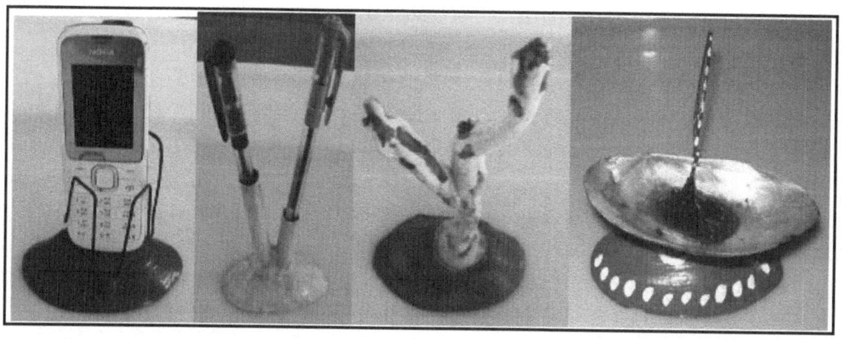

BIOLOGICAL INDICATOR

The bivalve mollusks are sedentary filter-feeding aquatic invertebrates which can bioaccumulate pollutants, thus considered ideal species for investigating the effects of environmental contaminants on aquatic invertebrates (Wootton *et al.*, 2003; Ray *et al.*, 2013). Bivalves often studied as models to assess and evaluate the effects of exposure to various toxins and heavy metals (Zhou *et al.*, 2008).They are commonly labeled as "good" indicators of biological integrity and water quality. Their potential decline in an area could indicate that pollution is spreading and affecting the decline of the water quality. The Rainbow mussels (*Villosa iris*) have been used extensively as a surrogate to evaluate the effects of various toxic contaminants (Mummert *et al.*, 2003; Wang *et al.*, 2007a, b). Augspurger (2006) and March *et al.* (2007) placed this mussel among the most sensitive aquatic organism to copper and ammonia. Some studies have shown that radio nucleotides and metals like uranium and lead etc. significantly concentrate in the outer periostracal layer of the shells exposed to the environment, concentrated with these elements (Widdows and Donkin, 1992). Also, studies have been made that some anti-fouling agents like tributyl tin (TBT), cause shell deformities creating cavities in it. Gorinstein *et al.* (2006) reported changes in the mussel protein profile as a reaction of water pollution, which can be used as an indicator of water pollution. Recently Chakraborty *et al.* (2013) reported that freshwater mussel, *L. marginalis* act as a model organism for biomonitoring of the freshwater arsenic contamination.The mantle of mussels plays a vital role in the bioaccumulation of metal and organic contaminants in addition to the gills, kidneys and digestive glands. Generally kidneys eliminate the contaminants converting to different metabolites into the special protein, metallothioneins in gills and mantle helps to eliminate the heavy metals (Widdows and Donkin, 1992; Roesijafdi, 1996).

BIOFILTERS OR LIVING FILTERS

Freshwater mussels play a number of important roles in aquatic ecosystems. As sedentary suspension feeders, they remove a variety of materials from the water column, including sediment, particulate organic matter, bacteria, and phytoplankton(Vaughn and Hakenkamp, 2001). The removal of suspended matter from water is often considered desirable, in order to reduce algal blooms and in the treatment of drinking water. It is reported that individual mussel can filter up to half a litre of water per hour. Calculations of the filtration rates of mussel populations in four British rivers indicate that mussel filtering removes between 7% and 30% of the particulate matter in a parcel of water travelling 10 km downstream. This implies that mussels play an important role in the removal of suspended particulate matter in river ecosystems (McIvor, 2004). As bio-filters, mussels perform an important ecosystem service, by removing phytoplankton and suspended particulate matter from the water.

The novel use of mussels in drinking water treatment was investigated by placing mussels in large flow-through drinking water treatment plant and observed that they reduced the concentration of chlorophyll *a* and suspended solids in the water flowing through tanks, and increased sedimentation through the production of feces and pseudo- feces. Therefore mussels behaved as flocculates, and could be used in the early stages of drinking water treatment.

Finally, mussels can enrich the freshwater environment in several ways. As mussels burrow into the sediment, they mix-up the lower layers, which reintroduces deposited nutrients and dissolves oxygen back into the water column (Vaughn and Hakenkamp, 2001). Nutrient cycling is one of the fundamental processes in the freshwater ecosystem. Mussels can be labeled 'ecosystem engineers' because of their shell production. Shells requires a large amount of calcium carbonate, which does not break down easily after the mussel dies, so shells become a refuge for other organisms or as a substrate for fouling mussels (Guiterrez *et al.*, 2003).

REFERENCES

Álvarez-Rodríguez E, M J. Fernández-Araujo and A. Nuñez (2009): Utilización de la concha de mejillónendiferentestamañoscomoencalante: efectossobre el suelo y la producción de pratenses. *Actas de la XXVII ReuniónCientífica* del Suelo, 7.*American Zoologist*33, 599-609.

Anthony, J.J. and J.A. Downing (2001): Exploitation Trajectory of a Declining Fauna: A Century of Freshwater Mussel Fisheries in North America. *Canadian Journal of Fisheries and Aquatic Sciences* 58(10): 2071-2090.

Augspurger, T., Dwyer, J., and C. Ingersoll (2006): Implications of including Freshwater Mussel Toxicity Data in Water Quality Criteria Derivation Datasets. Presentation # 724 at the 27th *Annual Meeting of the Society of Environmental Toxicology and Chemistry*, Montreal, Quebec, November 2006.

Chakraborty, M., S. Bhattacharya, R. Mishra, D. Mukherjee and R. Mishra (2012): Antioxidant Content and Activity of the Indian Freshwater Pearl Mussel in the Prevention of Arthritis in an Experimental Animal Model. *British Journal of Nutrition*, 108: 1346-1350.

Chakraborty, S., M. Ray and S. Ray (2010): Toxicity of Sodium Arsenite in the Gill of an Economically Important Mollusk of India. *Fish and Shellfish Immunology*, 29: 136-148.

Chakraborty, S., M. Ray and S. Ray (2013): Cell to Organ: Physiological, Immunotoxic and Oxidative Stress Responses of *Lamellidens marginalis* to Inorganic Arsenite. *Ecotoxicology and Environmental Safety*, 94: 153-163.

Coker, R.E. (1919): Fresh-water Mussels and Mussel Industries of the United States. *U.S. Bureau of Fisheries Bulletin*, 36: 13-89.

Gorinstein, S., P.A. Avila, S. Moncheva, F. Toledo, S. Trakhtenberg, A. Gorinstein, I. Goshev and J. Namiesnik (2006): Changes in Mussel *Mytilus galloprovincialis* Protein Profile as a Reaction of Water Pollution. *Environment International*, 32: 95-100.

Guiterrez, J.L., C.G. Jones, D.L. Strayer and O.O. Iribarne (2003): Mollusks as Ecosystem Engineers: The Role of Shell Production in Aquatic Habitats. *Oikos*, 101: 79-90.

Janakiram, K. (2003): Freshwater Pearl Culture Technology Development in India. *Journal of Applied Aquaculture*, 341-349.

Jha, G.N., B.A. Dar, P. Sarkar and V. Singh (2014): Freshwater Bivalves of Commercial Importance in Western Ghats. *Indian Farming*, 64(2): 113-114.

Kim, S-K and R. Pallela (2012): Medicinal Foods from Marine Animals: Current Status and Prospects. In: Advances in Food and Nutrition, Vol. 65, Marine Medicinal Foods: Implications and Applications-Animals and Microbes (S-W Kim, ed.). *Academic Press, USA*, pp. 1-9.

March, F.A., F.J. Dwyer, A. Augspurger, C.G. Ingersoll, N. Wang, and C.A. Mebane (2007): An Evaluation of Freshwater Mussel Toxicity Data in the Derivation of Water Quality Guidance and Standards for Copper. *Environmental Toxicology and Chemistry* 26(10): 2066-2074.

Marin F. and G. Luquet (2004): Molluscan Shell Proteins. *Comptes Rendus Palevol*, 3, 469-492.

McIvor, A.L. (2004): Freshwater Mussels as Biofilters. Ph.D. Thesis, Dept. of Zoology, University of Cambridge.

Moncheva, S., S. Trakhtenberg, E. Katrich, M. Zemser, I. Goshev, F. Toledo, P. Arancibia-Avila, V. Doncheva and S. Gorinstein (2004): Total Antioxidant Capacity in the Black Mussel (*Mytilus galloprovincialis*) from Black Sea Coasts. *Estuarine, Coastal and Shelf Science*, 59: 475-484.

Mummert, A.K., R.J. Neves, T.J. Newcomb and D.S. Cherry (2003): Sensitivity to Juvenile Freshwater Mussels (*Lampsilis fasciola*, *Villosa iris*) to Total and Un-ionized Ammonia. *Environmental Toxicology and Chemistry*, 22(11): 2545-2553.

Naidu, S.J. and M.K. Misra (1998): Production and Consumption of Wild Date Palm Sap and Country Liquor in Two Tribal Village Ecosystems of Eastern Ghats of Orissa, India, *Biores Techno*, 67: 267.

Padro, J., E. Gutierrez, C. Saez, M. Brito and L.O. Burzio (1990): Purification of Adhesive Proteins from Mussel. *Protein Expression and Purification*, 1(2): 147-150.

Panda, A. and M.K. Misra (2007): Traditional Methods of Mollusc Shell Collection for Lime Preparation in East Coast of India. *Indian Journal of Traditional Knowledge*, 6 (4): 549- 558.

Parmalee, P.W. and W.E. Klippel (1974): Freshwater Mussels as Prehistoric Food Resource. *American Antiquity*, 39.3: 421-434.

Pattnayak, P.K. and M.K. Misra (2004): Energetics and Economics of Traditional *gur* Preparation: A Case Study in Ganjam District, Orissa, India. *Biomass Bioenergetics*, 26: 79.

Prabhakar, A.K. and S.P. Roy (2009): Ethno-medicinal Uses of Some Shell Fishes by People of Kosi River Basin of North-Bihar, India. *Ethno-Med*, 3: 1-4.

Ramkrishna and A. Dey (2007): Handbook on Indian Freshwater Molluscs: Zoological Survey of India, pp. 1-399.

Ray, M., A.S. Bhunia, N.S. Bhunia and S. Ray (2013): Density Shift, Morphological Damage, Lysosomal Fragility and Apoptosis of Hemocytes of Indian Molluscs Exposed to Pyrethroid Pesticides. *Fish and Shellfish Immunology*, 35: 499-512.

Roesijafdi, G. (1996): Environmental Factors; Response to Metals. In: The Eastern Oyster *Crassostrea virginica* (V.S. Kennedy, R.I.E. Newell and A.F. Eble, eds.), *Maryland Sea Grant, College Park, Maryland*, pp. 515-37.

Strayer, D.L., J.A. Downing, W.R. Haag, T.L. King, J.B. Layzer, T.J. Newton and S.J. Nichols (2004): Changing Perspectives on Pearly Mussels, North America's most Imperiled Animals. *Bioscience*, 34.5: 429-439.

Subba Rao, N.V. and A. Dey (1989): Freshwater Molluscs in Aquaculture. In: Handbook: Freshwater Molluscs of India. *Zoological Survey of India, Calcutta*, pp: 225-282.

Vaughn, C.C. and C.C. Hakenkamp (2001): The Functional Role of Burrowing Bivalves in Freshwater Ecosystems. *Freshwater Biology*, 46: 1431-1446.

Wang, N., C.G. Ingersoll, I.E. Greer, D.K. Hardesty, C.D. Ivey, J.L. Kunz, W.G. Brumbaugh, F.J. Dwyer, A.D. Robers, T. Augspurger, C.M. Kane, R.J. Neves and M.C. Barnhart (2007b): Assessing Contaminant Sensitivity of Early Life Stages of Freshwater Mussels (Unionidae): Chronic Toxicity Testing of Juvenile Mussels with Copper and Ammonia. *Environmental Toxicology and Chemistry*, 35pp.

Wang, N., C.G. Ingersoll, I.E. Greer, D.K. Hardesty, C.D. Ivey, J.L. Kunz, W.G. Brumbaugh, F.J. Dwyer, A.D. Robers, T. Augspurger, C.M.Kane, R.J. Neves, and M.C. Barnhart. (2007a): Assessing Contaminant Sensitivity of Early Life Stages of Freshwater Mussels (Unionidae): Acute Toxicity Testing of Copper, Ammonia, and Chlorine to Glochidia and Juvenile Mussels. *Environmental Toxicology and Chemistry*, 38pp.

Widdows, J. and P. Donkin (1992): Mussels and Environmental Contaminants: Bioaccumulation and Physiological Aspects. In: The Mussels Mytilus: Ecology, Physiology, Genetics and Culture (E.M. Gosling, ed.), *Elsevier Science Publishers B. V., Amsterdam*, pp. 383-424.

Wootton, E.C., E.A. Dyrynda, R.K. Pipe and N.A. Ratcliffe (2003): Comparisons of PAH-induced Immunomodulation in Three Bivalve Molluscs. *Aquatic Toxicology*, 65: 13-25.

Zhou, Q., J. Zhang, J.Fu, J.Shi and G. Jiang (2008): Biomonitoring: An Appealing Tool for Assessment of Metal Pollution in the Aquatic Ecosystem. *Analytica Chimica Acta*, 606: 135-15.

Pages: 38-66

FISH HABITAT AND AQUACULTURE
Edited by: Dr. Sanjay Kumar Gupta; Dr. Pawan Kumar 'Bharti'
ISBN: 978-93-5056-744-9
Edition: 2015
Published by: Discovery Publishing House Pvt. Ltd., New Delhi (India)

3

Farming of *Macrobrachium rosenbergii* – A Prospectful Alternative to Tiger Shrimp having Attributes of Environmental Concerns

Subrato Ghosh and **Himadri Chandra**

ABSTRACT

Environmental impact of tiger shrimp farming has become a major issue in many countries with developing shrimp culture industries. Deterioration of state of effluent receiving natural water bodies in vicinities of shrimp farms, conflicts with agriculturists, heavy loss of production and earnings due to viral diseases has led farmers to realize that it is a non-profit-making venture. In this context, culture of the high-valued freshwater crustacean *Macrobrachium rosenbergii* has been thought to be environment-friendly, sustainable and prospectful. The obstacles that shrimp farming has faced can be overcome by the adoption of freshwater giant prawn farming as an alternative to the former in suitable locations where adequate freshwater is available. In India, *M. rosenbergii* farming has received considerable attention of the fish farmers in recent years due to higher profit realization from unit area. Its high demand in domestic market and the ever-increasing demand in international market further provide enormous scope for expansion of its cultivation. In this communication, problems that have come up in relation to commercial tiger shrimp culture practices have been reviewed, management practices of *M. rosenbergii* farming in India along with a case study have been discussed comprehensively and some newer trends in its farming and research have been highlighted.

Key words: *Macrobrachium rosenbergii*, monoculture, monosex, polyculture, production status, production rate.

INTRODUCTION

The giant freshwater prawn *Macrobrachium rosenbergii* (Decapoda : Palaemonidae) is a high-valued delicious food item and one of the most important crustacean species produced in inland aquaculture in many tropical and sub-tropical countries worldover. It has been introduced into every continent as an eco-friendly candidate species for aquaculture. Out of all 49 commercial freshwater prawn, *Macrobrachium* (Bate, 1868) species, *M. rosenbergii* (De Man, 1879) is the largest and fastest growing species. Adult males have been reported with a total body length of upto 33cm and adult females of upto 29cm. This species can be distinguished from other species in the genus by some characteristics like: (a) it possess a very long sword-shaped rostrum with 12-14 dorsal teeth and 10-13 ventral teeth; (b) the tip of its telson reaches distinctly beyond the posterior spines of the telson; (c) the adult male has very long second chelipeds (chelate legs) in which all segments are elongate and have blunt spines; (d) the movable finger of the second chelipeds of the adult male is covered by a dense velvet-like fur (except the extreme tip) but this fur is absent from the fixed finger and the rest of the cheliped; (e) the second pair of periopods (walking legs) in the male is thicker than in other species; (f) the carpus segment of the periopods is longer than the merus. The body colour is usually of greenish to brownish grey, sometimes more bluish colour which is darker in larger specimen. There are irregular brown, grey and whitish streaks often placed somewhat longitudinally (New *et. al.*, 2010). The closely-related cultivable species *Macrobrachium malcolmsonii* possess a rostrum with 9-11 dorsal teeth and 4-7 ventral teeth.

In the juvenile stage of *M. rosenbergii* (21-90mm), characteristic parallel horizontal lines varying from 1 in smaller and 7-8 in bigger specimens are present on carapace. These lines disappear beyond 90mm size. Rostrum is sharply upturned. Older juveniles become distinctively blue, sometimes brownish (Chondar, 1999). Adult breeders migrate from freshwater to brackishwater and sometimes in marine, and return to freshwater after breeding. The freshwater zones of rivers Rupnarayan, Ichhamati and Hooghly in West Bengal and Valapattanam in Kerala are very good natural habitats with large population of *M. rosenbergii*.

Environmental Impact of Fish Farming Practices with Respect to Shrimp Culture

Tiger shrimp, *Penaeus monodon* farming plays an important but controversial role in the economic development of many countries in Asia because of the catastrophic environmental impact of shrimp production in coastal areas. Its development in coastal states of India has been controversial. Considerable environmental and social problems include water pollution, salinisation of drinking-water wells and paddy fields, destruction of early stages of wild fish and crustacean species and various social conflicts related to land conversion and conversion of mangrove areas to shrimp farms. The scenario witnessed during 1994-1995 in shrimp farming in India led to be connoted as one among several potential polluters of aquatic environment causing degradation of mangroves and other water resources (Balakrishnan Nair, 1998).

(a) Impact of shrimp farming on mangrove ecosystems

Regarding selection of site and establishment of shrimp farms, the mangrove water bodies and estuarine wetlands are looked upon as highly conducive habitat for profitable shrimp farming projects due to the availability of brackishwater and other ecological parameters favourable for the growth of shrimps. In coastal Andhra Pradesh, 2850ha of mangrove areas have been converted to shrimp farms. Ecologically mangrove ecosystems form the feeding grounds of over fifty commercially important finfish and shellfish species. With destruction of such productive water bodies and establishment of farms, loss of habitat will adversely have considerable impact upon natural replenishment/recruitment of these fishes, their natural repository will decline. Exploitation of natural shrimp seed from estuaries, backwaters and creeks in a significant proportion in West Bengal, threat to the conservation of natural resources and ecosystem associated to uncontrolled collection of natural seeds of tiger shrimp and damage to seeds of other finfishes have been reported (Vasudevappa and Seenappa, 2002).

(b) Alterations in flowing water systems

Shrimp farms are constructed by altering the structure of flowing and non-flowing water bodies in the area as per requirement to suitable culture systems. Bunding and diversion of tidal creek, canal and river tributaries carrying brackishwater and change in their flow pattern will cause change in current patterns, drainage systems and percolation of water and leaching of minerals and salts into the soil.

(c) Salinisation of ground water

Salinisation of groundwater resource due to leaching of salts underneath via soil is an important problem to be taken into consideration. Chloride content of 80 - 300ppm has been recorded in potable groundwater resources and aquifers in human settlements in the vicinity of shrimp farms, whereas the permissible limit is 250ppm. In certain areas of Tamil Nadu, chloride content in groundwater has reached upto 667.4ppm (Menon, 2001). High levels were also noticed in drinking water from tubewells in adjoining villages of the state. Seepage of saline water from shrimp aquaculture ponds is an environmental problem since it results in salinisation of soil in nearby agricultural land and drinking water resources (Varadaraju *et al.*, 2014).

(d) Water quality deterioration

In semi-intensive shrimp farming systems, highly effective fertilizers, chemical microbicidal agents, herbicides, fungicides, algicides, pesticides (to kill insects, parasites and all unwanted organisms), disinfectants and antibiotics (with feed) are used in culture ponds to favour the growth and prevent pest and microorganism attack on shrimps. But when water exchange is done in ponds, portion of existing water mass is let out; then residue of the above-mentioned non-biodegradable compounds, shrimp excreta and unutilized feed matter find their way into nearby natural water bodies. Due to contamination of waters by discharged pond effluent, the non-biodegradable elements enter and accumulate into the natural food web (Menon, 2001). This results in biomagnification of such elements up above the trophic level from the primary producers phytoplankton. Water quality gets deteriorated, indigenous naturally dwelling immature finfishes and shellfishes do not survive in such conditions. The process of shrimp farming leads to the release of various farm effluents in the aquatic ecosystem. Water bodies like coastlines get severely affected as the waste produced from shrimp farms and hatcheries gets contaminated therein.

Residual fertilizers via effluent discharge contaminate the shallow regions of natural water bodies and facilitate hyper-nutrification and finally eutrophication, which is undesirable. Suspended organic solids decompose and increase the Biological Oxygen Demand load of the concerned aquatic environment. The negative effects of effluents from intensive and semi intensive shrimp farms on the environment of receiving water, self-pollution of ponds, deteriorating water quality, eutrophication of water bodies which receive farm waste, impact of shrimp pond waste on the farming system in terms of reducing Dissolved Oxygen, increasing BOD and COD, eutrophication, alteration of biological community structure, increased sediment load, changes in productivity, benthic community, etc. have been widely noticed (Vasudevappa and Seenappa, 2002). To reduce the risk of crop failure, farmers use a relatively large amount of feed, pesticides and antibiotics in shrimp farming. Several concerns have been raised about the use of toxic compounds, including their persistence in aquatic environments, the possibility of residues in non-cultured seafood, the toxicity to non-target (off farm) species and the possible effects on the health of farm workers (Anh *et. al.*, 2010).

In Udupi and North Canara districts of Karnataka, even though shrimp farming is primary occupation for majority of the farmers, majority of the farmers are not willing to depend on shrimp farming because at any point of time they may lose the crop due to disease outbreaks. So as alternative source of income they depend on agriculture and other business. Number of constraints and risks has been reported by the farmers which were low price for the produce, labour scarcity, high labour charges, occurrence of White Spot Syndrome Virus, high electricity cost, no credit facility. The largest problem reported by 81% of respondents was low price for the produce and occurrence of WSSV (Leo Cyril *et. al.*, 2014). In addition to these, one of the concerns for Indian shrimp farmers is, for 5 months of the year during monsoon the rain lowers down the water salinity level below the standards in which shrimp culture is practically not possible. In Bangladesh also, white spot is a common symptom and is frequently reported from the shrimp *Penaeus monodon* farms especially in Khulna region which is caused by a DNA virus of White Spot Syndrome Virus (WSSV). This virus causes serious economic losses of tiger shrimp and incidence of the disease is prevalent in the farms (Zamal *et. al.*, 2012).

Growth of Giant Prawn Farming

Following the setback to brackishwater shrimp farming in mid-1990s and consequent regulations on expansion and intensification of the activity, farmers in both coastal and land-locked (inland) states in India have gone for large scale farming of *M. rosenbergii*. Production of farmed freshwater prawns in India and Bangladesh picked up more recently, following the reduced production and near collapse of shrimp *Penaeus monodon* farming. The giant prawn *M. rosenbergii* has a very wide distribution in most of the river system of the country and even in some of the independently flowing smaller rivers of peninsular India. It has a key role to play in improving economic status of people in addition to increasing food production. It has capacity to adjust to varying environmental condition, ready acceptability of artificial feeds, has fast growth rate. India is one of the few targeted countries best suited for freshwater prawn production (Vasudevappa, 2002). Freshwater giant prawn farming had developed in India in 1999 due to a sudden rise in demand in response to the devastation made by White Spot Syndrome Virus in farmed tiger shrimp production. The infrastructure available to produce shrimp seed and process the shrimp was helpful in providing support to giant freshwater prawn farming. Average productivity from *M. rosenbergii* farming activities in India is 1.05 tonnes/ha/year (Nair and Salin, 2006).

In India, *M. rosenbergii* farming has received considerable attention of the fish farmers in recent years due to higher profit realization from unit area. Its high demand in domestic market and the ever-increasing demand in international market further provide enormous scope for expansion of its cultivation. Besides monoculture, the compatibility with major carps makes the species suitable for its large-scale adoption under composite fish culture. Other than conventional culture water bodies (earthen ponds, pen enclosures and net cages), this species can also be grown in low saline brackishwater areas having salinity less than 10ppt and is suitable for incorporation in paddy-cum-fish culture system (Pillai *et. al.,* 2007). Along with the boom in the aquaculture of giant prawn has come a corresponding growth in the demand for viable seed, which has topped six billion throughout India. Culture of *M. rosenbergii* is done in most of the coastal states of India (Andhra Pradesh, West Bengal, Orissa and Kerala are leading ones); recently Madhya Pradesh, Haryana, Punjab, Bihar, Chhattisgarh, Tripura have also initiated giant prawn culture. The main freshwater prawn producing countries are China, India, Bangladesh, Brazil, Thailand, Taiwan, Vietnam, Ecuador and Malaysia. It has begun to expand in Iran, Sri Lanka, Indonesia. While the farmed production of prawns in China and Thailand are directed principally for local consumption, South Asian (India and Bangladesh) production is targeted mainly for export. USA, Belgium, United Kingdom, Canada, UAE, Germany, Mauritius, Malaysia, Japan, Indonesia are major buyers of Indian *M. rosenbergii*. While carp and other finfishes are grown for the domestic market, a large proportion of freshwater prawn production is exported.

Two serious problems in shrimp farming concern environmental degradation and shrimp health. Another major conflict is groundwater salinization that could seriously affect the environment; the provision of good-quality water for human use and for agriculture in the community will no more exist. The other major issue of concern to shrimp farmers is the unpredictability of collapse or near collapse of farms owing to White Spot Disease, a devastating viral (WSSV) infection. The obstacles that shrimp farming has faced can be overcome by the adoption of freshwater prawn farming as an alternative to shrimp farming in suitable locations where adequate freshwater is available. This change would not cause the salinisation of soil and water and could lead to smoother interactions with other sectors, especially public health and agriculture (Kutty, 2005). In China, the rapid increase in production of cultured freshwater prawn is the result of growth in the area under culture, improved culture techniques and decline in the production of cultured marine shrimps. By the year 2000, culture of *M. rosenbergii* had expanded to 24 provinces, with 0.64% contribution in total freshwater aquaculture production (Weimin and Xianping, 2002).

About 4 million hectare of impounded freshwater bodies in various states of India offer great potential for *M. rosenbergii* farming. In India, freshwater prawn production has increased to 8000tonnes by the turn of the century with over 50% of the production coming from Andhra Pradesh wherein about 7000 hectare water area are under monoculture farming of

M. rosenbergii (Vasudevappa, 2002). In this state, production as high as 1.5-1.8 tonnes/ha is commonly achieved. According to Nair and Salin (2006), Andhra Pradesh holds 76% of the production area generating 89% of the total *M. rosenbergii* production. Water resource covered under mono- and polyculture of *M. rosenbergii* are 3500ha in West Bengal, 2000ha in Gujarat, 1000ha in Orissa, 170ha in Tamil Nadu, 50ha in Punjab. In Andhra Pradesh, there are hatcheries exclusively producing *M. rosenbergii* seeds and many tiger shrimp hatcheries are partially converted for production of giant freshwater prawn seeds. Farmers generally practice monoculture of *M. rosenbergii* in ponds undertaking repeated cull-harvesting schedules after 3-4 months of rearing. In Gujarat, seeds of *M. rosenbergii* are collected in large numbers from rivers. Every year more than 19 million prawn juveniles are collected from river Narmada and its tributaries using bundles of branches of Babool trees during October-November and January-February. Seed collected is of good quality with *M. rosenbergii* forming 60-80% of the lot. In Maharashtra, monoculture prawn production varies between 250 to 800kg/ha/year. In Tamil Nadu, although the focus is still on tiger shrimp farming, results of semi-intensive and monosex culture ('all-male' system) have demonstrated the profitability of *M. rosenbergii* farming (Vasudevappa, 2002). In West Bengal and Kerala with giant prawn *M. rosenbergii* production area of 3500ha and 710ha respectively, annual production of giant prawn are 1820 tonnes and 450 tonnes respectively (Nair and Salin, 2006).

Production Trend

As has been discussed, for the past two decades, the culture of giant freshwater prawn spread quickly as an alternative to shrimp culture due to the decline of the shrimp industry. From 1993-2002, the world production of giant freshwater prawn increased from 17,000 tonnes to 195,000 tonnes. The global annual production of freshwater prawns in 2003 was about 280,000 tonnes, of which China produced some 180,000 tonnes, followed by India and Thailand with some 35,000 tonnes each. In 2004, the total world farmed *M. rosenbergii* volume reached more than 194,000 tonnes with an estimated market value that exceeded US 810 million dollars, of which 99% was produced in Asia. In 2008, total quantity of *M. rosenbergii* produced in the world was 214,849 tonnes, that produced in China and Thailand were 127,788 tonnes and 28,500 tonnes respectively (New, 2011).

India is the third largest producer of freshwater prawns after China and Vietnam. During 2003-2004, total country's production of freshwater prawns (*M. rosenbergii* and *M. malcolmsonii*) was 35,870 tonnes with total culture area of 41,870ha. Culture area dropped down to 36,990ha in 2004-2005. Giant freshwater prawn *M. rosenbergii* production in India had increased from less than 178 tonnes in 1996 to 42,870 tonnes in 2005. However, reduction in productivity in major culture areas reduced total production of *M. rosenbergii* to 12,806 tonnes in 2008. In 2010, production reached an unprecedented low point yielding only 3721 tonnes in our country. Productivity decline has also been reported in Taiwan and Thailand and was attributed to inbreeding depression in this species (Aflalo *et. al.*, 2012). In 2007, farmed *M. rosenbergii* production in India was 27,300 tonnes. Production declined to 6568 tonnes during 2009; it was mostly due to stunted growth and diseases in ponds because of poor seed quality and the broodstock which had been inbred over several generations. Besides these, there were pond water quality issues and increased cost of production on account of feed and labour that were mostly unaffordable.

Aspects of Monoculture

Size of the most easily-managed giant prawn grow-out culture earthen village ponds range between 0.2-0.6ha. If the width is 30mt, a 0.6ha pond will have to be 200mt long. In West Bengal farms, length of pond is maintained at 2.5-3.0 times of its width. The depth of water is maintained between 0.75 - 1.20mt. A slope of 1:500 is suggested for ponds of 0.4ha in area towards the outlet, where drain harvesting occurs. Derris root powder or Mohua oilcake are used to kill predatory fishes. After initial liming, application of TSP @25kg/ha, mixture of TSP-Urea @ 8:24kg/ha before stocking and monthly application of the mixture @ 16:36kg/ha is essential during culture period. Normal paddlewheels or long shaft engine-run paddlewheel aerators are used to maintain Dissolved Oxygen levels in pond water above 4ppm. Routine liming (at low dose; 100kg/ha/month) should be sufficient to increase total pond alkalinity to about 40 mg/lit. Some freshwater prawn farms make a standard application of 1000 kg/ha of agricultural limestone every time a pond is drained.

The giant freshwater prawn exhibits aggressive behaviour; the provision of additional substrates to increase surface area on pond berm/slope improves production by reducing mortalities from cannibalism as well as increasing natural algal food production (periphyton) which can also be utilized by the prawns. The substrates may also provide shelter for freshly moulted prawns which make them less vulnerable to aggression by other non-moulting prawns. Hollow PVC pipes of 2-4inch diameter, plants like *Hydilla* sp., *Elodea* sp., *Ipomoea* sp., coconut/date palm tree leave bunches are used over pond water. For a 1 bigha (33 decimal) pond, 40-50 palm tree leaves are required. Folded coconut leaves are commonly placed as hide-outs in nursery ponds.

Stocking post-larvae in grow-out ponds is not much profitable because most would be lost through predation. In West Bengal, the 12-14mm post-larvae (two weeks old after metamorphosis; 8-10mg) obtained from hatchery facilities are reared in separate 0.02ha nursery ponds at a density 20nos./m^2 for about seven weeks, finally they attain the juvenile stage (30 - 40mm; 3gm size). Juveniles are stocked in grow-outs; in first three months, they attain sub-adult stage (7-8cm; 10gm size) and in next three months, most attain marketable size (adult: 17-18cm; 35-40gm body weight). The culture period under monoculture is generally 6-8 months starting at the beginning of southwest monsoon (June-July, 27-30°C). It is 8-12 months under polyculture system and composite fish culture. The average growth of *M. rosenbergii* may range from 40 to 160gm. In monoculture system in earthen ponds, production ranges between 1000-1800kg/ha/6-7 month crop in Indian conditions, 800-1200kg/ha in Brazil, 600-750kg/ha in Vietnam, 900-3150kg/ha/crop in Malaysia, 2000kg/ha in Taiwan Province of China, 1500kg/ha in Thailand without aeration facilities and 3100kg/ha/crop with paddlewheel aeration device.

Cull harvesting is used to harvest market-sized prawns from pond and sold at intervals and removes the faster growing prawns. The rest of the prawns are kept for further growth (smaller ones and soft-shelled animals) and are caught when the ponds are drained (after about 8-11 months) at the end of the grow-out cycle. It is drain harvesting. In tropical grow-out ponds, cull-harvesting usually starts 5-7 months after post-larvae have been stocked, or sooner if juveniles have been stocked. In farm ponds with aeration facilities without substrates on pond berm/slope, juveniles are stocked @ 40,000nos / ha water body. In West Bengal conditions, in the 'batch' system of culture, i.e., stocking each pond once, allowing the animals to grow until prawns achieve the average market size, and then totally draining and harvesting it (selective harvesting/culling is not done); under 60-75% survivability in grow-out ponds and each attaining 40gm on average, a production of 960-1200kg/ha/crop is obtained. When post-larvae are stocked, it is @ 40,000-200,000nos./ha. In Philippines, *M. rosenbergii* grow-out culture looks promising since fish farmers can earn a net income of at least Php 100,000 per year for a total farm area of 5,000sqmt with 70% survival rate. The post-larvae are grown for 4-5 months with a stocking density of 10-15nos./sqmt. The average harvest size of prawn is 25-35 grams.

Supplementary feeding with on-farm-made feed (in the form of dough balls) or commercial pelleted (2-3mm diameter) feed is done with protein-rich plant and animal ingredients maintained at 1:3. For juveniles, the feeding rate might be 20-10% of body weight and it would decline gradually to about 2% by harvest time. In different prawn farms, plant ingredients used are: boiled rice, boiled pulses, green coconut flesh, soyabean meal, cottonseed meal, groundnut meal, coconut oil cake, sesame cake, moist pressed brewers' grains, dry sugarcane yeast, distillers' dried grains, broken rice, rice bran and polish, corn (maize) meal, corn silage, wheat meal, wheat bran, wheat middling, cassava/tapioca flour, fresh leaves, Alfalfa, grass meal, orange flesh, peeled sweet potatoes, frozen peeled bananas, butternut squash, yellow squash, turnip greens, carrot tops. The animal ingredients used are: fish meal, shrimp shell meal, molluscan flesh, marine shrimp meal, trash fish, squid meal, brewers' yeast, meat meal, beef liver, dusted chicken bones, dried silkworm pupae, silkworm litter, earthworms (New, 2002). In Indian conditions, according to an estimate the total investment cost (cost of prawn juveniles, fertilizers, lime, feed, electricity, harvesting and accessory expense) in monoculture system in 1ha pond sums up to Rs. 1,66,625/- and the gross income after sale of big-sized and small-sized prawns sums up to Rs. 2,25,000/-. A net income/profit of Rs. 58,375/- is achievable at end of six months (Source: Aquaculture Technology for Farmers, ICAR Publication). Scientists of WB University of Animal and Fishery Sciences have given an estimate of a possible net income of Rs. 1,49,225/- from a 1ha giant prawn monoculture pond at the end of 8-10 months (one crop), aiming at a production level of 1500kg/ha/year; with total investment cost of Rs. 2,15,775/- and gross income of Rs. 3,75,000/-.

In our country, shallow areas of derelict water bodies, lakes and floodplain wetlands can be used for raising *M. rosenbergii* in enclosure (pens). The pens may be stocked with bigger fingerlings of IMC and prawn at 6-8cm length @ 20,000-30,000nos./ha. An average production of 400kg of IMC and 80kg of prawns can be realized from pens of 0.10-0.15 ha area in four months of rearing. During Oct-Nov 2005, Kerala Fisheries Department had stocked 600,000nos *M. rosenbergii* post-larvae in Malampuzha reservoir in Palakkad district. Cull harvesting started from April 2006. Stocked prawns showed exceptional growth; males and berried females ranged between 200-350gm and 100-150gm respectively. As on September 2006, a total of 6374kg of prawns were harvested that earned a return of more than Rs 1600000/-. This fishery had brought considerably higher income to 122 regional tribal families (including 47 SC/ST communities) residing in hill tracts (Kutty *et al.*, 2008).

Adoption of nursery rearing of post-larvae to juveniles instead of direct stocking in grow-out ponds for better pond management has been felt desirable. Semi-intensive (stocking @ 150-200PL/m^2) and intensive (800-1000PL/m^2) rearing technology with a survivability rate of above 80% are found to be effective in getting prawn juveniles of about 0.3-0.5gm in 40-50 days (Vasudevappa, 2002). Sometimes, PL obtained from hatcheries are reared for 4-5 weeks till they attain 40-50mm (1-3gm). In nursery ponds stocked @ 2,50,000 PL per ha area (25nos./m^2), survivability rate was found to be 70-80% after 45-60 days (Nair and Salin, 2006). Crumbled feed (0.5mm diameter) with 35% crude protein level is best suited for this purpose. Using good quality supplementary feed, feeding strategies, frequent cull-harvesting schedules and proper water quality management, semi-intensive prawn production technology with a stocking density of 5 juveniles per square metre could produce 800-1500kg/ha in 6-8 months. With proper extension programmes, such technologies should be demonstrated to farmers by undertaking large-scale trials in village ponds. From a domestic sewage-fed fish pond of 0.4ha area in West Bengal, 499.8kg/ha *M. rosenbergii* production could be obtained in 8 months (Ghosh *et.al.*, 1985). In giant prawn monoculture grow-out ponds, *Catla catla* may be stocked @ 100-150 bigger fingerlings/ha so that growth of algal bloom in excess is controlled.

Polyculture System

Mixed farming of giant freshwater prawn along with carps is also accepted as a technologically-sound culture practice and a viable option for enhancing farm income. Such a system holds the potential to increase the total value of a crop by the inclusion of a high-valued species. Prawns are known to consume fish faeces. Grow-out stocking densities range from 0.5-2.5nos giant prawn juvenile/sqmt in polyculture system (Mitra and Mukhopadhyay, 2005). In West Bengal conditions, in usual six species (3 IMC and 3 exotic carps) composite culture system of 1000nos carp fingerling stocking in 1 bigha pond (7.5bigha = 1ha; 1 bigha = 33 decimal), bigger juveniles of *M. rosenbergii* (50-60mm) may be stocked @ 500nos./bigha. If bottom dwelling major carps Common carp and Mrigal are avoided, then stocking density of prawn juveniles may be increased to 1200nos./bigha. After one year, prawn production to the tune of 225-260kg/ha is achievable with each attaining 100gm weight. A production of 40-50kg from 1 bigha pond may be achieved under scientific management practice. In rural West Bengal in 1 bigha pond, total investment (including cost of carp fingerlings, prawn juveniles, pond preparation, liming, fertilizer, netting and other accessories) has been estimated to be Rs 15,000/- and monetary output (including sale of table-sized carps and giant prawn) Rs. 26,000/-. Thus a net profit of Rs. 11,000/- may be achieved at the end of one year of culture (Dr Ashis Panigrahi: personal communication). Polyculture of *M. rosenbergii* juveniles at densities 3000-4000/ha alongside major carps (10000-15000/ha) has been demonstrated to be economically viable.

Freshwater prawns are grown with silver carp and bighead carp in China. Prawn production upto 200-300kg/ha in Bangladesh and 200-500kg/ha in India has been achieved in composite culture systems. Fermented chicken manure is applied to the ponds @ 750-1500kg/ha, 7-10 days before stocking to maintain good benthic algal growth. In China, rearing period of prawns is only 4-6 months and are harvested at 20gm size. In polyculture systems of China, when prawn juveniles are stocked at a high density, production of 1200-1800kg/ha/crop has been obtained. When prawns are stocked at a lower rate with finfishes as the primary crop, the yield was typically 300-900kg/ha/crop of prawns (New and Valenti, 2000). In Vietnamese polyculture system, total aquaculture production is 2.1-3.0tonnes/ha, of which about 10% comprise freshwater prawns, the rest being finfishes including silver carp, silver barb, tilapia, river catfish and common carp.

For small and medium sized village ponds in our country, polyculture would be effective with stocking densities of 5000/ha of major carp fingerlings (with *Labeo rohita* and *Catla catla* in 3:2 ratio) and *M. rosenbergii* juveniles 20,000/ha, which will yield a production of 2500-3000kg/ha of finfishes and 700-800kg/ha of *M. rosenbergii* in a culture period of 8-10 months. In this system, greater than 80% of the prawns will be large in size. Pelleted feed containing 30% crude protein level containing about 75% plant protein have been found to be cost-effective and efficient in terms of feed utilization. In mixed culture with major carps where the faecal matter of carps might be an added source of direct and indirect food of prawn, it has given a yield of 3895kg/ha of *M. rosenbergii* in 5 months of culture in freshwater ponds, in addition to production of carps (Rajyalakshmi, 1979). An experiment was conducted to evaluate the effects of stocking density of tilapia on water quality and production in organic prawn farming system over a period of 122 days at the Bangladesh Agricultural University. It was concluded that grow-out polyculture of prawn *M. rosenbergii*, tilapia and silver carp at stocking densities of 30,000nos., 20,000nos. and 1250nos. per hectare water body respectively will provide high net production and economic benefit (Roy *et. al.*, 2012).

Production in Paddy Fields

Culture of high-valued crustaceans has been developed recently in the rice fields; *M. rosenbergii* in trenched rice fields in south-west Bangladesh and in southern Vietnam, where the post-larvae are raised concurrently with rice and then in rotation after rice harvest as rains flood the fields (Edwards, 2011). In Mekong delta of Vietnam, *M. rosenbergii* is successfully reared in paddy fields without depressing rice production. It has been shown that the income from prawns in integrated rice-prawn culture can be 2-3 times as great as that from rice cultivation. When deeper areas in form of peripheral canals (water level above 1mt, 2-3mt wide) where prawns can shelter when the ricefield is dry are constructed, introduction of freshwater prawns reduces the area devoted to rice paddy by about 15%. It also reduces weeding costs (prawns eat weeds) by about 33% and fertilization costs by 28% without reducing rice yield. Prawn juveniles (3-5gm) collected from wild sources are stocked in paddy fields @ 0.5-2nos./sqmt. They are fed with rice bran mash. Rice fields are 0.5-2.0 ha in area, of which 15-20% of the space consists of internal canals. Prawn production of 100-300kg/ha has been achieved from Vietnamese rice fields in one year. Prawns remain in the irrigation ditches during the first rice harvest and are allowed back into the main paddy plots (second crop) for a total of 8-12 months rearing period. In association with cucumber culture over split-bamboo fences/platforms around paddy plots on peripheral dykes, 200-300kg/ha prawn production is achievable.

In Vietnam, prawns are reared in both rice - prawn systems and in garden trenches supplying fruit trees and vegetables. A prawn yield of 354kg/

ha could be obtained from a single annual crop (Van Nguyen, 1993). Integrated prawn culture with monsoon season rice farming is ecologically sound and a good method for culture diversification. Prawns predate on insects and improve soil fertility. In Puerto Rico, Japan and Southern Brazil, prawns had been shown not to depress rice production when grown together. Technical and economic feasibility of cultivating *M. rosenbergii* post-larvae either alone or with Nile Tilapia have been evaluated in rice fields of Egypt. The maximum net return was obtained in rice-prawn culture with stocking density @ 2 post-larvae/sqmt. Rice alone gave a much lower return. In integrated prawn culture in deep-water rice fields, rice production is increased in the presence of fishes and prawns (Roy *et. al.*, 1991). In China, *M. rosenbergii* post-larvae @ 150,000nos./ha or early juveniles @ 60,000-75,000nos./ha are stocked in rice-prawn farming systems. One crop of prawn is produced in a year; 300-450kg of prawn can be produced through supplementary feeding and good management in addition to normal rice production. It has been a very effective approach to improve the economic return of traditional rice cultivation.

Single crop paddy - prawn production systems in the low-lying fields of Kerala, India have helped gradual transformation into a sustainable, organic mode of farming of both rice and prawns, which is suitable for other states of India. In Kuttanad, Kerala, although paddy cultivation in rice fields is being practiced on a regular basis, the successful integration of *M. rosenbergii* in the rice fields had in fact evoked much response among farmers as a means for improving their economic status. Due to phenomenal increase in the cost of rice production in past decade and due to the diminishing returns, there is a strong tendency among the farmers to abandon rice cultivation and look for alternative uses of their fields. The integration of paddy farming with prawn/fish culture has turned out to be the only viable alternative to effectively utilize the vast expanse of fertile derelict water bodies available in the district (Kurup and Ranjeet, 2002). For many years *M. rosenbergii* has been farmed in integration with paddy as a means to utilize the flooded seasons which helped in gaining an additional income. Weedicides, pesticides and insecticides need not be applied in paddy cultivation. In Kuttanad, the "Society for Culture of Aquatic animals and good Management Practices in Kuttanad" has been formed to promote freshwater prawn culture as a means of rural livelihood in the region. In low lying paddy fields of Kerala, one crop of rice is cultivated during dry periods and prawns are grown after the monsoon rains when the fields are submerged. High production is achieved in this system with minimum inputs (Courtesy: Dr C. Mohanakumaran Nair).

In rice fields, freshwater prawn *M. rosenbergii* can be stocked at lower densities of 0.5nos./sq.mt. (Devaraja *et. al.*, 2014). In the domestic sewage-fed paddy plots (wetlands) in the estuarine upper Sunderbans region of

North 24 Pgs., West Bengal, during monsoon season, kharif paddy cultivation is possible simultaneously with freshwater fishes and *M. rosenbergii*; through selective stocking, freshwater aquacrop production upto 500-600kg/ha has been obtained comprising *M. rosenbergii* 40% and major carps 60% (Chakraborti, 1998). A farmer of Mahisara village in Jajpur district, Odisha, India has developed a large rice-fish farm of 35 acres (14ha) following the technology developed at CRRI, Cuttack. He grows semi-deepwater rice varieties along with around 3,00,000nos juveniles of *M. rosenbergii* and 2,00,000nos fry of Rohu and Catla. Vegetables, tuber crops and Pigeon pea are being grown on wide bunds all around. The farmer gets a net income of Rs 16,00,000/- from rice-fish-prawn and other crops. In the year 2007-'08, the farmer expanded and renovated the culture area to a total area of 65 acres; it includes three farms in which rice-fish farming is done in two farms of 35 and 20 acres and *M. rosenbergii* is being grown in 10 acre area.

M. rosenbergii Farming in Bangladesh

Freshwater prawn farming industry and contribution of prawn production in Bangladesh has been very important in supporting a thriving local economy, livelihood of many peoples, income and generating foreign exchange earnings. It is currently one of the most important sectors of national economy (Ahmed, 2008). About 0.04 million people in the country are involved in freshwater prawn sector, with 75,000 prawn farmers involved in 'gher' systems and 30,000 prawn farmers in pond system. There exists 105,000nos freshwater prawn farms in Bangladesh. In 2008, total quantity of farmed *M. rosenbergii* production was 23,377 tonnes. Along with pond polyculture of carps, a current focus is on promoting culture of *M. rosenbergii* due to its export potential. In Mymensingh district, few sub-district areas have become important areas for prawn farming because of the availability of hatchery-produced post-larvae, availability of low-lying agricultural land, fertile soil, cheap and abundant labour.

Livelihoods of a considerable number of small and marginal farmers are associated with polyculture and integrated prawn farming. Pond area ranges from 0.06-0.11ha. Juveniles are preferred for stocking (19760nos./ha/year) for high survival rate, along with fingerlings of Rohu and Catla. Farmers found that Catla-Rohu-Giant prawn combination was economically and ecologically the best culture practice. They prefer commercial pelleted supplementary feed for prawn production instead of home-made feeds. Rice bran and GNOC were used for the two carps. Average annual yield of prawn was estimated to be 552kg/ha. Average annual yield in south-west Bangladesh (Khulna, Bagherhat districts) was 432kg/ha; fish farmers at Mymensingh obtained better production owing to technical assistance and training received from project personnel. Average farm gate price of prawn was found at US dollar 5.0 per kilogram (Ahmed *et. al.*, 2007).

On the pond dyke, different crops like cucumber, gourd, beans, leafy vegetables are cultivated. In the scenario of prawn farming in paddy fields, rice production has been reported to have increased by 10-15% due to enhanced fertility and environment of rice fields due to simultaneous culture of prawn and fish in the monsoon season. In the Greater Noakhali Aquaculture Extension Project in Bangladesh, after experiencing that improved carp polyculture in small ponds was unable to increase household income significantly, the export-oriented culture of *M. rosenbergii* has been promoted; it has remarkably lifted some farming households out of poverty level within two years. In small homestead seasonal ponds and ditches (typical seasonal ditch in rice field) in rainy season, women-headed households stock prawn post-larvae and rear them for two months to juvenile stage, which are sold to better-off farmers for grow-out culture. Two prawn nursery cycles give a huge average net return of Taka 8000 for the two crops. The Project is also promoting prawn grow-out culture practice in polyculture system with carps in community ponds. About 30 or more households farm and manage a culture pond of 4000sqmt in area. Within nine months, prawns are harvested at a size of more than 250gm, that worth Taka 730/kg. Input supply of feed and seed is carried out through the farmer managed community-based organizations. The Upakul Freshwater Prawn Hatchery has been established at Noakhali, catering post-larvae to the farmers (Edwards, 2006).

Due to the scarcity of wild giant prawn post-larvae supply, a prawn hatchery sector has emerged in Bangladesh over last few years. Many hatchery owners have stated that the primary reason of producing post-larvae was profitability. About 95% of hatchery owners would like to continue this venture in the future because of high profit. Small-scale fish farmers in Philippines practice the hatchery seed production of giant freshwater prawn. They utilize plastic drums (cut into half) as larval rearing tanks. A plastic drum can be converted into two 50-litre capacity larval rearing tanks. The stocking density for larval rearing is 50-100 larvae/lt and in nursery systems, 1,000 post-larvae/sqmt are stocked and raised to juvenile stage. With a total hatchery area of 150sqmt, a farmer can have a net income of about Php 400,000 per run/cycle (estimated four runs per year) with a post-larvae survival rate of 70% at 15th day. In India, *M. rosenbergii* seeds are transported by aerial route to commercial prawn farming sites from hatcheries of Tamilnadu, Andhra Pradesh and Orissa. Considering the huge gap between the demand and supply of seeds, there exist enormous scope for establishment of hatchery that can be undertaken as a profitable enterprise (Jena *et.al.*, 2005). In Bangladesh, *M. rosenbergii* fishing (capture fishery) is done throughout the year from estuaries and during winter months from beels and rivers.

Morphological Variations

A study was conducted during June-November 2011 to determine morphological variations of *M. rosenbergii* at local market of Batiaghata, Dist.

Khulna in Bangladesh. Samples of prawn were collected directly from the different local markets. Two types of male morphotypes were found in local markets; blue clawed male (BC) and orange clawed male (OC). They differed in cheliped morphology and some morphometric characters. OC had large orange claws on their second chelate leg. OC males later might transform into the third and final stage, the 'blue claw' (BC) males. These had blue claws, and their second chelate leg might become twice as long as their body. The total length (22.28±2.96cm in BC and 21.42±2.77cm in OC), chelate length (8.96±3.92cm in BC and 6.21±1.03cm in OC), body length (12.28±3.16cm in BC and 14.42±2.19cm in OC), carapace length, weight (132.88±53.52gm in BC and 146.13±57.16gm in OC) and rostrum length had been found to be significantly different between the two morphotypes (Akter *et. al.,* 2012).

Farming Practice in Dist. Midnapore East, West Bengal – A Case Study

In Midnapore East district of West Bengal, which is the major district where *M. rosenbergii* is cultured in monoculture systems on a commercial scale, the main producing areas include Bhagabanpur, Moina, Sabang, Pingla and Junput Police Stations/Blocks. In 25-30 villages of the aforesaid Blocks, presently there are about 1250-1300 professional prawn farmers. During April, quarter of an inch sized 5-6PL stage *M. rosenbergii* are collected from rivers Kansabati, Rupnarayan, Keleghai and are stocked in nursery ponds. Seeds are available from two hatcheries namely Bengal Scampi Private Limited, located at Duttapukur, Digha and the hatchery owned by Lotika Seafood Private Limited at Contai in same district. Riverine seed are mostly preferred by farmers for stocking as those are more healthy and strong. Nursery ponds are mostly 1-5 decimal in area with 4.5-5 feet water level. Seeds are reared for a period of 45 days till juvenile stage.

In old ponds meant for nurseries, before seed stocking, complete dewatering is done followed by sundrying. Bottom soil cracks, then 2-3inch top soil is sliced off and removed. In case of black soil with good deposition of organic sediment, 5-6inch thick layer of top soil is removed. In newly excavated pond, this function need not be done. Subsequently soil pH is checked which has to be preferably above 6.5. Lime in dry state is applied over dry soil. The dosage of lime according to soil pH is mentioned below:

Range of Soil pH	Dosage of Lime
4.5-5.0	300kg/ha of CaO (quick lime)
5.0-5.5	200kg/ha of CaO (quick lime)
5.5-6.0	150kg/ha of CaO (quick lime)
6.0-6.5	100kg/ha of CaO (quick lime)
6.5-7.0	100kg/ha of $CaCo_3$ (limestone powder)
7.0-7.5	–
7.5-8.0	500kg/ha of $CaSo_4$ (gypsum)

After 6-7 days of application of lime on dry soil, water from a canal source or beel/wetland is let into the pond. At inlet, inflowing water is screened with 80-100 mesh screen. Water level is increased to 4-4.5 feet. After this, an organic mixture called 'Juice' is added to water to increase phytoplankton productivity and favour pH balance. For a one decimal ($40m^2$) nursery pond, this mixture comprises 500gm molasses, 2kg mustard oil cake and 10-12gm bakery yeast. After adding water, it is fermented in small cemented tanks for 48 hours and then the liquefied mixture is applied over water body. On next day, after 24 hours, dolomite is applied into pond @ 200gm/decimal water body. Again after 24 hours, the 'Juice' preparation is applied. In this manner on every alternate day, application of dolomite and Juice is continued for 5 days. On 6th day, water turns greenish as desired, having pH range of 7.8-8.2.

In this condition, 5-6PL stage *M. rosenbergii* are stocked @ 40nos./m^2, i.e., 1600nos. per decimal. Feeding to growing PL is very important; it is done with commercially available crumble-type pelleted feed (Starter stage), which costs Rs. 1600-1650/- per 25kg pack. A simplified daily feeding schedule is mentioned below:

Days	Stocking Density			
	1000nos./dec	**2000nos./dec**	**3000nos./dec**	**4000nos./dec**
Every 1st-8th day	8gm/1000nos.	7gm/1000nos.	6gm/1000nos.	5gm/1000nos.
Every 9th-17th day	10gm/1000nos.	9gm/1000nos.	8gm/1000nos.	7gm/1000nos.
Every 18th-20th day	12gm/1000nos.	11gm/1000nos.	10gm/1000nos.	9gm/1000nos.
Every 21st-40th day	4gm increase/ day/1000nos.	3gm increase/ day/1000nos.	2.5gm increase/ day/1000nos.	2gm increase/ day/1000nos.

In nursery ponds, the growing early stages are fed four times a day at 8 hours interval. Rearing period of 45 days is a must in nurseries. Regular pH checking is done. Prawns attain 3.0-4.0gm body weight individually at the end of this period, these are termed as juveniles. These are stocked in grow-out ponds. For the first one month, limestone powder is not applied in nursery ponds, only dolomite is applied.

Regarding pond preparation in grow-outs, same process is followed as like nursery ponds. Broken asbestos sheet, sun-dried date palm or palm tree leaves, broken earthen pots are provided in grow-out ponds so that growing juveniles may take shelter after moulting to avoid predation of non-moulted prawns. Area of grow-out *M. rosenbergii* monoculture ponds ranges between 1 bigha (33 decimal) to 1 hectare (250decimal). Agricultural fields with high embankment on four sides after paddy harvest are utilized as grow-out ponds. Juveniles are stocked @ 4-5nos./m^2 in mixed sex culture (160-200nos./ decimal) and 3nos./m^2 in 'all-male' culture system. At the 3.0-4.0gm stage of *M. rosenbergii*, the gap that exists between the base points of the two legs of

5th pair of walking leg has been found to be less in case of males, and more in case of females. In males, blunt point headed small muscular tubercle is observed at the base of two legs of 5th pair of walking leg. Based on these distinguishing features, the male juveniles are segregated and selected for stocking in 'all-male' monoculture system.

Regarding supplementary feeding management, growing juveniles are fed four times at six hours interval in grow-out ponds. To growing juveniles, commercial pelleted feed 'Grower' type of 1-2mm diameter is fed upto 25gm size and 'Finisher' type pelleted feed of 2-3mm diameter is fed thereafter till time of harvest. The feeding schedule in grow-out ponds is mentioned below:

Age	Average Body Weight	Feed Applied Each day (in % of Total Body Weight)
1-15 days	3-7gm	7-4%
16-30 days	7-10gm	4.0-3.6%
31-44 days	10-16gm	3.6-3.2%
45-59 days	16-22gm	3.2-2.8%
60-74 days	22-29gm	2.8-2.4%
75-89 days	29-34gm	2.4-2.0%
90-105 days	34-39gm	2.0-1.5%
106-145 days	40-50gm	1.5-1.0%
Above 145 days	Above 50gm	1.0%

Commercially available bakery yeast (supplemented with binder and feed attractants) is added to feed, which facilitates bodily growth. In grow-out ponds, 25% of the total daily feed is applied at 5.00am in morning 20% at 11.00am, 30% at 5.00pm and 25% at 11.00pm. Sometimes the feed which is applied at 11.00pm is replaced by muscle meat of the freshwater bivalve *Lamellidens marginalis*. The flesh portion from collected adult mussels is sliced out with scalpel, it is finely chopped, salt and turmeric are added to it according to requirement and is cooked/boiled. Mussel meat is softened and made easily digestible and then it is spread in the feeding zone of ponds by hand. In grow-out ponds, the feeding zone refers to a distance of 8 feet from bank towards inside of pond on all four sides. Farmers who do not excavate new grow-out ponds, they utilize agricultural fields with 3.5 feet high embankment. After the Rabi crop of paddy (December-January to April-May) is harvested, then the impoundments are filled with water and juveniles are stocked therein. Soil pH is checked, which should preferably be of the range 6.5-8.5. Commercially available water probiotic is applied to nursery and grow-out ponds before seed stocking.

If advanced juveniles and sub-adults of *M. rosenbergii* in grow-out culture systems do not moult normally, then whitish algal deposit is found over their shell/exoskeleton. It causes retardation in growth. In such conditions, 'forced moulting' is done. At 7.00pm of a particular day, a mixture of Gas Remover @ 10gm/decimal (a commercial product in dust form) and Zeolite @ 100gm/decimal is applied in the pond. After 24 hours, Dolomite @ 200gm/decimal is applied. Again after 24 hours of it, a mixture of limestone powder (@ 100-200gm/decimal) and sand is applied to pond. At last, commercially available water probiotic is added. This entire process facilitates moulting of prawns. Gas Remover causes elimination of toxic gases like H_2S, NH_3 from pond bottom. Zeolite incorporating different metal oxides supplies oxygen into the system. Dolomite facilitates softening of the prawn shell. Mixture of LSP and sand causes irritation to the prawns and finally they moult. Many farmers use Multi-Vitamin supplier (a commercial product) along with supplementary feed (@ 10gm/kg feed) during this 'forced moulting' process.

Grow-out culture of *M. rosenbergii* is a practice of 7 months in this district. Juveniles are mainly stocked during April-May and marketable-sized prawns are harvested in November-December. In mixed sex culture, *M. rosenbergii* attain 40gm body weight on average, but in 'all-male' system, body weight has been observed to be 45-50gm at time of harvest. Repeated drag netting and subsequently dewatering is done at time of harvest. In auction fish markets of the district, 'first grade' *M. rosenbergii* ranging between 50-70gm is sold @ Rs. 420-450/- per kilogram. Those between 30-50gm in size are sold @ Rs. 300-350/- per kilogram. Since *M. rosenbergii* prefers the zooplankter *Cyclops* sp. as food, some farmers use a commercial product that includes readily available stored and fresh *Cyclops* sp. Limestone powder is applied in ponds as per requirement upto a maximum of 400gm/decimal area. Accumulation of unconsumed excess feed, moulted and shed-off shell, crushed plankton, dead insects, tree leaves and faecal matter over pond bottom causes in increase in organic load which is undesirable. To overcome this, Zeolite is applied to pond @ 40-50kg/ha. After conditions of heavy rain, dolomite is applied in ponds @ 400gm/decimal, i.e., 100kg/ha to maintain pH balance.

Culture and presence of *M. rosenbergii* blue-clawed males in monoculture ponds is undesirable to farmers. If it is observed that males are growing with blue coloured chelate legs (one pair), then such prawns are taken out from pond by farm staff, hold in upright position individually with head on top and the pair of legs are hold on palm. It is then given a gentle shake so that the chelate legs are broken/detached at their base point. Prawns without chelate leg pair are then dipped in $KMnO_4$ solution so that no infection arises from the base point (detached) area with minor wound and are released back into pond. These prawns attain a higher growth rate in comparison to those having blue claws.

In agricultural fields (0.5-1.5ha) which have been converted to *M. rosenbergii* grow-out systems after paddy harvest and farming of the species have been undertaken for 7 months, after this period of time, planting of paddy saplings is done again and paddy farming is initiated as usual in same plot. Deposition of faecal matter of *M. rosenbergii,* unconsumed feed materials during prawn farming prior to paddy act as manure thereby making the soil nutrient-rich and fertile; it has been observed that normal production of paddy occurs in the plot as expected without use of any kind of inorganic fertilizers. Many farmers opined that if the body of a freshly-killed goat obtained from a butcher shop is kept in submerged condition in *M. rosenbergii* grow-out ponds (using inclined bamboo or other support), within a day, growing prawns will devour away the meat portion of goat body leaving only the bones and vertebrae.

Farming of *M. rosenbergii* in Cemented Tanks

In West Bengal and other states, prawn farmers can rear this species in concrete or cemented rectangular tanks constructed in own home premises. Size of the tank should be 20 feet × 18 feet × 3 feet. Two openings (inlets) should be situated at the base of two opposite walls of the tank where plastic or iron mouths should be installed, which should have 90° bent on one side. When water is let into the chamber in a strong rush via these mouths, it will move around the inner base of the tank, lift the water table and water will exit out through the two outlets (having plastic/iron mouths and 90° bent on one side), which will be positioned on the other two opposite walls at their top margins. It will maintain the water level. Very fine-meshed bolting silk cloth/net piece should be placed at the mouth of the two outlets at the upper margin of the chamber, so that planktonic food matter will not be able to move out of the chamber. Nylon net should be placed and spread above covering the entire water area of the tank, so that preying birds will not pose any harm to the growing prawns. The chamber should be constructed under a roof provided with asbestos sheet or polythene, to prevent tank water from scorching sunshine and heavy rainfall.

Prawn juveniles can be stocked during May and marketable size prawns weighing 45-50gm can be harvested during October-November. After one crop, the chamber should be cleaned and treated with sunshine for a week. Again juveniles should be stocked during November-December and harvesting should be done during April-May. Under good management practices, with provision of high quality feeds and facilities for oxygenation, growth of *M. rosenbergii* can be increased upto 75-80gm in one crop.

In order to ensure sufficient growth of planktonic organisms that will serve as natural food of the prawn species, 1kg lime and 5kg cowdung should be applied into the 360 sq. feet water area before stocking of juveniles. After that, 250gm lime and 500gm mustard oil cake should be applied every month. Total 2500 juveniles of 1.5-2.0 inch size should be stocked into the tank in one time. Balanced supplementary feed can be prepared by mixing ingredients like rice bran (50%), mustard oil cake (20%), fish meal (10%), soyabean dust (10%) and wheat flour (10%). Feeding should be done twice a day in late evening and night as these are nocturnal organisms. Daily feeding should be done @ 3-4% of body weight of prawns; every month their body weight should be recorded.

Proper attention should be given towards keeping the water pollution-free. If water temperature rises above 29°C, then comparatively cooler normal tubewell water should be poured into the tank. Deep tubewell water is ideally suited for such a farming practice. During fog-infested winter months, particularly in morning, dissolved oxygen concentration in tank water depletes. So provision of aerating device should be kept. Once in a month $KMnO_4$ should be applied in water @ 1mg/lit. If 75% of 2500 juveniles survive, then 1875 marketable-sized *M. rosenbergii* will be harvested. About 80kg production will be obtained in a crop, considering 45gm average body weight at time of harvest.

CONCLUSION

Of late, culture of giant freshwater prawn is getting tremendously popular in rural India owing to its increased seed availability both from natural waters and hatcheries. In major carp polyculture system, incorporation of *M. rosenbergii* alone in moderate to low stocking density could raise the farmer's income manifolds (Tripathi, 2002). In Punjab and Haryana, vast areas of agricultural lands that became unsuitable for agriculture due to excessive fertilization have been found useful for prawn farming. Many farmers of Vadodara District, central Gujarat have recently opted for *M. rosenbergii* farming. In 2008, the total quantity of freshwater prawns produced globally has reached 58% of the level of tiger shrimp production. It is understood that freshwater prawns are immediately recognizable and valued commodities in the markets, restaurants and homes of most Asian countries. Its demand can only be satisfied through farming. Some notable technical problems in freshwater prawn farming are being addressed at research laboratories.

Diseases and water quality problems have been responsible for a decline in the Indian production of *M. rosenbergii* in near past. With increasing popularity in the culture of the species, some bacterial diseases both in hatcheries and grow-out ponds have been reported. In Vibriosis disease, black/brown cuticular lesion, muscle opacity, black lymphoid organ, melanisation of appendage tips have been observed. Control measures like proper water quality management, good nutrition, use of filtered sea water can be adopted. In the shell disease/black spot/brown spot disease, pitted and eroded exoskeleton leading to melanisation (blackening) at the site of infection is observed, disease produced focally on the gills, carapace, appendages, uropods. Poor water quality and high organic load are associated with shell lesions in severe cases. In conditions of bacterial necrosis, bluish body colouration, empty stomach, weak larvae falling to the bottom of the tank, brown spots on antennae and newly formed appendages are observed. Black gill disease is caused by precipitation of chemical and nitrogenous waste products which are implicated in melanisation of the gills. It is caused by increasing levels of ammonia, nitrate and nitrite concentration in grow-out ponds. Protozoan epibiont *Zoothamnium* sp. has been reported to preferentially locate on the gill lamellae of *M. rosenbergii*, while hard water with high calcium content has been reported to be associated with an increase in *Epistylis* sp. infestation of the prawn species (Shankar and Mohan, 2002). Luminiscent bacteria pose major threat in hatcheries. Proper cleaning of waste food, disinfection of water, periodic water exchange, treatment with recommended antibiotics, less organic loading, use of good quality feeds have become essential components in both hatchery and pond water management.

Freshwater prawn production could make a substantial contribution to sustainable poverty alleviation, particularly when integrated with rice and/ or pig farming, and prawn farming is thought to be less risky than brackishwater shrimp production. The TraVinh provincial authorities of Vietnam, with the support of the UNDP, are exploring the possibilities of encouraging the expansion of giant freshwater prawn production as an income diversification strategy for rice farmers in freshwater areas (Ref: M. B. New. Responsible aquaculture: Is this a special challenge for developing countries?). In Bangladesh, the organization 'CARE' is seeking to improve the education of poor prawn farmers and to reduce risk, to enable the poorest to benefit from aquaculture projects. A freshwater prawn farming project managed by 'CARE' has helped to alleviate poverty in some areas of Bangladesh (Nandeesha and Alam, 2001).

Future Directions

(a) Selective breeding at CIFA, Bhubaneswar

Giant prawn *M. rosenbergii* has become an important cultured species in the pond aquaculture system in commercial terms but dishearteningly in last few years, prawn farmers have reported about decreasing productivity from 500-750kg/ha to 250-300kg/ha mainly due to inferior quality prawn seed and low survivability rate in nursery and grow-out ponds. Heavy mortality has been caused due to White Tail Disease (caused by *M. rosenbergii* Nodavirus) and Appendices Deformities Syndrome. Aiming to produce an improved breed, provide genetically-improved superior quality prawn seed to the farmers and improve growth performance of the species in farm ponds, CIFA (ICAR), Bhubaneswar in collaboration with World Fish Centre, Penang, Malaysia have been conducting a systematic selective breeding programme of *M. rosenbergii* since July 2007. Development of quality broodstock and production of quality seed for the farmers is very important; this could be ensured through selective breeding. Initially juvenile *M. rosenbergii* (3gm size) were collected each from Narmada river, Gujarat (G), Brahmani river, Orissa (O) and hatcheries and backwaters of Kerala (K) and the stocks were separately reared in CIFA experimental ponds as base population till they attained sexual maturation (35-40gm). In each of two successive batches, diallele cross-breeding design was followed and single pair mating was done. Matured males (M) and females (F) were transferred to rectangular ferro-cement tanks to facilitate natural breeding; the crosses done in first batch were KMxKF, KMxGF, KMxOF, GMxKF, GMxGF, GMxOF, OMxKF, OMxGF and OMxOF. Crosses done in subsequent batch were KMxKF, KMxGF, GMxGF, GMxOF and OFxGF. After mating, fertilized egg-bearing females from different crosses were reared individually in circular FRP tanks throughout incubation period (18-19 days). Hatched-out larvae of each full sib family of each batch were obtained (first generation offspring) and reared separately in indoors till they attained post larva stage and further the PL of each full sib family were reared separately in cloth hapa fitted in nursery ponds in next three months.

By this time, the PL had attained "taggable" size. For the next 120-125 days for first batch and 145-160 days for second batch, these 90-day old post larvae or juveniles of all full sib families were reared in grow-out ponds (400sq.mt.) with proper feeding in unsegregated manner in 'communal rearing' system but in the beginning, before being released into ponds, all individuals (90 day old PL) of all families of two batches of first generation were tagged with VIE tags and VIA tags for specific identification of all prawns for the family it belongs to at time of harvest. After 120-125 days of rearing, prawns of first batch were harvested, their survivability rate, morphomeristic characters were recorded, all prawns were observed for presence or absence of tags, tag numbers were noted, percentage of tag retention in prawns of the two tags separately, final body weight of individual prawns, average final body weight of prawns of each of the nine diallele crosses, growth performance, breeding values of individuals, total magnitude of effect of heterosis/hybrid vigour on harvest body weight were estimated and recorded. Community rearing of juveniles of full sib families of second batch was on progress, as information obtained till July-August 2011.

Based on the results, the families and individuals of first batch have been given ranking, the first round of selection and mate allocation was on progress in order to produce second generation offspring. It is expected that in near future, increase of production of *M. rosenbergii* in farm ponds will be restored through implementation of the Project. According to Project investigators, due to shorter generation length and complete occurrence of life cycle in captive conditions, selective breeding is advantageous in *M. rosenbergii* but unlike finfishes, it needs lot of care for transplantation of VIA tags in proper abdominal position of prawn juveniles. CIFA had initiated genetic improvement of *M. rosenbergii* through selective breeding in 2007 to improve the growth rate and come out with a faster growing strain of *M. rosenbergii*. The project has so far shown encouraging result with a cumulative selection response of 16% in four generations. Further the 3rd and 4th generation prawns have undergone on-farm testing at farmer's field in different districts of Odisha with promising results (Source: Official website of Central Institute of Freshwater Aquaculture, Bhubaneswar. Courtesy for information: Director, CIFA, Dr K. D. Mahapatra and Dr. B. R. Pillai, Principal Scientists, CIFA).

(b) 'All-male' M. rosenbergii culture

Since males of *M. rosenbergii* grow faster and reaches a larger size at harvest than females, production of monosex (male) population and their culture in ponds would be economically advantageous. Sexual differentiation in prawns is regulated by the androgen gland and its peptide hormone. In PL-30 stage, if androgenic glands of the immature males are removed through microsurgical intervention, it will lead to sex reversal with complete female differentiation and production of functional neo-females. These neo-females would subsequently be mated with normal males to produce all-male progeny. In a study, total production at 3nos./m^2 stocking density of monosex male *M. rosenbergii* was found to be significantly higher over the other stocking densities (1 and 2nos./m^2) and it was inferred that this treatment could effectively be introduced in the culture of mono-sex giant fresh water prawn for optimum benefit (Nure Alam Siddique *et. al.*, 2012). Whereas in mixed culture in grow-out ponds, stocking density is maintained at 20000-25000nos./ha and reared for 8-10 months but in monosex 'all-male' culture, stocking is maintained @ 12500-15000nos./ha. Farm yields in the latter system amount to 500-1500kg/ha (Nair and Salin, 2006).

In India, Andhra Pradesh dominates the giant prawn monoculture sector with over 86% of the total production in India with more than 60% of the total water area dedicated to prawn farming, followed by West Bengal. Andhra farmers have evolved many innovative *M. rosenbergii* culture strategies ('All-male' culture, Claw ablation) based on their experiences. 'All-male' culture has been found to yield better than mixed culture of both sexes. More than 60% of prawn farmers in Andhra Pradesh practice 'all-male' culture. Advantages of 'all-male' monosex culture include: increased yield and survivability, bigger size at harvest, better profit margin, shortened crop period, lower feed consumption and FCR, improvement in overall output from farming (Nair *et. al.*, 2006). In farms located at Nellore, East and West Godavari districts of the state, skilled women are involved in manual segregation of male and female juveniles (with 95% accuracy) from nursery ponds after 45 days of rearing and separate stocking in grow-outs.

(c) Organic prawn and other aspects

In November 2008, there was an announcement of what is claimed to be the world's first organic aquaculture harvest of the giant prawn *M. rosenbergii* in the backwaters of Kerala. In Giant Prawn 2011 Conference at Kochi, Kerala it was discussed that issues that are responsible for a decline in giant prawn production, viz., poor quality of the seed stocked, poor genetic quality of the broodstock used, pond water quality issues, diseases, poor growth in ponds, increased cost of production on account of feed, labour can be overcome by utilizing sustainable farming systems like organic prawn farming. Sustainability is the key concept and it was hoped that, while the production levels are presently low, the sector would streamline for sustainability in the near future (Source: *Fishing Chimes, March 2011 issue*). Another important paper on "Potential of *Macrobrachium rosenbergii* in poverty alleviation - examples from Asia" was presented in the Conference, authored by eminent fisheries professional Prof. M. C. Nandeesha and others. Examples of several successful small-scale farmers earning substantial income through prawn aquaculture were highlighted, particularly in Bangladesh, India, Thailand and Vietnam. It was discussed about the innovations of farmers in the coastal areas of the south-western part of Bangladesh; who have shown practices which could be used for poverty alleviation and have developed the technology for rearing Macrobrachium species in impounded waters using the naturally available wild seed.

Hatchery managers need to give special attention to feeding management of early stages, *viz.*, use of good quality egg custard, Artemia nauplii enrichment, production of freshwater zooplankton, other live feeds and water quality management. Strengthening of extension linkages through large-scale demonstration of seed rearing and production technologies, on-site training, field days, meetings on important aspects of prawn farming is essential for spread of prawn farming technology. In India, the saline (soil less than 15 exchangeable sodium percentage, pH 7.5-8.5), alkaline (soil more than 15 exchangeable sodium percentage, pH 8.5-10.0) and low-lying water-logged areas under various reservoir commands constitute the major resource for establishing commercial *M. rosenbergii* farms.

Finally, a research achievement is worth mentioning. In northern India, *M. rosenbergii* is normally cultured during June to December, depending on the water temperature (optimum range 27°-31°C). Fresh prawn-crop is not available to consumers after December. In Bihar, the species has been successfully cultured during post-monsoon winter season for the first time. The scientists of ICAR Research Complex at Patna could succeed in its farming by providing suitable shelters in ponds and trenches at its Walmi Farm, from August to February. This adaptive research work has paved way for giant prawn farming beyond December. The farmers and entrepreneurs will be highly benefited from the new approach of prawn farming in the seasonally waterlogged areas of Bihar (*Source*: ICAR Newsletter, April-June 2009).

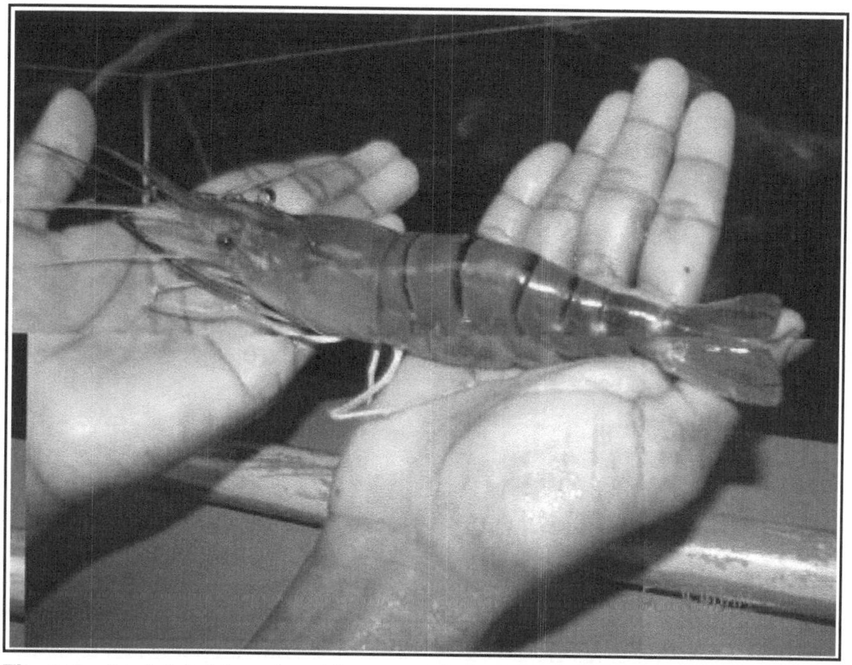

Fig. 3.1: An Adult *Macrobrachium rosenbergii* Harvested in a Prawn Farm in Midnapore East, West Bengal (Photograph: Sri Himadri Chandra)

Fig. 3.2: An adult *Macrobrachium rosenbergii* with Blue Claw in a Prawn Farm at Midnapore East, West Bengal (Photograph: Sri Himadri Chandra)

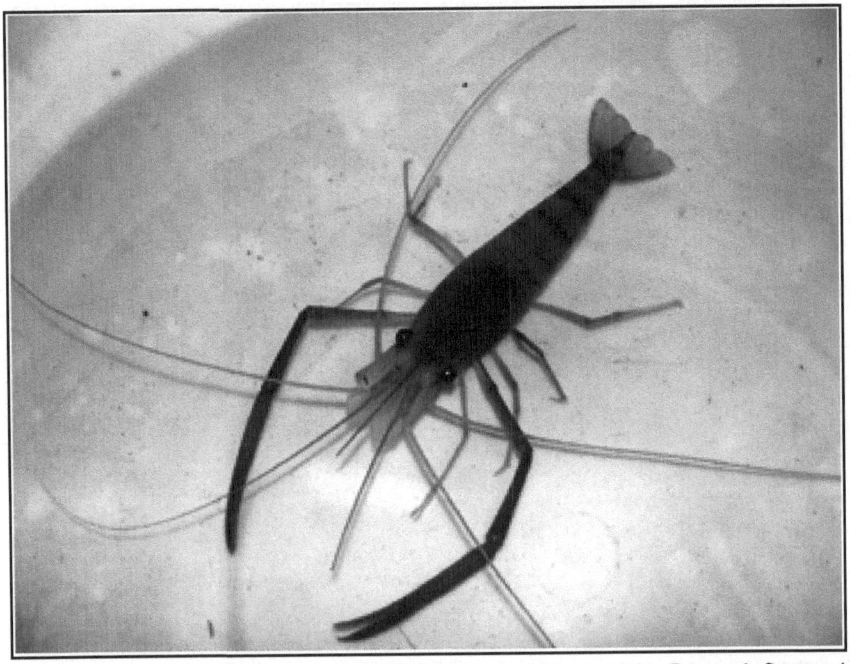

Fig. 3.3: *Macrobrachum rosenbergii* Brooder Reared in Bengal Scampi Hatchery, Digha, Midnapore East (Photograph: Sri Himadri Chandra)

REFERENCES

Aflalo, Eli D., D. V.S.N. Raju, N.A. Bommi and J.T. Verghese. (2012). Towards a Sustainable Production of Genetically Improved All-male Prawn *Macrobrachium rosenbergii*: Evaluation of Production Traits and Obtaining Neo-females in Three Indian Strains. *Aquaculture*, 338-341: 197-207.

Ahmed, N., M.A. Wahab and S.H. Thilsted. (2007). Integrated Aquaculture-agriculture Systems in Bangladesh. *Aquaculture Asia*, 12 (1): 14-22.

Ahmed, N. (2008). Freshwater Prawn Hatcheries in Bangladesh: Concern of Broodstock. *Aquaculture Asia*, 13 (3): 22-26.

Akter, N., A.K. Ghosh, K.A. Huq and S.M.B. Rahaman. (2012). Morphological Variations of Freshwater Giant Prawn (*Macrobrachium rosenbergii*) at Local Markets in Batiagata, Khulna. Book of Abstracts, 5th Fisheries Conference and Research Fair 2012. *BFRF, Dhaka, Bangladesh*: pp 4.

Anh, P.T., C. Kroeze, S.R. Bush and A.P.J. Mol. (2010). Water Pollution by Intensive Brackish Shrimp Farming in South-east Vietnam: Causes and Options for Control. *Agricultural Water Management*, 97: 872-882.

Balakrishnan Nair N. (1998). Impact of Aquaculture on Coastal Ecosystems and Suggested Mitigating Measures. In Natarajan P. *et al.*, Ed. Advances in Aquatic Biology and Fisheries. Prof. Balakrishnana Nair Felicitation Committee, University of Kerala, Trivandrum, India: pp. 11-30.

Chakraborti, P.K. (1998). Scope and Prospects of Fisheries in Estuarine Wetlands of West Bengal. *Meenbarta Wetland Day issue*: 66-68.

Chondar, S.L. 1999. Biology of Finfish and Shellfish. *SCSC Publishers, Howrah*: pp. 460-473.

Devaraja, T.N., S. Magada and A.V. Swamy. (2014). Fish cum Paddy Farming. In. Souv. Nat. Sem. Strategies for Bridging the Yield Gap in Fisheries and Aquaculture. PFGF Publication: pp. 24-31.

Edwards, P. (2006). Poor Households Raise Prawns for Export. *Aquaculture Asia*, 11 (2): 25-27.

Edwards, P. (2011). Aquaculture for Enhancing Nutritional and Economic Improvement in Asia. In. Compendium of Asian-Pacific Aquaculture 2011. *College of Fisheries, Panangad*: pp. 1-11.

Ghosh, A., S.K. Mukhopadhyaya, P.K. Chakraborti, , G.N. Chattopadhyaya, A.K. Dutta and A.K. Roy. (1985). Culture of *Macrobrachium rosenbergii* in a Sewage-fed Pond. *Ibid.*, 17 (1-2): 54-61.

Jena, J.K. (2005). Aquaculture Technology for Farmers. *ICAR Publication*: pp. 31-36.

Kurup, B.M. and K. Ranjeet. (2002). Integration of Freshwater Prawn Culture with Rice Farming in Kuttanad, India. *NAGA, World Fish Centre Quarterly*, 25 (3-4): 16-19.

Kutty, M.N. (2005). Towards Sustainable Freshwater Prawn Aquaculture - Lessons from Shrimp Farming with Special Reference to India. *Aquaculture Research*, 36: 255-263.

Kutty, M.N., C. Mohanakumaran Nair and K.R. Salin. (2008). Reservoir Fisheries of Freshwater Prawn - A Success Story at Malampuzha Dam. *Aquaculture Asia*, 13 (2): 40-42.

Leo Cyril A. R., S. Immanuel, B. Thongam, B.T. Naveen Kumar and Sathish Rama Poojary. (2014). Assessment of the Livelihood Status of the Shrimp Farmers in Karnataka. In. Souv. Nat. Sem. Strategies for Bridging the Yield Gap in Fisheries and Aquaculture. *PFGF Publication*: pp. 32-39.

Menon, N.R. (2001). Shrimp Culture: Its Ecological Imperatives and Eco-ethical Solutions. In. Souvenir of Fish for Nutritional Security in the 21st Century. *CIFE (ICAR) Publication, Mumbai*: pp. 70-79.

Mitra, G. and P.K. Mukhopadhyay. (2005). Nutrition and Feeding in Freshwater Prawn *Macrobrachium rosenbergii* Farming. *Aqua Feeds: Formulation and Beyond*, 2 (1): 17-19.

Nair, C.M., K.R. Salin, M.S. Raju and M. Sebastian. (2006). Economic Analysis of Monosex Culture of Giant Freshwater Prawn *Macrobrachium rosenbergii* De Man: A Case Study. *Aquaculture Research*, 37: 949-954.

Nair, C.M. and K.R. Salin. (2006). Freshwater Prawn Farming in India: Status and Prospects. *Global Aquaculture Advocate*, Nov-Dec 2006: 33-37.

Nandeesha, M.C. and R. Alam. (2001). Scaling up the Impact of Aquaculture: The CARE Experience in Bangladesh. In. Utilizing Different Aquatic Resources for Livelihoods in Asia: A Resource Book. *World Fish Center, Malaysia*: pp. 95-100.

New, M.B. and W.C. Valenti. (2000). Freshwater Prawn Culture: The Farming of *Macrobrachium rosenbergii*. *Blackwell Science Publishing*: pp. 192-198.

New, M.B. (2002). Farming Freshwater Prawns. *FAO Fisheries Technical Paper No. 428.*

New, M.B., W.C. Valenti, J.H. Tidwell and M.N. Kutty. (2010). Freshwater Prawns: Biology and Farming. Wiley Blackwell Publishing: pp. 760.

New, M.B. (2011). Freshwater Prawn Farming. In. Compendium of Asian-Pacific Aquaculture 2011. *College of Fisheries, Panangad*: pp. 13-17.

Pillai, B.R., S.C. Rath, S. Sahu and N. Sarangi. (2007). Grow-out Technology of Giant Freshwater Prawn. *Indian Farming*, 56 (10): 3-6.

Rajyalakhsmi, T. (1979). The Role of Macrobrachium Species in Freshwater Aquaculture Systems. In. Symp. on Inland Aquaculture, *CICFRI, Barrackpore*: pp. 119.

Roy, B., D.N. Das and P.K. Mukhopadhyay. (1991). Rice-fish/prawn-vegetable Integrated Farming: Viable Proposition in Deepwater Rice Ecosystem. Proc. Nat. Sym. New Horizons in Freshwater Aquaculture, *CIFA (ICAR), Bhubaneswar*: pp. 24-25.

Roy, H.C., M.A. Wahab and M. Jashim Uddin. (2012). Organic Prawn in Polyculture: Effects of Stocking Density of Tilapia on Environment and Production. Book of Abstracts, 5th Fisheries Conference and Research Fair 2012. *BFRF, Dhaka, Bangladesh*: pp. 76.

Shankar, K.M. and C.V. Mohan. (2002). Common Diseases of Giant Freshwater Prawns. In. Fish and Shellfish Health Management. *College of Fisheries, Mangalore*: pp. 54-56.

Siddique, M.N.A., K.A. Huq, W. Sabbir and M.L. Rahi. (2012). Impact of Stocking Density on Growth of Mono-sex (Male) Giant Freshwater Prawn (*Macrobrachium rosenbergii*). Book of Abstracts, 5th Fisheries Conference and Research Fair 2012. *BFRF, Dhaka, Bangladesh*: pp. 82.

Tripathi, S.D. (2002). Small-scale Farming Systems for Rural Development. Souv. Sixth Indian Fisheries Forum. *CIFE, Mumbai*: pp. 67-77.

Van Nguyen, Q.T. (1993). Integrated Rice-prawn Farming in the Mekong Delta, Vietnam: A Route Towards Sustainable and Profitable Farming Systems? *Naga, the ICLARM Quarterly*, 16 (2-3): 18-20.

Varadaraju S., B. Hanumanthappa and H. Badami Shashidhar. (2014). Impact of Shrimp Culture on Adjacent Source Water Quality Along the Coastal Line of Dakshina Kannada and Udupi Districts. In. Souv. Nat. Sem. Strategies for Bridging the Yield Gap in Fisheries and Aquaculture. PFGF Publication: 129.

Vasudevappa, C. (2002). Status and Scope for Enhancing Giant Freshwater Prawn Production in India. In. S. Ayyappan Ed. Souv. Int. Symp. Fish for Nutritional Security in 21st Century. *CIFE, Mumbai Publication*: pp. 154-162.

Vasudevappa C. and D. Seenappa. (2002). Literature Review of Shrimp Farming in India. Individual Partner Report for the Project: Policy Research for Sustainable Shrimp Farming in Asia. *University of Agricultural Sciences, Bangalore*: pp. 48.

Weimin, M. and G. Xianping. (2002). Freshwater Prawn Culture in China: An Overview. *Aquaculture Asia*, 7 (1): 9-12.

Zamal, M.M. and G.R. Banu. (2012). Detection of White Spot Syndrome Virus (WSSV) in Brackishwater Cultured Shrimp (*Penaeus monodon*) in Khulna District Using PCR with Different Primer. Book of Abstracts, 5th Fisheries Conference and Research Fair 2012. *BFRF, Dhaka, Bangladesh*: pp 38.

Pages: 67-82

FISH HABITAT AND AQUACULTURE
Edited by: Dr. Sanjay Kumar Gupta; Dr. Pawan Kumar 'Bharti'
ISBN: 978-93-5056-744-9
Edition: 2015
Published by: Discovery Publishing House Pvt. Ltd., New Delhi (India)

4

Organic Fertilizers and Organic Fish Farming System
An Approach Towards Sustainability

M.K. Datta and Subrato Ghosh

ABSTRACT

Fertilization is an important step in fish farm management practices; proper application of fertilizers increases pond productivity and consequently production of fish under culture. Although inorganic fertilizers are more efficient and quick in functioning, still in present day conditions, organic fertilizers are preferred over inorganic ones and the former is recommended for application for sustainable fish farming and production. The main objective of 'organic fish farming' approach is to optimize the health and production potential of pond water and soil, fishes under culture and human beings. Over time, ponds treated only with synthetic chemical fertilizers lose organic matter and the living organisms that help to build a quality bottom soil. Organic fertilizers seek the survivability of beneficial microorganisms and worms living in the soil, creating a healthy ecosystem that is sustainable and conducive to long-term use. Likewise organic fertilizers have proved to be superior and beneficial in other aspects also. The characteristic features of different kinds of animal manures and other organic fertilizers and their utility in fish production have been comprehensively reviewed in this communication.

Key words: Organic fertilizers, Manures, Organic aquaculture, Sustainability.

INTRODUCTION

Organic agriculture is an ecological production management system that promotes and enhances biodiversity, biological cycles and soil biological activity. It is based on minimal use of off-farm inputs and on management practices that restore, maintain and enhance ecological harmony. Organic agriculture is a system of farm design and management that creates an ecosystem which can achieve sustainable productivity without the use of artificial external inputs such as chemical fertilizers and pesticides.

PRINCIPAL GUIDELINES FOR ORGANIC PRODUCTION

- To use materials and practices that enhance the ecological balance of natural systems and that integrate the parts of the farming system into an ecological whole.
- Organic agriculture practices cannot ensure that products are completely free of residues; however, methods are used to minimize pollution from air, soil and water.
- Organic food handlers, processors and retailers adhere to standards that maintain the integrity of organic agricultural products.
- The primary goal of organic agriculture is to optimize the health and productivity of interdependent communities of soil life, plants, animals and people.

ORGANIC AQUACULTURE

Diminishing fishery harvests, wild fish food-safety issues, environmental concerns, increased fish consumption, and the increasing market share of organic foods have combined to focus attention on "organic aquaculture." Consumer demand may well drive the organic production of finfish, shellfish, and other aquatic species into the mainstream during the next decade. Organic aquaculture has attracted the attention of researchers from several academic disciplines as well as that of environmental advocates and entrepreneurial innovators. A small number of "certified" and non-certified organic fish and microalgae products have made it to the retail market place in the developed countries. While the regulatory specifics still need to be addressed, this new organic market niche has significant potential for growth in the future (Boehmer *et al.*, 2005). Management techniques must be governed by the physiological and ethological needs of the organisms in question. The organisms should be allowed to meet their basic behavioural needs.

Management techniques, especially when applied to influence production levels and speed of growth must maintain and protect the good health and welfare of the organisms. When introducing non-native species, special care must be to avoid permanent disruption to natural ecosystems. Breeding strategies and practices in organic aquaculture interfere as little as possible with natural behaviour of the animals. Natural breeding methods are used. Organic aquaculture production provides a good quality diet balanced according to the nutritional needs of the organism. Feed is only offered to the organisms in a way that allows natural feeding behaviour, with minimum loss of feed to the environment. Feed compromises by-products from organic food processing and wild marine feed resources not otherwise suited for human consumption. Fish feed is one of the most important factors in aquaculture production. It is widely anticipated that global aquaculture expansion will encounter an inevitable future shortfall of non-renewable resources such as fishmeal and fish oil, necessitating the exploration of alternative strategies for fish feeds. The principles of organic aquaculture encourage the development of feeds that do not deplete global fish stocks. Fish discard and cut-offs may be potential alternative ingredients, but this conflicts with the Danish environmental regulations because of their high phosphorus content. Intuitively, partial substitution of fishmeal and fish oil by sustainable organic plant protein and oil sources seems a good alternative, since fish feed (including organic) contains more than 60 % fishmeal on a fat-free basis

ORGANIC PRODUCTION IN AQUACULTURE

"Organic" in the context of food production connotes standards and certification – a verifiable claim for the production process and production practices – as well as more elusive characteristics such as consumer expectation for food quality and safety and general environmental, social, and economic benefits for farmers and for society. The variety of species produced in aquacultural systems and vast differences in cultural requirements for finfish, shellfish, mollusks, and aquatic plants add to the complexity of defining this sector. In India there is an ample opportunity to boost organic crop, livestock and fish production to catch the organic food market of the world. The north-eastern region can become a major organic farming of the world. In N-E region of India, particularly the hill States, have already started moving towards organic agriculture. In the eastern region, it is estimated that about 1.8 million ha already existing as 13 million organic by default. It is obvious that large quantity of FYM, compost, vermi-compost, feeds, biopesticides and other organically produced inputs and biomass would be required to compensate for the fertilizers and pesticides (Datta, 2008). For the sustainability of organic farm, it is important to note that a certified organic farm(s) has to produce most of these inputs in-situ. But that is lacking in the region.

NON-DEPENDENCE ON INORGANIC FERTILIZERS

Use of manure (Organic fertilizers) in aquaculture specially in earthen pond system for carps is age old practice. Organic fertilizers are usually animal manures or plant wastes and cuttings ("green manure").Manure from chickens, goats, sheep, ducks, pigs, rabbits, cattle and horses are excellent fertilizers for fish ponds. Organic fertilizers decompose and release nitrogen, phosphorous and potassium which are used by phytoplankton for growth and reproduction. In this way more natural food organisms are produced for fish to eat. Organic fertilizers, especially animal manures, provide nutrients and attachment sites for bacteria and other microscopic organisms. These organisms provide nourishment for fish even though in some cases the manure itself may have no direct food value when eaten. Many "green manures" and the undigested food in animal manures are digestible and provide direct nutrition when eaten by fish. This is in addition to their effect as fertilizers and attachment sites for fish food organisms as described above. The result is enhanced fish production.

Many professional fish farmers of India specially in West Bengal have reported that the routine wise monthly application of inorganic fertilizers urea and single superphosphate in composite carp culture system in grow-out ponds during the entire 10-12month period do lead to nutrient enhancement and vigorous proliferation of phytoplankton and subsequently zooplankton, but at the time of harvest, table-sized fishes loses the 'tightness' of body flesh, becomes somewhat flaccid, soft-textured and the original taste of such fishes is lost. They become less acceptable to buyers in market who have become aware about the nature of 'urea-treated' fishes. Farmers have also opined that dependence on incessant use of such mineral fertilizers to restore/improve the productivity status of fish ponds will lead to complete loss of their normal biological productivity potential; ponds will be incapable of generation of their normal productivity/fertility in near future and will demand larger quantities of fertilizers to be used.

Before stocking of fingerlings in grow-out ponds, many fish farmers use the two chemical fertilizers to cause an initial phytoplankton production, liberation of toxic accumulated gases from pond bottom *via* subsequent raking, release of nutrients from bottom soil and elimination of turbid nature of water due to mud suspension, but those are not applied during the culture period. As a substitute they use different organic manures to raise the level of nitrogen, potassium, carbon, potassium in pond water and soil upto sufficiency and maintain the biological productivity therein. Inorganic fertilizers are formulated using various chemicals containing nitrogen, phosphorus and potassium. Such fertilizers leave harmful residues in food crops. Long-term use of such food materials can be seriously harmful to health.

In recent times, in order to maintain the sustainability of fish production from farm ponds and wipe-out the long-term potential adverse effect of artificial inorganic fertilizers on pond ecology and environment quality, fish and human health; alternative means of fish farming have been thought of and the use of such external inputs to its minimum extent or their complete avoidance in commercial pond aquaculture have been suggested. Fishery scientists recommend the application of 10 kg urea and 15 kg single superphosphate in combination in a 1 hectare pond once in a month during the entire culture period, but many fish farmers are reluctant to follow this practice; and in context of the above circumstances, their belief is considerably relevant and significant.

ORGANIC AND INORGANIC FERTILIZERS

Fertilization is an essential step or procedure in efficient fish farm management to increase pond productivity. Fish production can be increased with accurate application of fertilizers and supplementary feeds in different culture systems. The main purpose of pond fertilization is to augment the production of plankton which serves as natural food of the fishes; because fertilization stimulates both the autotrophic and heterotrophic levels which increase fish production (Sayeed *et al.*, 2007). Briefly going through the two terms, inorganic fertilizers are synthetically prepared; they have a definite chemical composition of nutrient elements and are instantly soluble in water. In low productive soils, any one of the inorganic fertilizers may be used: Calcium ammonium nitrate @ 500-650kg/ha/year, Urea @ 225-290 kg/ha/year, SSP @ 315-405kg/ha/year, TSP @ 110-145kg/ha/year. In high productive soils, fertilizers that may be used are Urea @ 112-156 kg/ha/year, Ammonium sulphate @ 225-330 kg/ha/year, SSP @ 156-219 kg/ha/year, TSP @ 54-76 kg/ha/year. They have a high concentration of nutrients that are rapidly available for plant uptake.

On the other hand, organic fertilizers are derived from animal or vegetable matter. They have a very beneficial effect on pond bottom. Besides nitrogen and phosphorus, they contain other minerals which have beneficial effect on plankton growth. They contain protein, fat and fibre (Das and Jana, 1996). The defecated excreta of goats, sheep, farmed pigs, cattle (bullock and dairy cows), horses, rabbit, chicken, ducks and goose serve as excellent sources of nutritional elements in fish culture ponds and consequently increases fish production. These are the animal manures, and other materials like plant wastes, plant cuttings, green manure (grass, leaves or whole plant), compost manure, silkworm faeces, diluted night soil (human excreta and urine/domestic sewage), in addition to the faeces and urine of livestock and farmed birds may be collectively termed as organic fertilizers (Vinod and Basavaraja, 2007).

Both chemical (inorganic) and organic fertilizers act by directly stimulating phytoplankton production within the pond. Inorganic fertilizers act through the primary production of the pond while organic manures can, in addition, directly stimulate higher trophic levels supplying organic matters and detritus (Source: Aquaculture Feed and Fertilizer Resources Information System, FAO).

EMPHASIZING ON ORGANIC FERTILIZERS – A BETTER ALTERNATIVE

With due consideration of the economic status of mostly small-scale marginal professional fish farmers of our country having less-to-moderate water resource and investment capability, it has been proposed to promote fish farming practice based on on-farm, low-cost, easily and locally available natural organic resources. Attention has been concentrated on maximizing protein food production through optimum and productive utilization of available resources and recycling of farm wastes that can provide maximum return to the fish farmer. Giant prawn culture is heavily dependent on use of a combination of urea and triple superphosphate in pre- and post-stocking period for achieving a good production level. Time has arrived to think about an alternative approach. In November 2008, there was an announcement of what is claimed to be the world's first organic aquaculture harvest of the giant prawn 'scampi' in the backwaters of Kerala.

Along with organic manure, some extension officers recommend a monthly application of single superphosphate at a low dose i.e., 1kg/bigha (7-8kg/ha) to fish farmers in post-stocking period in grow-out carp culture ponds, but application of urea should not be prescribed. The input cost in way of nutrient supply in the scientific fish farming technology pose problem especially to the small-scale fish farmers, leaving every scope of substantial rise as the subsidy on inorganic fertilizers is being proposed to be partially or fully withdrawn. Again shortage of inorganic fertilizers at an increasing rate has been felt in the last decade of twentieth century. Fertilizers' News (1980) viewed that the anticipated gap between production and consumption of nitrogenous and phosphatic fertilizers during 2000-2001 will be far more than that of 1980-1981. It has been reported that zooplankton population in ponds treated with inorganic fertilizers often lags far behind than that in ponds treated with organic manure. In most chemically-fertilized ponds, the predominant phytoplankton belong to family Chlorophyceae, which is less nutritious in comparison to the predominant phytoplankton groups Chrysophyceae, Bacillariophyceae and Cryptophyceae, produced in ponds treated with organic manure. Such manures are especially efficient in increasing the abundance of zooplankton and benthic organisms in pond.

Live plankton and benthic invertebrates are preferred prey for young fish and shrimp and provide high quality protein as well as other essential nutrients. An important advantage of the use of organic fertilizers is that a shorter production cycle is possible than that obtained with inorganic fertilizers, especially for production of zooplankton in rearing ponds. Organic fertilizers bring about a favourable action on pond soil and phytoplankton growth is increased through decomposition of organic materials and subsequent release of carbon dioxide.

THE ORGANIC FARMING APPROACH

The main objective of the 'much-discussed term' organic fish farming is to optimize the health and production potential of pond water and soil, fishes under culture and human beings. It emphasizes on human health. This system has become more important as consumers have become aware about the effects of artificial inorganic fertilizers and other chemical inputs on environment; they are concerned about the undesirable impacts of pond aquaculture and doubtful about the safe nature of farmed consumable aqua-products. In many rural sectors, the wide practice of application of organic manures for fertilizing fish ponds provide adequate amount of primary (N, P, K) and secondary (Ca, Mg, S, Zn) nutritional elements for phytoplankton reproduction, who are the 'producers' in pond ecosystem. These in turn are eaten by primary consumers like planktonivorous fishes and zooplankton. Organic manures are extremely important for use in ponds to produce fish for family and domestic markets by small-scale fish farmers (Diwan and Ayyappan, 2004; Singh *et al.*, 2011).

Organic manures lead to natural live microscopic fish food production; it is essential for sustainable inland pond aquaculture and to reduce expenditure on costly fish feeds and pond fertilizers which account for more than half of the total input cost. Such a farming and management system creates an ecosystem which can achieve sustainable productivity without the use of artificial external inputs like chemical fertilizers (calcium ammonium nitrate, ammonium sulphate, ammonium sulphate-nitrate, SSP, TSP, urea, rock phosphate, diammonium phosphate, potassium sulphate), pesticides (to kill aquatic insects), agrochemicals and antibiotics. Antibiotics and growth enhancing hormones are used in input-intensive fish farms to increase the bulk of fish; their use have adverse effects on environment and other species. Increasing market share of organic foods, food safety issues over fertilizer-treated fishes, environmental concerns have combined to focus attention on organic fish farming. In India, many agro- and aqua-farmers are shifting to organic farming due to domestic and international demand for organic foods.

Organic fish farms rely on the use of local natural resources and management of the ecosystem. It is need of the hour that the organic principles of health, ecology, fairness and care are applied to fish farming, in the way that organic principles are applied to farming of food crops on land. Supposedly, in order to achieve a satisfactory amount of fish production at the end of one year from a productive grow-out pond of 1 bigha area

(7.5bigha = 1hectare), it is required to supply a total amount of 11kg nitrogen and 5kg phosphorus in it during the entire culture period. It is expected that proper application of different kinds of organic fertilizers in recommended doses will help fish farmers to reach this target of nutrient level and incessant planktonic production will persist in pond all throughout the period.

ORGANIC MANURES AND FISH CULTURE

Non-toxic organic wastes generated from human and mostly from farmed animal sources have proved to be potentially rich in easily transformable nutrients and are widely used in pond fish culture in China. Their efficacies in pond aquaculture have been appraised. In India, the total waste in form of excreta generated from human sources, cattle and poultry birds annually has been estimated to be 314.60 million tonnes; the total nutrient potentiality has been worked out to be 9.72 million tonnes of nitrogen, 2.98 million tonnes of phosphorus (P_2O_5) and 4.05 million tonnes of potassium (K_2O) (Hossain *et al.*, 2006). Total excreta generated from sources like pigs, goat and sheep annually has been estimated to be 39.0 million tonnes. This huge nutrient reserve as fish pond fertilizer has remained largely unexploited. The average yearly weight of manure produced by various farm animals per 100kg of live weight is as follows: 2920kg for pig, 2555kg for each of poultry bird and sheep, 2190kg for dairy cow. According to FAO training manual, maximum amount of fresh solid manure safely applicable per day in 100 sq,mt. of tropical fish pond is of the order: 6kg for each of pig and cattle, 3.4kg of sheep/goat, 2.8kg and 4.8kg of duck and chicken respectively.

The releases of nutrients from organic manures are slow and their availability remains for a longer period depending on the rate of decomposition. Regarding either of cattle, goat/sheep or horse/donkey excreta, total amount of manure needed to fertilize a 100 sqmt pond in one week time is 10kg; while that of chicken, duck or pig excreta is 6-8kg. These are the application rates, and the number of reared animals from which the material may be obtained is 10-15nos. for each of chicken and ducks, 0.3nos. for cattle, 0.5nos. for horse/donkey, 0.8nos. for pig and 4nos for goat/sheep. In one year, manure obtained from a dairy cow cause 100-200kg fish biomass production, that obtained from a beef cattle cause 90-160kg, that obtained from a sheep, a laying hen and a broiler bird cause 10-17kg, 6-8kg and 3-4kg respectively. Even 8kg of silkworm dregs is known to produce one kilogram of fish. If fish farming is combined with mulberry cultivation, sericulture and silk extraction from cocoons, it will allow the pupae to be used as fish feed and the worm faeces and wastewater from the processing factory to be used as pond fertilizers.

OTHER ORGANIC FERTILIZERS AND ECOLOGICAL PROCESS

Digested semi-decomposed sludge (i.e., slurry) from biogas generators, molasses from sugarcane factories (mainly for shrimp ponds), wastewater from animal slaughter houses (cattle rumen contents, blood, bones and enriched wastewater), treated domestic sewage, composted vegetation, compost farmyard manure, vermicompost, dried blood meal - all may be used in ponds to improve fish production level. Cassava tubers of the bitter species form an excellent and cheap way to fertilize small ponds. Aquatic vegetation cropped from the pond itself, such as the water hyacinth, water ferns and water lettuce *Pistia* sp. may be profitably used in ponds.

Through decomposition by microorganisms, mineralized fraction of the organic fertilizers are converted to nutritional elements which are absorbed and assimilated by microscopic plant matter and macro algae/duckweeds. Non-mineralized fraction is used as the food base for bacteria and protozoa and becomes attached to bottom mud. Bacterial decomposition of organic fertilizers facilitates release of essential nutrients, which enriches the pond water and which contributes to nutrients for producing phytoplankton and zooplankton and finally fish. The manure organic matter provides dissolved and particulate substrates for bacteria. Particles of organic matter serve as surfaces for growth of decomposing bacteria, which increase the nutritional value of particles. After application, firstly rapid multiplication of decomposing bacteria is facilitated. After manure application every time, nutrient content of the water increases; phytoplankton reaches a production peak after 4 days of application and zooplankton within 4-7 days. Zooplankton appear to ingest small manure particles, digest the bacteria with which the particles are surrounded. Greater abundance of microscopic plant and animal life in ponds support larger populations of the desired fish species(s). Besides carbon dioxide, water and sunlight for carbohydrate synthesis, phytoplankton need mineral elements including nitrogen, phosphorus, potassium, calcium, sulphur, iron, manganese, copper and zinc for their growth and nutrition. To promote phytoplankton growth and to maintain the optimum natural productivity of ponds, the water must contain adequate amounts of these nutrients (Datta, 2008; El-Ebiary, 1998).

GOAT AND PIG DUNG

In our country, the packages of practices for fish farming using farmed animal and bird excreta have been developed and verified extensively for economic viability and feasibility at the farmers' level. The goat excreta contain nitrogen upto 2.70%, with 1.78% phosphorus and 2.88% potassium and its urine is also equally rich in the nutrients. At least 50-60 goats are essential to fertilize 1ha fish pond. The manure production of goat/sheep is equivalent to 800kg fresh manure/animal/year or 290kg dry matter/animal/year. The sweepings of goat/sheep sheds are placed in pits for decomposition and it is applied later to the pond.

An adult pig weighing 50kg discharges 10kg faeces everyday. From piglet to adult stage, a farmed pig discharges 1000kg faeces and 1200kg urine in a period of 8 months that is utilizable in fish culture ponds in same period. A young pig produces 4.0 - 6.0kg and 4.5 - 6.5kg faecal matter and urine respectively in a day. The Carbon-Nitrogen ratio in pig dung is 14:1. Fishes also feed directly on the pig excreta which contains more than 70% digestible fish feed. Excreta discharged by 35-40 pigs is adequate to fertilize 1 hectare water area under composite fish culture system. Pig dung, urine and spilled feed from pig sties may be channeled into the pond everyday. In comparison to Indian variety, exotic stock of pigs such as 'Large-white Yorkshire' and 'Hampshire' are suitable for raising. The monthly application rate of dry-form pig manure is 400kg/ha for 12 times in a year. The waste produced by 20-30 pigs is equivalent to 1000kg of Ammonium sulphate applied to the soil. Both pig and cow dung contains 0.6% nitrogen, 0.5% and 0.4% phosphorus and potassium respectively.

COW DUNG AND SLURRY

In cow dung, the Carbon-Nitrogen ratio is 25:1. The average daily excreta for each cow is 25kg with dung - urine ratio of 3:2. Total amount of excreta discharged by a healthy cow in a year is 8000-9000kg, comprising 4000-5000kg dung and 3500lit urine. Roughly half of excreted nitrogen is in faeces and half in urine. Urine nitrogen is especially subjected to rapid volatilization loss when urea in the urine is enzymatically hydrolyzed to ammonia (Boyd, 1998).

About 5-6 cows can provide adequate manure for 1ha pond. In composite fish culture ponds, a basal application of cow dung @ 5000-6000kg/hectare area before stocking of fingerlings and a monthly application of 750kg/ha has been recommended to maintain the pond productivity throughout 10-12 months. Unlike inorganic fertilizers, cow manure supply valuable humus to ponds. Some farmers do have an indigenous model of manure-based aquaculture system in that the washings of the cow-shed on pond dyke are drained into the pond. Application of bio-gas slurry is more advisable; applied @ 100k/ha/day, it results in substantial plankton production. The slurry that comes out after gas generation is highly composted and extremely nutrient-rich. Continuous use of bio-gas slurry checks seepage and improves the water retentivity of ponds in semi-porous soils. About 20000-30000kg of biogas slurry is recycled in a 1 hectare fish pond to get a rich harvest in one year. Creditability of cow dung application lies in the generation of a standing crop of zooplankton within a short period of manuring. One-hundred kg organic manure (cow dung, duck and chicken droppings) contain 8kg carbon which can produce 15-16kg algae and 3-4kg fish. By applying 12,500kg cow dung/ha/annum, we can obtain 500kg fish from 1ha pond (FAO, 1983).

POULTRY LITTER

Poultry excreta is generally accompanied with litters like straw, saw dust or leaves upto depth of 8-12 inches. Deep litter resembles to dry compost manure. In one year, 25-30 poultry birds can produce 1000kg deep litter. Before application, it is necessary to dry the excreta of poultry birds preferably under shade (or can be composted/fermented) to neutralize its harmful impact and eliminate uric acid from it. About 500-600 birds of 'White Leghorn' or 'Rhode Island' breed produce excreta (litter) adequate enough to fertilize 1 hectare water area under composite fish culture system (Hoq *et al.*, 1999). Manurial value is about three times more than that of cattle manure. One hundred farm hens consume about 9kg duckweed *Azolla* sp. everyday.

Raw/fresh poultry dung contains 1.63% nitrogen, 1.54% phosphorus. The litter contains about 3% nitrogen. Each chicken produces about 40gm of excreta per day (14-15kg droppings/year). In Bangladesh, the average fresh manure discharge has been quantified as 96.7gm/chicken/day. Application of 250kg/ha of dry poultry droppings once in a month maintains the pond productivity in composite culture system. To preserve the fertilizer value, poultry manure should be dried to about 10-12% moisture content before storage. This will retain the maximum nitrogen content for fertilizer value. Fully built-up deep litter is removed from poultry pens which are applied in fish ponds in daily doses of 40-50kg per hectare. One kg of fish may be produced by using 15-17kg of chicken manure. The manure production of a chicken is equivalent to 25kg fresh manure/animal/year or 6-11kg dry matter/animal/year. Poultry excreta ferments very quickly and about half of nitrogen content is lost within a month if left exposed under sun. A total of 2,500 laying hens with living weight 5,000kg will excrete 33,000kg waste/day comprising 495kg nitrogen, 170kg phosphorus and 145kg potassium.

DUCK DROPPINGS

In a year, each duck excretes 40-50kg of wet manure. It contains 0.91-1.14% nitrogen, 1.44% phosphorus, 0.62% potassium. A laying duck (mean weight 1.45 kg) has been found to produce 20.6kg dry manure/animal/year. Fish ponds may be fertilized with the spilt duck feed and duck manure falling directly into the ponds (when kept in houses). During daytime, duck excreta easily mix with water and fertilize it. About 10,000-15,000kg of duck droppings is recycled in a 1 hectare pond every year. About 200-300nos of ducks of the improved breeds 'Indian runner' or 'Nageswari' are sufficient to produce manure adequate enough to fertilize 1ha of water area under fish culture. One duck discharges about 125-150gm excreta in a day. By stocking 250-300 ducklings/ha water area, the required quantity of duck excreta may be obtained. Fishes get their major nutrition by feeding on duck waste, duck feed and from natural fish food organisms produced in the pond through duck faeces manuring. It is estimated that 20,000 ducks produce 1000 tonnes of manure in a year.

Being an excretory product, fresh animal manures may contain pathogenic organisms with low pH content. Animal manures, when properly composted, is completely safe for use in fish ponds and does not bring any adverse impact. It is more recommended to compost them for few months before use. It has been discussed about fermentation of poultry manure before use. Occasional development of unhygienic conditions in the pond may be avoided by using pre-decomposed organic manure. In many parts of Asia, organic manures and wastes are first biologically stabilized by aerobic composting or by anaerobic fermentation prior to application as pond fertilizers. Both these stabilization processes rely on the controlled microbial decomposition of an organic waste substrate; the former (composting) in the presence of atmospheric oxygen, and the latter (fermentation) in absence of oxygen. In many places, cow dung (accompanied by urine and waste straw) is collected after cleaning cowshed in a nearby pit and is allowed to decompose over a period of time. Every month this manure (compost) is applied to fish ponds as farm-yard manure.

COMPOST MANURE

The practice of *'composting'* involves *intensive decomposition of organic materials by micro-organisms,* generally under controlled conditions. This process makes it possible to utilize a wide range of cheap wastes, residues and natural vegetation for the production of a clean, dry material rich in organic matter. Compost is particularly useful as organic manure which contains nitrogen, phosphorous and potassium as well as micro-nutrients which can be utilized for the growth of microscopic plants (Coche *et al.*, 1996). Compostable materials rich in nitrogen include animal husbandry products, slaughterhouse wastes, vegetable residues, aquatic weeds, grass cuttings, legume leaves, oilseed cake, neem, fruit wastes, molasses and biogas slurry, and those poor in nitrogen include cereals, stalks and leaves of potato, groundnut, soyabean (excluding maize), sugar-cane stalks and leaves, rice husks, peat, straw from barley, wheat, rice and sawdust.

Compost manure is suitable for plankton reproduction in ponds. It may be prepared using a mixture of green grasses, cattle dung and lime (lime is added to neutralize the effect of organic acids produced during decomposition in pits) in the proportion 1:1:0.02, allowed to decompose in dugged-out pits near pond. Water is added to soak it. The compost can be removed for use in small heaps after 10-20 days of fermentation. In another method, vegetable matter, grasses, leaves, garden weeds, spoiled fruits and vegetables, plant wastes are chopped to pieces and mixed to a compost pile. Lime is added @ 2.5kg/100kg compost mixture. It is moistened to decompose in pits, and may be applied at a rate 20-25kg in a 100sq.mt. fish pond once in every ten days. In West Bengal villages, a 100kg compost pile is prepared comprising cow dung 25kg, mustard oil cake 5kg, water hyacinth ash 20kg, lime 25kg, submerged aquatic weeds "Jhaujhaji" 10kg and pond bottom sediment 15kg. It is kept inside a pit under complete anaerobic condition and after one month water is added to it. This liquefied compost may be added to fish ponds @ 600-800kg/ha/month. Compost may be prepared using cattle dung, aquatic weeds, green plants and oilseed cakes in the ratio 50:25:20:5, it may be used in ponds within 1.5-2 months. In the decomposed organic matter in composts, pathogens are destroyed and nutrients become readily available. The Carbon-Nitrogen ratio in such preparations is 20:1. In newly excavated ponds, an application of a mixture of 'Jhaujhaji' (40%), old thick silt (25%), raw cow dung (25%) and limestone powder (10%) @ 400kg per acre will lead to increase in fertility/productivity of pond bottom soil. Huge quantity of water hyacinth can be collected from beels/wetlands, dried and burnt, then the ash produced can be mixed with cow dung and allowed to rot for 4-5 days. Finally the compost mixture obtained can be applied to fish ponds; it will lead to proliferation of zooplankton, particularly *Moina* sp.

HUMAN EXCRETA AND GREEN MANURE

In China, night soil (human faeces and urine) is diluted two times and applied evenly in fish ponds along pond dyke. First it is allowed to ferment under anaerobic condition, stored for 2-3 weeks and 1-2% quicklime is added to it before application. The Carbon-Nitrogen ratio in it is 3:1. Treated (sludge removal, oxygenation and organic matter decomposition) and diluted domestic wastewater gives rise to enormous growth of phytoplankton and duckweeds, and its use in fish culture ponds has been proved to be lucrative. Farmers around East Kolkata wetlands have developed a technique of using domestic sewage for fish culture almost a century ago, that is widely used to meet the growing demand for fish. The stem and leaves of broad bean, Alfalfa, wild grass, water hyacinth, water lettuce (*Pistia* sp.), seaweeds may serve as green manure. Some of the common legume-bearing crops having nodule bacteria that serve as green manure are sunhemp, dhanicha, cowpea, blackgram, greengram (mungbean), sada methi, wild indigo, cluster bean, horsegram and barseem. In West Bengal, some fish farmers cultivate 'Dhanicha', green pea in sun-dried soil base of nursery and rearing ponds. In grown-up stage, the plants are uprooted, laid down, mixed with soil and water is filled into the ponds. The plants decompose and produce green manure, increasing the nitrogen content in water body (Satpati, 2006).

Duckweed *Azolla* sp. containing about 3.5-4.5% nitrogen, 1-1.5% phosphorus and 2-3% potassium can be cultured in rectangular tanks and used as a potential manure in composite fish culture systems @ 40,000kg/ha/year. In such a situation, the pond receives 100kg nitrogen, 25kg phosphorus and 90kg potassium. *Azolla* sp. fixes nitrogen symbiotically with the blue-green algae *Anabaena* sp., which is responsible for the fixation and assimilation of atmospheric nitrogen. *Azolla* sp., in turn, provides the carbon source and favourable environment for the growth and development of the algae. It may be used as green manuring crop. In one month, a maximum of 2500kg *Azolla* sp. can be produced from a 1 bigha pond area (7.5 bigha = 1 hectare) using 5kg seeds of *Azolla* sp. as the initial material. This 2500kg *Azolla* sp. will provide 6.25kg nitrogen, 4.5kg phosphorus and 6.0kg potassium to agricultural fields and pond soil; which is a substitute to 15kg urea, 28kg single superphosphate and 12kg 'muriate of potash' respectively. Also it will provide 10kg organic carbon to soil. It can be applied as organic fertilizer in fresh, dried or composted form. If composted alone, decomposition takes about two weeks. Many green manures and undigested food in animal manures are digestible and provide direct nutrition to fish. Prof. B. B. Jana at School of Ecological Engineering and Department of Zoology, University of Kalyani, West Bengal is investigating on the possible use of treated human urine in fish culture ponds.

AGRO-INDUSTRIAL WASTE

Such examples include cotton seed, molasses, mahua oilcake, oil-palm sludge (with 4-5% nitrogen). The agro-industrial waste mainly the oil-cakes from both edible and non-edible oilseeds have immense nutritional value and are found to be highly useful in fish culture. The edible oilseed cakes from groundnut, rapeseed, mustard, linseed, sesamum mostly are used as supplementary fish feed which may also serve as manures. The production of non-edible cakes from cottonseed, karanj (both with 3.9% nitrogen), neem, mahua, castor, undecorticated safflower have established to be effective to produce non-conventional energy and huge volume of slurry. These cakes have been found to be highly useful manures in fish ponds, may be applied @ 8kg/100sq.mt. pond in a week.

Before stocking of fish seeds in culture ponds, 2500kg mahua oil cake may be used in a 1ha pond of 1mt. depth and 1500kg in a 1 ha pond of 60cm depth. After killing predatory fishes, it fertilizes the pond. Mahua cake contains 2.5% nitrogen. Production of fish in ponds can be increased by the use of organic fertilizers such as cottonseed meal and soyabean meal. Nutrients present in oil cakes, after mineralization, are made available to pond 7-10 days after application. Oilcakes need to be well-powdered before application for even distribution and quicker decomposition. Animal manures and agricultural byproducts contain 0.5-2.5% nitrogen while soyabean meal, cottonseed meal, corn meal contain 1.5-7.0% nitrogen. Groundnut oil cake contains about 7.29% nitrogen, 1.53% phosphorus and 1.33% potassium; it is used as chief ingredient to fertilize nursery ponds in combination with cow dung and single superphosphate. Half of the mixture is applied before stocking of carp spawn and rest in two doses in fifteen day period.

INDIA ORGANIC AQUACULTURE PROJECT

The "India Organic Aquaculture Project" was started in 2007, with the signing of a Memorandum of Understanding between MPEDA and the Swiss

Import Promotion Programme, Switzerland. Under this Project, M/s. Naturland, Germany has been certified as the Certification Body, under which M/s. INDOCERT, Alwaye, Kerala is entrusted with the inspection of the entities. The aquaculture systems identified for organic farming have to be managed scientifically to promote ecological sustenance and biodiversity. The culture systems should have specific standards, for which there is a separate mechanism for validation. The management of the farm should target for the good health and welfare of the farmed animals, so that their natural behavioural patterns are unaffected by interventions. The inputs required for farming should come from certified sources of organic production. The processing factory is also required to follow a set of separate code of procedures for organic processing of the material. The product is expected to be from chemicals, contaminants and to be certified so, after suitable verifications. In Kerala, progress has been achieved in organic production of freshwater prawns during 2008-2009, and this is stated to be the pioneer attempt by any country. At present, India has organically certified shrimp and giant freshwater prawn farms, hatcheries, feed mills and processing plants (Bhat and Vinod, 2009).

CONCLUSION

In European countries, the Atlantic salmon, Atlantic cod, carps, sea bream, sea bass and rainbow trouts have been begun to be produced organically, using recycled processing wastes. Certified organic mussels, tiger shrimp, white shrimp, pangasid catfishes and tilapia are cultured in countries like Vietnam, Peru, Ecuador, Chile, New Zealand and Israel (Oribhabor and Ansa, 2006). At present, the production rate of organic fishery products in the world is about 25,000 tonnes per year. The same in Asia is about 8,000 tonnes. In organic fish farming system, even chemical medicines and antibiotics are never used in disease management; Indian aquaculturists have accepted the use of medicinal extracts obtained from neem oil and cake, turmeric, garlic, Euphorbia and other plants to kill bacterial fish pathogens and parasites. Extension officers now have to think twice before recommending the application of Fe_2O_3 in giant prawn monoculture ponds for liberation of toxic gases from bottom soil. Animal manures and other organic fertilizers if applied properly in recommended doses in fish ponds will not lead to any harmful impacts like depletion of dissolved oxygen level, proliferation of fish ecto-parasites or lowering of pond pH value. Manure applications can be monitored and adjusted according to pond conditions.

Organic fertilization is known to stimulate the growth of decomposers such as bacteria and fungi which are critical to the breakdown of the toxic waste products that can accumulate with the use of prepared feeds. Over time, ponds treated only with synthetic chemical fertilizers lose organic matter and the living organisms that help to build a quality bottom soil. Organic fertilizers seek the survivability of beneficial microorganisms and worms living in the soil, creating a healthy ecosystem that is sustainable and conducive to long-term use. It also stores higher levels of carbon in the soil. Increase in the awareness of farmers as well as the consumers with regard to potential of organic aquaculture, organic farming technologies and market to be developed in India through appropriate extension services would be beneficial to the stakeholders.

REFERENCES

Bhat, V. and Vinod, P.N. 2009. Status of Indian Aquaculture Sector with Reference to Organic Aquaculture. In. PFGF's VII Annual National Meet 2009. Souvenir, Ed. Riji John, PFGF Publication, Mumbai: pp. 67-72.

Boehmer, S., Gold, M., Hauser, S., Thomas, B., and Young, A. (2005). Organic Aquaculture, *AFSIC Notes 5.* Alternative Farming Systems Information Center, National Agricultural Library, U.S. Department of Agriculture. January 2005.

Boyd, C.E. 1998. Organic Fertilizers for Fish Ponds. Publication of International Centre for Aquaculture and Aquatic Environments, Auburn University.

Coche, A.G., Muir, J.F. and Laughlin, T.L. 1996. Fertilizing Fish Ponds. In: Management for Freshwater Fish Culture. 1. Ponds and Water Practices. FAO Training Series No. 21/1.

Das, S.K. and Jana, B.B. 1996. Pond Fertilization Through Inorganic Sources – An Overview. Ind. J. Fish., 43 (2j): pp. 137-155.

Datta, S. 2008. Organic Aquaculture – A New Approach in Fisheries Development. CIFE Kolkata Centre Publication.

Diwan, A.D. and Ayyappan, S. 2004. Organic Fish Farming. Fishing Chimes 24(6): pp. 11-13.

El-Ebiary, E.H. 1998. The Use of Organic Manures in Polyculture Systems of Tilapia, Mullets and Carps. Egypt. Jour. Aquatic Biology and Fisheries, 2 (3): pp. 133-147.

FAO Corporate Document Repository. 1983. Review of Recycling of Animal Wastes as a Source of Nutrients for Freshwater Fish Culture within an Integrated Livestock System.

Hoq, M.E., Das, G.B. and Uddin, M.S. 1999. Integration of Fish Farming with Poultry: Effects of Chicken Manure in Polyculture of Carps and Freshwater Prawn. Indian J. Fish., 46(3): pp. 237-243.

Hossain, M.Y., Begum, M., Hoque, M.A., Karim, M.A. and Wahab, M.A. 2006. A Study on the Effects of Iso-phosphorus Fertilizers on Plankton Production in Fish Ponds. South Pacific Studies, 26 (2).

Oribhabor, B.J. and Ansa, E.J. 2006. *Organic Waste Reclamation, Recycling and Re-use in Integrated Fish Farming in the Niger Delta. Journal of Applied Sciences & Environmental Management, 10 (3): pp. 47-53.*

Satpati, P. 2006. Organic Farming: Resurgence of Traditional Agriculture. Regional Centre of Organic Farming Publication, Bhubaneswar, Orissa.

Sayeed, M.A., Alam, M.T., Sultana, S., Ali, M.S. and Islam, M.A. 2007. Effect of Inorganic Fertilizers on the Fish Growth and Production in Polyculture System of Bangladesh. Univ. J. Zool. Rajshahi Univ., 26: pp. 77-80.

Singh, S., Shaya Devi, M. and Singh, A.A. 2011. Organic Aquaculture: Sustainable and Superior Production. World Aquaculture: pp. 62-66.

Vinod, B. H. and Basavaraja, N. 2007. Organic Aquaculture. Fishing Chimes 27(4): pp. 37-41.

Pages: 83-95

FISH HABITAT AND AQUACULTURE

Edited by: Dr. Sanjay Kumar Gupta; Dr. Pawan Kumar 'Bharti'

ISBN: 978-93-5056-744-9

Edition: 2015

Published by: Discovery Publishing House Pvt. Ltd., New Delhi (India)

5

Sustainable Composting of Aquatic Weeds and Animal Excreta for Utilization in Aquaculture

Madhumita Das, Biswajit Dash

ABSTRACT

In order to compost and utilize aquatic weeds along with different organic manures in aquaculture different combination of substrate macrophytes and animal excreta (i) cow manure (ii) poultry manure (iii) *Salvinia* + cow manure (0.5:0.5) (iv) *Eichhornia* + cow manure (0.5:0.5) (v) *Eichhornia* + poultry manure (0.5:0.25:0.25) (vi) *Eichhornia* + cow manure + poultry manure (0.625:0.250:0.125) were mixed with 20% moisture and incubated at room temperature for sustainable composting for a period of four months and samples were drawn at bimonthly intervals and resultant slurry samples collected from the containers were analyzed for moisture, chemical and bacterial populations. An increase in the available nutrient component from the organic substrates was clearly observed in the present study. The mean heterotrophic bacterial populations and amylolytic bacterial populations were in the ranges of 8.54 - 14.34×10^8/g and 4.5-6.0×10^7/g. Cellulolytic and pectinolytic bacterial populations did not show much difference. The mean counts of methanogenic bacterial populations were in the ranges of 5.4-9.9 × 10^6/g with higher counts in cow manure.

Key words: Aquatic Weeds, Compost, *Eichhornia*, *Salvinia*, Manure.

INTRODUCTION

Pond fertilization is widely used in India and other countries to increase plankton production and fish growth (Wohlfarth and Schroeder, 1979; Atay and Demir, 1998). Fertilizing fish ponds with manure is a way to increase production and utilization of both raw and processed organic material in carp culture is common in aquatic systems (Das, 1996; Hargreaves, 1998). Prolonged use of organic manures reduces production efficiencies and cause microbial and parasitic diseases. With increasing costs of chemical fertilizers as well as awareness regarding the possible environmental hazards of continued application of both organic and chemical fertilizers, bioprocessed composite fertilizers are proposed in aquaculture practices.

Composting involves treatment of biodegradable wastes through microbial activity of bacteria, fungi and actinomycetes to upgrade and increase their usability (Gray *et al.*, 1971; Gaur, 1982; McCarthy and Williams, 1992; Gaur and Sadasivam, 1993; Ghazifrad *et al.*, 2001; Neklyudov *et al.*, 2008). In developing countries it is an important technology for technologists and rural farmers as well as a treatment option for utilization of biological wastes. Composting organisms need carbon for energy, nitrogen for growth, oxygen and sufficient moisture levels. Raw materials used for composting vary significantly in their carbon and nitrogen levels. It is the best method to produce organic fertilizer. Composting of animal wastes is a common phenomenon in both plant culture and fish culture activities (Gray and Sherman, 1969; Poincelot, 1974; Khalil, 1996; György Füleky and Szilveszter Benedek, 2010). In agriculture to restore the productivity crop waste biomass recycling and compost application is a good alternative (Gajdos, 1992; Gaur and Singh, 1993; Gaind and Nain, 2007). Applying composted soil conditioners and mulches to land has many benefits. The organic matter and nutrients in soil conditioners can increase soil fertility, provide a benefit to plant nutrition and promote revegetation. Mulches provide surface cover, reduce runoff, erosion (Wong *et al.*, 2005) and conserve soil moisture. Sewage treatment and composting of municipal solid waste involves reduction and changes in the microbial community (Herrmann and Shann, 1997; Khalil *et al.*, 2001). Similarly aquatic weed composting along with animal excreta is of great use in organic and low input aquaculture (Biddlestone and Gray, 1985: Chanalya *et al.*, 1992; Insam *et al.*, 1996).

Crawford (1983) gave an elaborate review on composting of agricultural wastes. Different types of raw materials are recycled in compost preparations

(Gray and Biddlestone, 1981; N'dayegamiye and Isfan, 1991; Gaur, 1997; Laine *et al.*, 1997; Ryckeboer *et al.*, 2003). Numerical model of organic matter decomposition and practical aspects of compost engineering were described Nkasaki and Ohtaki (2002) and Haug (1993). Chemistry and microbiology of different types of wastes and their composting have been studied by several workers (Bernal *et al.*, 1998; Goyal *et al.*, 2005). Inbar *et al.* (1990, 1993) studied different approaches to compost maturity process and its characterization. Kwon *et al.* (2011) monitored antibiotic residues in manured-based composts. Dolliver *et al.* (2008) opined that antibiotics present in raw materials get degraded during composting. Forgarty and Tuovinen (1991) studied the microbiological degradation of pesticides in yard waste composting. Recycling of rural and urban wastes was studied by Gaur and Singh (1995). Composting is carried out in open or closed piles and reactors at normal or high temperatures (Pedro *et al.*, 1999). Wolverton (1975) and Amon *et al.* (1999) studied the emission of NH_3, N_2O and CH_4 from composted and anaerobically stored farmyard manure and water hyacinth. Use of compost for peat substitution has a large potential for emission savings and from a global warming perspective it could be preferable to use compost on land (Boldrin *et al.*, 2009). Nutrient, carbon and mass loss during composting of beef cattle feedlot manure was studied by Eghball *et al.* (1997). Yu *et al.* (2007) studied microbial community succession and lignocellulose degradation during agricultural waste composting. Carpenter-Boggs *et al.* (1998) and Klamer and Bath (1998) used phosphlipid fatty acids and carbon source utilization patterns to track microbial community succession in developing compost.

AQUATIC WEEDS EICHHORNIA AND SALVINIA, CONTROL METHODS AND UTILIZATION

The aquatic weeds are major menance in rivers, lakes and ponds leading to low productivity due to their invasion and destroy the livelihoods of the communities that depend on them. *Eichhornia* and *Salvinia* are important free floating aquatic weeds have high growth rate and ability to infest a wide range of freshwater habitats have created many ecological, economical to social problems (Williams, 1956; Gopal, 1976; Henderson and Cilliers, 2002). *Salvinia* is a slow flowing fresh water fern and regarded as a weed because of its rapid growth and it becomes difficult to control. Infestation of *Eichhornia* and *Salvinia* disrupts aquatic ecosystems and affects native animals and plant life. In different water bodies and waterways they decrease the quality of water leading to accumulation of organic matter and also stagnate waterways (Gopal, 1987; Dorahy *et al.*, 2009). *Salvinia* mats are also habitats for mosquitoes. Edwards and Clayton (2002) opined that aquatic plants are environmental indicators of lake health. Heavy metal pollution is a global problem and if these metals are present in sediments of different types of water bodies then they reach the food chain through these plants and aquatic animals. In small quantities, certain heavy metals are nutritionally essential for a healthy life, but large amounts of any of them may cause acute or chronic toxicity. Phytoaccumulation of these trace elements by wetland plants may reduce heavy metal pollution (Salt *et al.*, 1995; Zhu *et al.*, 1999).

Methods for controlling water hyacinth include conventional control (manual or mechanical removal) and chemical control, but both approaches have proven generally inadequate and very expensive to apply in areas of high infestation. Reduction or elimination of aquatic weeds is possible through well planned management strategies which includes preventive and control (biological, physical, chemical, eco-physiological) measures. Higher aquatic weeds are controlled by properly selected herbicides that include bispyribac-sodium, carfentrazone-ethyl, diquat dibromide, endothall compounds, flumioxazin, fluridone, 2, 4-D, glyphosate, imazamox, imazapyr, triclopyr, penoxsulam, sodium carbonate peroxyhydrate, and nutrient reducers (Durbow, 2014). The Chironomus larvae can dig into the bulbiform petiole of water hyacinth, the petiole will be broken and decomposed soon and also the canker of water hyacinth will fall off. So this larva will be a native natural enemy of water hyacinth for controlling its invasion (Gao and Li, 2006). The West Indian Manatee (*Trichechus manatus*) has been widely suggested as a means of biological control of aquatic weeds (Haigh, 1991). Singh *et al.* (1967), Thompson *et al.* (1988) and Sheikh and Zaragar (2008) utilized grasscarp for control of aquatic weeds. A successful weed control programme depends on the resources available, the weeds present and the ability to carry out effective control methods. Herbicides have the added disadvantage of causing possible adverse environmental effects, and they must be applied carefully and selectively (Bateman, 2001).

Effective utilization of huge biomass of *Eichhornia* and *Salvinia* has to be used for waste water treatment, animal and fish feed, soil conditioner, heavy metal and dye remediation, electricity generation, substrate for bioethanol and biogas production, antioxidants, medicines and components in compost for sustainable aquaculture development (Wile and Niel, 1975; Mara, 1976; Rath and Dutta, 1991; Ray and Das, 1992; Dushenkov *et al.*, 1995; Barker, 1997; Faskin *et al.*, 1999; Joachim *et al.*, 2000; Reyes and Fermin, 2003; Williams, 2005; Singh *et al.*, 2012). These aquatic weeds usually occurring in organic rich eutrophic water bodies as weeds can be harvested manually, processed and utilized as organic manures in fish culture ponds. Composting of aquatic weeds allows safer reuse of the nutrients and organic matter contained in the weed material. These materials do not decompose easily because of higher carbon and low nitrogen levels. Keeping in view the importance of weed control and their reutilization as aquatic bioresources the present communication is based on the combination of substrates macrophytes and animal excreta. Microbial processing of these organic matters enhances the degradability of the substrates, faster nutrient release for which microbial inoculants are introduced in different forms (Finstein and Morris, 1975; Moriarty and Pullin, 1987; Ayyappan *et al.*, 1992; Chambers *et al.*, 2000). To make aquaculture sustainable, microbial processing of organic matter prior to application in an aquatic system renders the substrate less resistant to decomposition through conversion of complex molecules to simpler ones, in addition to providing biomass. Compost prepared from these aquatic weeds is lighter than ordinary soil.

COMPOSTING OF AQUATIC WEEDS AND ANIMAL EXCRETA

The manurial and macrophyte inputs like cow manure, poultry manure, *Eichhornia* and *Salvinia* were processed in glass containers in different combinations: (i) cow manure; (ii) poultry manure; (iii) *Salvinia* + cow manure (0.5:0.5); (iv) *Eichhornia* + cow manure (0.5:0.5); (v) *Eichhornia* + poultry manure (0.5:0.25:0.25); (vi) *Eichhornia* + cow manure + poultry manure (0.625: 0.250: 0.125). The above ingredients were mixed with 20% moisture and incubated at room temperature for a period of four months, with samples drawn at bimonthly intervals. The resultant slurry samples collected from the containers were analyzed for moisture, chemical and bacterial populations.

METHODS OF ANALYSIS

Chromic acid method was used for analyzing carbon content of sediment samples and the final values were expressed as percentages. The total nitrogen content of the sediment samples was estimated by Kjeldhal's method of digestion, distillation and titration and the final values were expressed as percentages. Bray's technique with ammonium fluoride as extract was used for analyzing available phosphorus with measurements in UV-Vis Spectrophotometer (Hitachi, 150-20) at 660 nm. The final concentration was calculated from the standard graph and values expressed as mg PO_4/100g of sediment (Allen, 1989).

The dilution plate count technique was employed for enumerating aerobic heterotrophic bacteria and amylolytic bacteria in both water and sediment. The colonies, after incubating for 48 hours were counted and populations calculated. The Most Probable Number (MPN) method was employed for enumerating aerobic and anaerobic cellulolytic bacteria (Imshenetskii medium) and pectinolytic bacteria (medium) in water and sediment with potato as the pectin source. The medium was inoculated with successive dilutions of the samples in triplicates. Observations on the number of positive tubes in each dilution were used for computing the bacterial counts from MPN tables (Rodina, 1972; Collins and Lyne, 1976). Roll tube method was employed for enumerating the methanogens in water and sediment samples with 1ml of inoculum mixed with 4ml of Baker's medium and further incubated with an atmosphere of carbon dioxide. The colony-forming units on the walls of the test tube were counted and populations computed (Jones *et al.*, 1987).

RESULTS

The result of the laboratory analysis helped to assess the nutrient status of the processed substrates. The mean dry matter contents of the processed substrates (i) cow manure; (ii) poultry manure; (iii) *Salvinia* + cow manure (0.5:0.5); (iv) *Eichhornia* + cow manure (0.5:0.5); (v) *Eichhornia* + poultry manure (0.5:0.25:0.25); (vi) *Eichhornia* + cow manure + poultry manure (0.625:0.250:0.125) were 20.63, 36.14, 18.53, 15.71, 16.59 and 19.44% (Table 5.1). Poultry manure showed higher values of dry matter (36.14%), organic carbon (30.55%), total nitrogen (2.70%) and phosphorus (8.26%). The mixture of *Salvinia* and cow manure (0.5:0.5) showed low values of organic carbon and phosphorus. The nitrogen contents of the substrates were observed to increase with period of processing. The input nitrogen level had a clear effect on the resultant values as indicated in mixtures with poultry manure. An increase in the available nutrient component from the organic substrates was clearly observed in the present study (N'dayegamiye and Isfan, 1991).

Table 5.1: Mean Composition of Raw and Processed Organic Material

Sl. No.	Organic Substrate	Moisture (%)	Organic Carbon (%)	Total Nitrogen (%)	Phosphorus (%)
1.	Cow manure	79.37	35.14	1.44	0.80
2.	Poultry manure	63.86	30.55	2.18	1.6
3.	*Salvinia*+ Cowmanure (0.5:0.5)	81.47	31.5	1.22	0.76
4.	*Eichhornia*+Cow manure (0.5:0.5)	84.29	37.27	1.34	0.78
5.	*Eichhornia*+Cow manure +Poultry manure (0.5: 0.25: 0.25)	83.41	35.37	1.56	0.88
6.	*Eichhornia*+Cow manure +Poultry manure (0.5: 0.25: 0.25)	80.56	33.33	1.54	0.85

The corresponding mean heterotrophic bacterial populations were 8.54, 13.83, 13.80, 8.30, 14.34 and 13.26 × 10^8/g, suggesting the increased bacterial activity in resistant substrates on amendments with organic manure, resulting in conditions similar to manures with low carbon-nitrogen ratios like poultry manure. Similarly the mean counts of amylolytic bacteria in all the substrates were 4.5, 5.2, 6.0, 3.8, 4.8 and 4.5 x 10^7/g (Table 5.2). The variations in the counts of cellulolytic bacterial populations, both aerobic and anaerobic, were not considerable. The pectinolytic bacteria did not show much difference. The methanogenic bacterial populations were high in cow manure as compared to other substrates, with mean values of 9.9, 6.7, 6.9, 7.1 and 5.4 × 10^6/g owing to its high initial inoculum as also susceptibility to bacterial degradation (Zumft, 1992; Cotner and Biddanda, 2002; Riddech *et al.*, 2002; Narihiro *et al.*, 2003).

Table 5.2: Mean Bacterial Populations in Raw and Processed Organic Material

Sl. No.	Organic Substrate	Aerobic Heterotrophic Bacteria, No. x 10^8/g	Amylolytic Bacteria, No. x 10^7/g	Aerobic Cellulolytic Bacteria No. x 10^4/g	Anaerobic Cellulolytic Bacteria No. x 10^3/g	Pectinolytic Bacteria No. x 10^5/g	Methanogenic Bacteria No. x 10^6/g
1.	Cow manure	8.54	4.5	46	15	1.19	99
2.	Poultry manure	13.83	4.2	35	6	1.26	67
3.	*Salvinia*+ Cow manure (0.5:0.5)	13.8	6.0	46	9	1.19	64
4.	*Eichhornia*+Cow manure (0.5:0.5)	8.3	3.8	67	14	1.22	69
5.	*Eichhornia*+Cow manure+ Poultry manure (0.5: 0.25: 0.25)	14.34	4.8	40	13	1.22	71
6.	*Eichhornia*+Cow manure+ Poultry manure (0.625 : 0.250 : 0.125)	13.26	4.5	13	10	1.22	54

The study indicated the possibilities of recycling of aquatic macrophytes into the production process of aquatic ecosystems through substrate processing measures incorporating animal excreta both as sources of microbial inoculants as well as supplements to modify the nutrient composition of the substrates for higher nutrient availability.

CONCLUSION

Aquatic weeds infesting water bodies need to be harvested and potentially used for developing commercial feeds and in fertilization. Energy recovery from aquatic plants and animal wastes is important to satisfy the increasing demand for raw materials and resultant energy is of great use in agriculture, landscaping and aquaculture. The use of inorganic fertilizers can be reduced and large amount of organic matter gets added into the system. Composting process should be managed according to the requirement and availability of raw materials. The chemical and biological data provided by analysis of the different manurial and macrophyte inputs provides important information about the nutrient status of compost with different combinations and further utilization in aquaculture systems. Further studies are required to determine best methods for processing and supplying as manurial inputs for sustainable aquaculture and different other uses to develop weed based energy harnessing technology.

REFERENCES

Allen SE (1989). Chemical Analysis of Ecological Materials, Blackwell Sci. Publ., Second Edition, Oxford, Boston, Melborne, Inc. London, 368 pp.

Amon B, Amon T, Boxberger J and Pollinger A (1999). Emission of NH_3, N_2O and CH_4 from Composted and Anaerobically Stored Farmyard Manure. 8th RAMIRAN Int. Conf. on Management Strategies for Organic Waste Use in Agriculture, Rennes, France, 26-29 May, 1998, pp. 209-216.

Atay D and Demir N (1998). The Effects of Chicken Manure on the Phytoplankton Primary Production in Carp Ponds. Acta Hydrobiologica, 40: 215-225.

Ayyappan S, Tripathi SD, Basheer VS, Das Madhumita and Bhandari S (1992). Decompositon Patterns of Manurial Inputs in Aquaculture and Their Model-simulating Substrates. Int. J. Ecol. and Env. Sci., 18: 101-109.

Barker AV (1997). Composition and Uses of Compost. In: Rechigl J.E., Mackinnon H.C., Eds, Agricultural Uses of By-Products and Wastes. Amer. Chem. Soc., Washington, D.C.

Bateman R (2001). IMPECCA: An International, Collaborative Programme to Investigate the Development of a Mycoherbicide for Use Against Water Hyacinth in Africa. *In:* Julien M.H, Hill M.P., Center T.D. & Jianqing D., eds. Biological and Integrated Control of Water Hyacinth, *Eichhornia crassipes*. Proceedings of the 2nd Meeting of the Global Working Group for the Biological and Integrated Control of Water Hyacinth, 9-12 October 2000, Beijing, China. ACIAR Proceedings 102. Canberra: ACIAR.

Bernal MP, Paredes C, Sanchez-Monedero MA and Cegarra J (1998). Maturity and Stability Parameters of Composts Prepared with a Wide Range of Organic Wastes. Biores. Technol., 63: 91-99.

Biddlestone AJ and Gray KR (1985). Composting. In *Comprehensive Biotechnology,* eds. Robinson, C.W. & Howell, J.A. Vol. 4, pp. 1059-1070. Oxford, New York: Pergamon Press. ISBN 0–08–032512–2.

Boldrin Alessio, Andersen Jacob K., Møller Jacob, Christensen Thomas H. and Favoino Enzo (2009). Composting and Compost Utilization: Accounting of Greenhouse Gases and Global Warming Contributions. Waste Management & Research, 27: 800-812.

Carpenter-Boggs L, Kennedy AC and Reganold JP (1998). Use of Phospholipid Fatty Acids and Carbon Source Utilisation Patterns to Track Microbial Community Succession in Developing Compost. Appl. Environ. Microbiol., 64: 4062-4064.

Chambers BJ, Smith K and Pain BF (2000). Strategies to Encourage Better Use of Nitrogen in Animal Manures. Soil Use Manage, 16: 157-161.

Chanalya HN, Borgaonkar Sushama, Rajan MGC and Wahi M (1992). Two Phase Anaerobic Digestion of Water Hyacinth or Urban Garbage. Bioresource Techno., 42 (2), 123-131.

Collins CH and Lyne PM (1976). Microbiological Methods. Butterworth & Co. (Publ.) Ltd., London, 521 pp.

Cotner JB and Biddanda BA (2002). Small Players, Large Role: Microbial Influence on Biogeochemical Processes in Pelagic Aquatic Ecosystem. Ecosystems, 5: 105-121.

Crawford J (1983). Composting of Agricultural Wastes—A Review. Process Biochem., 18: 14-18.

Das Madhumita (1996). Microbial Ecology and Biological Productivity of Fish Ponds Fertilized with Biogas Slurry. Ph.D. Thesis. 389 pp.

Dolliver H, Gupta S and Noll S (2008). Antibiotic Degradation during Manure Composting. J. Environ. Qual., 37, 1245-1253.

Dorahy CG, Pirie AD, McMaster I, Muirhead L, Pengelly P, Chan KY, Jackson M and Barchia IM (2009). Environmental Risk Assessment of Compost Prepared from *Salvinia*, egeria densa and Alligator Weed. J Environ. Qual., 38(4): 1483-92.

Durbow Robert M (2014). Management of Aquatic Weeds. Recent Advances in Weed Management. 10th July 2014, 281-314.

Dushenkov V, Kumar PBAN, Motto H and Raskin I (1995). Rhizofiltration: the use of plants to Remove Heavy Metals from Aqueous Streams, Environmental Science and Technology, 29: 1239-1245.

Edwards T and Clayton J (2002). Aquatic Plants as Environmental Indicators of Lake Health in New Zealand. Proc. 11th Internat. EWRS Symp. on Aquat. Weeds, Moliets: 227-230.

Eghball B, Power JF, Gilley JE and Doran JW (1997). Nutrient, Carbon and Mass Loss during Composting of Beef Cattle Feedlot Manure. J Environ. Qual., 26: 189-193.

Fasakin EA, Balogun AM and Fasuru BE (1999). Use of Duckweed, *Spirodela polyrrhiza* L-Schleiden, as a Protein Feedstuff in Practical Diets for Tilapia, *Oreochromis niloticus* (L). Aquaculture Research, 30(5): 313-318.

Finstein MS and Morris ML (1975). Microbiology of Municipal Solid Waste Composting. Adv. Appl. Microbiol., 18: 113-151.

Forgarty AM and Tuovinen OH (1991). Microbiological Degradation of Pesticides in Yard Waste Composting. Microbiol. Rev., 55: 225-233.

Gaind S and Nain L (2007). Chemical and Biological Properties of Wheat Soil in Response to Paddy Straw Incorporation and its Biodegradation by Fungal Inoculants. Biodegradation, 4: 495-503.

Gajdos R (1992). The Use of Organic Waste Materials as Organic Fertilizers-recycling of Plant Nutrients. Acta Hortic., 302: 325-331.

Gao L and Li B (2006). A Potential Native Natural Enemy of Invasive Aquatic Weed-water Hyacinth. Biological Invasions, Volume 8, Issue 8, pp. 1689-1692.

Gaur AC (1982). A Manual of Rural Composting. Field Document No. 15, FAO, Rome.

Gaur AC (1997). Bulky Organic Manures and Crop Residues. In: Tandon H.L.S., Ed., Fertilizers, Organic Manures, Recyclable Wastes and Biofertilizers, FDCO, New Delhi, India, pp. 37-51.

Gaur AC and Sadasivam KV (1993). Theory and Practical Considerations of Composting Organic Wastes. In: Thampan P.K., Ed., Organics in Soil Health and Crop Production, Peekay Tree Crops Development Foundation, Cochin, pp. 1-22.

Gaur AC and Singh G (1993). Role of Integrated Plant Nutrient Systems in Sustainable and Environmentally Sound Agricultural Development. In: RAPA Publication: 1993/13, FAO, Bangkok, pp. 110-130.

Gaur AC and Singh G (1995). Recycling of Rural and Urban Wastes Through Conventional and Vermicomposting. In: Tandon H.L.S., Ed., Recycling of Crop, Animal, Human and Industrial Wastes in Agriculture, FDCO, New Delhi, India, pp. 31-35.

Ghazifard Akbar, Kasra-Kermanshahi Rouha and Etemadi Far Zahra (2001). Identification of Thermophilic and Mesophilic Bacteria and Fungi in Esfahan (Iran) Municipal Solid Waste Compost. Waste Manag. Res., Vol. 19, 3: pp. 257-261.

Gopal B (1976). A Note on the Growth and Ecology of *Salvinia molesta* Mitch. pp. 177-182. *In* C.K. Varshney and J. Rzoska, eds. Aquatic Weeds in S.E. Asia. W. Junk, The Hague.

Gopal B (1987). Water hyacinth. Amsterdam, The Netherlands: Elsevier.

Goyal S, Dhull S and Kapoor K (2005). Chemical and Biological Changes during Composting of Different Organic Wastes and Assessment of Compost Maturity. Bioresource Technol., 96: 1584-1591.

Gray KR and Sherman K (1969). Accelerated Composting of Organic Wastes. Birmingham Univ. Chem. Eng., 20: 64-74.

Gray KR and Biddlestone AJ (1981). The Composting of Agricultural Wastes. In: Stoneshose B (ed) Biological husbandry. Brutterworths, London.

Gray KR, Sherman K and Biddlestone AJ (1971). A Review of Composting - Part 1. Process Biochem., 6: 32-36.

György Füleky and Szilveszter Benedek (2010). Composting to Recycle Biowaste. Sociology, Organic Farming, Climate Change and Soil Science. Sustainable Agriculture Reviews, Volume 3, pp. 319-346.

Haigh MD (1991). The Use of Mantees for the Control of Aquatic Weeds in Guyana. Irrigation and Drainage Systems. Volume 5, Issue 4, pp. 339-349.

Hargreaves JA (1998). Nitrogen Biogeochemistry of Aquaculture Ponds. Aquaculture, 166: 181-212.

Haug RT (1993). The Practical Handbook of Compost Engineering. CRC Press, Boca Raton, FL, USA.

Henderson L and Cilliers CJ (2002). Invasive Aquatic Plants– A Guide to the Identification of the most Important and Potentially Dangerous Invasive Aquatic and Wetland Plants in South Africa. PPRI Handbook No. 16, Agricultural Research Council, Pretoria.

Herrmann RF and Shann JF (1997). Microbial Community Changes during the Composting of Municipal Solid Waste. *Microbial Ecology*, 33, 78-85.

Inbar Y, Chen Y, Hadar Y and Hoitink HAJ (1990). New Approaches to Compost Maturity. *BioCycle*, 31, 64-69.

Inbar Y, Hadar Y and Chen Y (1993). Recycling of Cattle Manure: The Composting Process and Characterization of Maturity. *Journal of Environmental Quality*, 22, 857-863.

Insam H, Amor K, Renner M and Crepaz C (1996). Changes in Functional Abilities of the Microbial Community during Composting of Manure. Microb. Ecol., 31: 77-87.

Joachim W, Hertrampf Dr. sc. agr., Dipl. agr., Dipl.-Ing., Felicitas Piedad-Pascual Ph.D. Nutr., M.S. Food and Nutr., B.S. Pharm.(2000). Handbook on Ingredients for Aquaculture Feeds. Water Hyacinth, pp. 525-530.

Jones WJ, Nagle DP Jr and Whitman WB (1987). Methanogens and the Diversity of *Archaebacteria*. Microbiol. Rev., 51: 135-177.

Khalil AI (1996). Composting and the Utilization of Organic Wastes: An Environmental Study. Ph.D. Thesis, Institute of Graduate Studies & Research, University of Alexandra, Alexandria, Egypt.

Khalil AI, Beheary MS and Salem EM (2001), Monitoring of Microbial Populations and Their Cellulolytic Activities during the Composting of Municipal Solid Wastes. World Journal of Microbiology and Biotechnology, Volume 17, Issue 2, pp. 155-161.

Klamer M and Bath E (1998). Microbial Community Dynamics during Composting of Straw Material Studied Using Phospholipid Fatty Acid Analysis. FEMS Microb. Ecol., 27: 9-20.

Kwon S-I, Owens G, Ok YS, Lee DB, Jeon W-T, Kim JG and Kim K-R (2011). Applicability of the Charm II System for Monitoring Antibiotic Residues in Manure-based Composts. Waste Manage., 31, 39-44.

Laine MM, Haario H and Jorgensen (1997). Microbial Functional Activity during Composting of Chlorophenol-contaminated Sawmill Soil. J Microbiol. Meth., 30: 21-32.

Mara MJ (1976). Estimated Values for Selected Water Hyacinth by-products. Econ. Bot., 30(4): 383-7.

McCarthy AJ and Williams ST (1992). Actinomycetes as Agents of Biodegradation in the Environment–A Review. Gene, 115: 189-192.

Moriarty DJW and Pullin RSV (Eds.) (1987). Detritus and Microbial Ecology in Aquaculture. In: D.J. W.Moriarty and Pullin (Eds.), Proc. Conf. Detritus and Microbial Ecology in Aquaculture, Aug. 26-31, 1985, Bellagio ICLARM Conf., 387, 420 pp.

Narihiro T, Yamanaka Y and Hiraishi A (2003). High Culturability of Bacteria in Commercially Available Personal Composters for Fedbatch Treatment of Household Biowaste. Microbes Environ.,18: 94-99.

N'dayegamiye A and Isfan D (1991). Chemical and Biological Changes in Compost of Wood Shavings, Sawdust and Peat Moss. *Canadian Journal of Soil Science*, 71, 475-484.

Neklyudov AD, Fedotov GN and Ivankin AN (2008). Intensification of Composting Processes by Aerobic Microorganisms: A Review. Applied Biochemistry and Microbiology, Volume 44, Issue 1, pp. 6-18.

Nkasaki K and Ohtaki A (2002). A Simple Numerical Model for Predicting Organic Matter Decomposition in a Fed-batch Composting Operation. J Environ. Qual., 31: 997-1003.

Pedro MS, Hayashi NR, Mukai T, Ishii M, Yokota A and Igarashi Y (1999). Physiological and Chemotaxonomical Studies on Microflora within a Composter Operated at High Temperature. J Biosci. Bioeng., 88: 92-97.

Poincelot RP (1974). A Scientific Examination of the Principles and Practice of Composting. *Compost Science,* 15, 24-31.

Rath SS and Datta H (1991). Use of the Water Hyacinth, *Eichhornia crassipes* as an Ingredient in the Feed of *Clarias batrachus*. Proceedings of the National Symposium on Freshwater Aquaculture. Bhubaneswar, India, pp. 98-99.

Ray AK and Das I (1992). Utilization of Diets Containing Composted Aquatic Weed (*Salvinia cuculata*) by the Indian Major Carp, rohu (*Labeo rohita* Ham.) Fingerlings. Bioresource Tech., 40: 67-72.

Reyes OS and Fermin C (2003). Terrestrial Leaf Meals or Freshwater Aquatic Fern as Potential Feed Ingredients for Farmed Abalone *Haliotis asinina* (Linnaeus, 1758). Aquaculture Research, 34(8): 593-599.

Riddech N, Klammer S and Insam H (2002). Characterisation of Microbial Communities during Composting of Organic Wastes. Microbiology of Composting, pp. 43-51.

Rodina AG (1972). Methods in Aquatic Microbiology. Tr. Rev. R.R. Colwell and M.S. Zambruski, Univ, Park Press, Baltimore and Butterworth Co, Ltd. London, 481 pp.

Ryckeboer J, Mergaert J, Coosemans J, Deprins K and Swings J (2003). Microbiological Aspects of Biowaste during Composting in a Monitored Compost bin. J Appl. Microbiol., 94: 127-137.

Salt DE, Blaylock M, Kumar NPBA, Dushenkov V, Ensley D, Chet I and Raskin I (1995). Phytoremediation: A Novel Strategy for the Removal of Toxic Metals from the Environment Using Plants. Biotechnology, 13: 468-474.

Sheikh FA and Zaragar R (2008). Growth of Grass Carp *(Ctenopharyndodon idella)* on the Different Macrophytes in Jammu and Kashmir: A Case Study. Fishing Chimes, 28(4): 14-15.

Singh SB, Pillai KK and Chakraborty PC (1967). Observation on the Efficacy of Grass Carp in Controlling and Utilizing Aquatic Weeds in Ponds in India. Proc. Indo-Pacific Fish Counc., 12 (2): 220-235.

Singh Divya, Tiwari Archana and Gupta Richa (2012). Phytoremediation of Lead from Wastewater Using Aquatic Plants. Journal of Agricultural Technology, 8(1): 1-11.

Thompson BZ, Underwood JL and Hestand RS (1988). Utilization of Triploid Grasscarp in Sewage Retention Ponds for Control of Floating Vegetation. Fla. Sci., 51: 115-119.

Wile I and Niel J (1975). Harvesting and Potential Uses of Aquatic Plants. 50th Anniv. Meeting A.S.A.E. Cornell University, Ithaca, N.Y.

Williams RJ (1956). *Salvinia auriculata.* Aubl.: The Chemical Eradication of a Serious Aquatic Weed in Ceylon. Trop. Agric. (Trinidad) 33: 145-151.

Williams PT (2005). Waste Treatment and Disposal, 2nd Edition. John Wiley & Sons Ltd, Chicester, UK.

Wohlfarth GW and Schroeder GL (1979). Use of Manure in Fish Farming: A Review. Agric. Wastes, 1, 279.

Wolverton BC, McDonald RC and Gorton J (1975). Bioconversion of Water Hyacinth into Methane Gas. Pt I & II. NASA Tech. Memo., Bay St. Louis, Mississippi.

Wong PTW, Gilmour MA and Pengelly P (2005).'Recycled Organics in Catchment Management'. Final Report Prepared by the NSW Department of Primary Industries for the Department of Environment and Conservation (NSW) (Project 02/371).

Yu H, Zeng G, Huang H, Xi X, Wang R, Huang D, Huang G and Li J (2007). Microbial Community Succession and Lignocellulose Degradation during Agricultural Waste Composting. Biodegradation, 18(6): 793-802.

Zhu YL, Bayed AM, Quean JH, De Souza M and Terry (1999). Phytoaccumulation of Trace Elements by Wetland Plants: II, Water Hyacinth, Journal of Environmental Quality, 28: 339-344.

Zumft WG (1992). The Denitrifying Prokaryotes. In: Balows A, Trüper HG, Dworking M, Harder W, Schleifer K-H (eds) The Prokaryotes, Vol. 1, 2nd edn. Springer, New York Berlin Heidelberg, pp. 554-582.

Pages: 96-121

FISH HABITAT AND AQUACULTURE
Edited by: Dr. Sanjay Kumar Gupta; Dr. Pawan Kumar 'Bharti'
ISBN: 978-93-5056-744-9
Edition: 2015
Published by: Discovery Publishing House Pvt. Ltd., New Delhi (India)

6

Water Treatment Technology

H.A. Kaoud and S.K. Gupta

ABSTRACT

Guidelines for Fresh Water Quality provide a large list of potential toxicants under the broad headings: metals and metalloids; non-metallic inorganic; organic alcohols; chlorinated alkanes; chlorinated alkenes; anilines; aromatic hydrocarbons and others. Water treatment is, collectively, the industrial-scale processes that make water more acceptable for an end-use, which may be drinking, industry, or medicine. Nanotechnology has promising perspectives for drinking water and waste water treatment as well. New and advanced treatment technologies developed with very specific targets than conventional technology. Reclaimed water or recycled water; is former wastewater (sewage) that is treated to remove solids and certain impurities, and used in sustainable landscaping irrigation or to recharge groundwater aquifers . The purpose of these processes is sustainability and water conservation. Although the best option varies from region to region, desalination is often superior economically, as reclaimed water usually requires a dual piping network, often with additional storage tanks, when used for non potable use. Other alternatives such as: grey water system, rain water harvesting system, atmospheric water generator and water remediation may be used in urban areas where climate change has threatened long-term water security and reduced rainfall over catchment areas.

Key words: Nanotechnology, Potential toxicants, Drinking water and waste water treatment, other Alternatives.

INTRODUCTION

Toxicants are chemical contaminants that may harm living organisms at concentrations found in the environment. The Anzecc/Armcanz (2000) Guidelines for Fresh and Marine Water Quality provide a large list of potential toxicants under the broad headings: metals and metalloids; non-metallic inorganics; organic alcohols; chlorinated alkanes; chlorinated alkenes; anilines; aromatic hydrocarbons (*e.g.* polyaromatic hydrocarbons, polychlorinated biphenyls and dioxins); phenols & xylenols; organic sulphur compounds; phthalates; miscellaneous industrial chemicals; organochlorine pesticides (*e.g.* DDT); organophosphorus pesticides (*e.g.* chlorpyrifos); carbamates (*e.g.* carbaryl) & other miscellaneous pesticides; pyrethroids; and herbicides and fungicides.

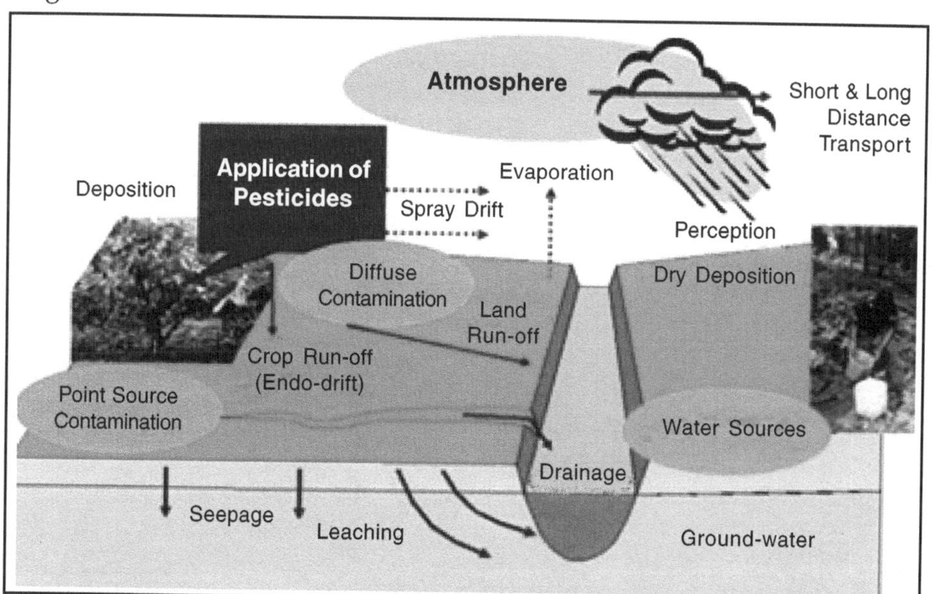

Fig. 6.1: Chemicals are Used Everywhere. Toxicants are Chemical Contaminants that may Harm Living Organisms at Concentrations Found in the Environment.(*Source:* Water technology/Tendency of Organic Aquatic Development.mht.

Chemicals are used everywhere, they are essential components in the production of the foods, equipment, fuels, goods, cosmetics, and medicines that maintain and improve our quality of life. When appropriately managed, they deliver major benefits to the community in the fields of agriculture, medicines, manufacturing and in and around the home. There are around 70,000 and 100,000 chemicals in use worldwide. Along with their many benefits, in some circumstances they can cause harmful impacts on the environment and public health, ranging from fish kills to potential long-term chronic impacts on children's health and development. Many metals and metalloids are essential to life (e.g. copper, zinc and chromium etc). However they become toxicants when they are present at higher concentrations.

Metal contaminants comprise metals and metalloids occur naturally in the Earth's crust, and are released to soils and the hydrologic cycle during physical and chemical weathering of igneous and metamorphic rocks.

Over large parts of the world, humans have inadequate access to potable water and use sources contaminated with disease vectors (Word Net, 2014). Arthropods form a major group of disease vectors with mosquitoes, flies, sand flies (Last, 2001), pathogens (Roberts et al., 2008), Microorganisms causing diseases that characteristically are waterborne prominently include protozoa and bacteria, many of which are intestinal parasites (Roberts et al., 2008; HELI, 2014) or invade the tissues or circulatory system through walls of the digestive tract. Various other waterborne diseases are caused by viruses (Parrish, 2014; Purlain, 2012) or unacceptable levels of toxins or suspended solids. Drinking or using such water in food preparation leads to widespread acute and chronic illnesses and is a major cause of death and misery in many countries. Reduction of waterborne diseases (Santa, 2012; Nwachcuku and Gerba 2004; Dziuban et al., 2006) is a major public health (Petrini 2006; Nwachuku et al., 2005) goal in developing countries.

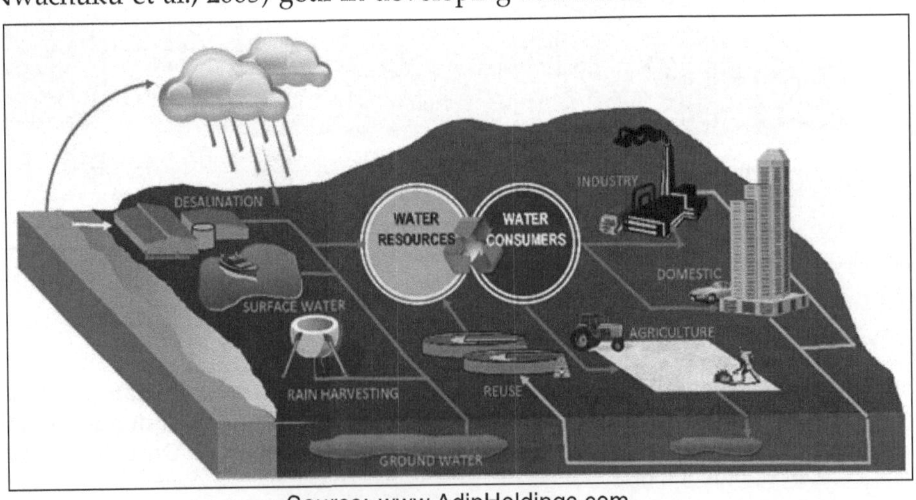

Source: www.AdinHoldings.com

Drinking water or potable water is water safe enough to be consumed by humans or used with low risk of immediate or long term harm. In most developed countries, the water supplied to households, commerce and industry meets drinking water standards, even though only a very small proportion is actually consumed or used in food preparation. Typical uses (for other than potable purposes) include toilet flushing, washing and landscape irrigation. The word potable came into English from the Late Latin potabilis meaning drinkable.

Water treatment is, collectively, the industrial-scale processes that make water more acceptable for an end-use, which may be drinking, industry, or medicine. Water treatment is unlike small-scale water sterilization that campers and other people in wilderness areas practice. Water treatment should remove existing water contaminants or so reduce their concentration that their water becomes fit for its desired end-use, which may be safely returning used water to the environment (Anzecc/ARmcanz, 2000).

SMALL-SCALE WATER STERILIZATION

Boiling

Boiling water will kill bacteria as well as other disease-causing microorganisms like *Giardia lamblia* and *Cryptosporidium parvum* which are commonly found in rivers and lakes. At high elevations, though, the boiling point of water drops. This reduces the time and energy required to bring water to a boil, but can increase the duration of boiling required to kill certain pathogens. Water temperatures above 70 °C (158 °F) will kill all pathogens within 30 minutes, above 85 °C (185 °F) within a few minutes, and at boiling point (100 °C (212 °F)), most pathogens will be killed, excluding certain pathogens and their spores, which must be heated to 118 °C (244 °F) (e.g.: botulism – *Clostridium botulinum*). This can be achieved by using a pressure cooker, as regular boiling will not heat water past 100 °C (212 °F) at sea level. It is worth noting that not all pollutants are removed from water by boiling, even in a pressure cooker. Boiling cannot remove chemicals having boiling points at or above 100 °C (212 °F), nor heavy metal contamination, e.g., colloidal metal pollutants. Activated charcoal, however, can remove many pollutants, but can't remove pathogens. A combination of rolling boiling for one minute at standard atmospheric pressure (i.e., not in a pressure cooker) plus filtering with activated charcoal can neutralize most pathogens and pollutants.

FILTRATION

Portable pump filters are commercially available with ceramic filters that filter 5,000 to 50,000 litres per cartridge, removing pathogens down to the 0.2-0.3 micrometer (μm) range. Some also utilize activated charcoal filtering. Most filters of this kind remove most bacteria and protozoa, such as *Cryptosporidium* and *Giardia lamblia,* but not viruses except for the very largest of 0.3 μm and larger diameters, so disinfection (Kahn and Visscher 1975; Jarroll et al, 1980; Zemlyn et al., 1981) by chemicals or ultraviolet light (Zemlyn et al,1981) is still required after filtration. It is worth noting that not all bacteria are removed by 0.2 μm pump filters; for example, strands of thread-like *Leptospira spp.* (which can cause leptospirosis) are thin enough to pass through a 0.2 μm filter. Effective chemical additives to address shortcomings in pump filters include chlorine, chlorine dioxide, iodine, and sodium hypochlorite (bleach). There have been polymer and ceramic filters on the market that incorporated iodine post-treatment in their filter elements to kill viruses and the smaller bacteria that cannot be filtered out, but most have disappeared due to the unpleasant taste imparted to the water, as well as possible adverse health effects when iodine is ingested over protracted periods.

While the filtration elements may do an excellent job of removing most bacteria and fungi contaminants from drinking water when new, the elements themselves can become colonization sites. In recent years some filters have been enhanced by bonding silver metal nanoparticles to the ceramic element and/or to the activated charcoal to suppress growth of pathogens.

CHEMICAL DISINFECTION

- *Iodine* (Zemlyn et al.,1981)

A potentially lower cost alternative to using iodine-based water purification tablets is the use of iodine crystals. A small amount of water is poured into a small glass bottle (with a capacity of approximately 1 ounce or 30 cubic centimeters), containing approximately 0.25 ounces (7 grams) of iodine crystals, and then shaken vigorously to produce a saturated solution of iodine. At 25 °C (77 °F), 12.5 cubic centimeters of this solution is added to one liter of water to be disinfected. In 15 minutes the water may be consumed.

- *Chlorine-based halazone*

Tablets were formerly popularly used for portable water purification. Chlorine in water is more than three times more effective as a disinfectant against *Escherichia coli* than iodine.

- *Silver ion/chlorine dioxide*
- *Solar water disinfection*

In solar water disinfection (SODIS), microbes are destroyed by temperature and UVA radiation provided by the sun. Water is placed in a transparent plastic PET bottle, which is first oxygenated by shaking partially filled capped bottles prior to filling the bottles all the way. The completely water-filled and capped bottles are exposed to sunlight, preferably on a corrugated metal roof, slanted slightly to maximize the exposure to solar radiation. In practice, the water-filled bottles are placed for six hours in full sun, or for two days in partial sunlight for weather conditions involving partially overcast days, which raises the temperature of the water and gives an extended dose of solar radiation to the water in the bottles, killing almost all microbes that may be present.

Large Scale Water Treatment

- The processes involved in treating water for drinking purpose may be solids separation using physical processes such as settling and filtration, and chemical processes such as disinfection and coagulation. Biological processes are employed in the treatment of wastewater and these processes may include, for example, aerated lagoons, activated sludge or slow sand filters.
- Aeration (also called aerification) is the process by which air is circulated through, mixed with or dissolved in a liquid or substance.
- Flocculation, in the field of chemistry, is a process wherein colloids come out of suspension in the form of floc or flake; either spontaneously or due to the addition of a clarifying agent. The action differs from precipitation in that, prior to flocculation, colloids are merely suspended in a liquid and not actually dissolved in a solution. In the flocculated system, there is no formation of a cake, since all the flocs are in the suspension.
- Sedimentation is the tendency for particles in suspension to settle out of the fluid in which they are entrained, and come to rest against a barrier. This is due to their motion through the fluid in response to the forces acting on them: these forces can be due to gravity, centrifugal acceleration or electromagnetism. In geology sedimentation is often used as the polar opposite of erosion, i.e., the terminal end of sediment transport. In that sense it includes the termination of transport by saltation or true bed load transport. Settling is the falling of suspended particles through the liquid, whereas sedimentation is the termination of the settling process.

A combination selected from the following processes is used for municipal drinking water treatment worldwide:

- Pre-chlorination - for algae control and arresting any biological growth.
- Aeration - along with pre-chlorination for removal of dissolved iron and manganese.
- Coagulation - for flocculation.
- Coagulant aids, also known as poly-electrolytes - to improve coagulation and for thicker floc formation.
- Sedimentation - for solids separation, that is, removal of suspended solids trapped in the floc.

- Filtration - removing particles from water.
- Desalination - Process of removing salt from the water.
- Disinfection - for killing bacteria.

There is no unique solution (selection of processes) for any type of water. Also, it is difficult to standardize the solution in the form of processes for water from different sources. Treatability studies for each source of water in different seasons need to be carried out to arrive at most appropriate processes.

Technologies for potable water treatment are well developed, and generalized designs are available that are used by many water utilities (public or private). In addition, a number of private companies provide patented technological solutions. Automation of water and waste-water treatment is common in the developed world. Capital costs, operating costs available quality monitoring technologies, locally available skills typically dictate the level of automation adopted.

Examples:

- **Aquazurvisa natural and economical water filtration solution**

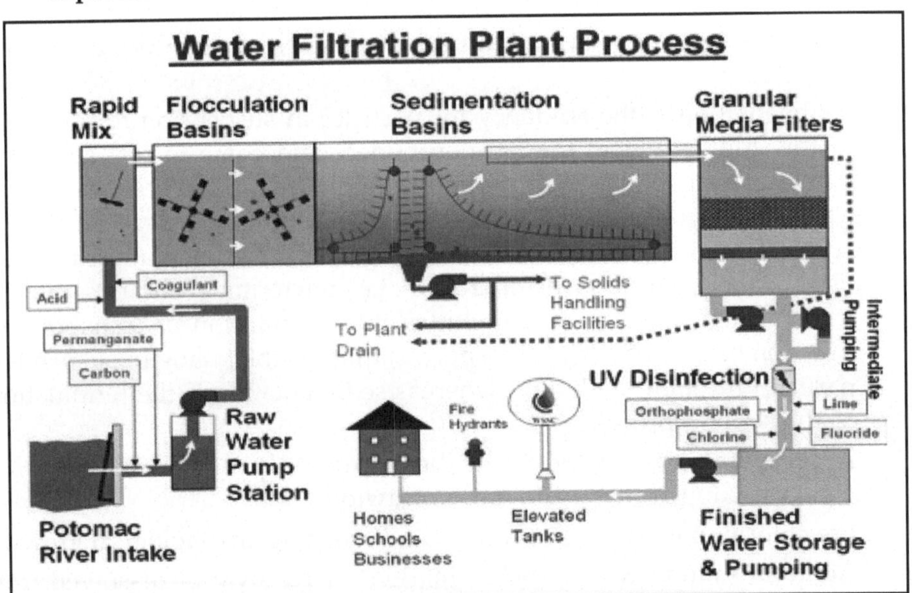

Fig. 6.2: Aquazurvisa natural and economical water filtration solution. Water is clarified via a process of filtration. Degrémont has therefore designed the Aquazur V, an open sand filter where a layer of sand retains suspended solids and particles by reproducing natural mechanisms. Besides providing fast filtration rates, the Aquazur V is simple to use, making it a process suitable for all water treatment plants. Placed either above or below a settling tank, the Aquazur V helps produce high-quality filtered water, essential for water intended for human consumption.(*Source:* http://www.degremont.com/en/homepage/).

- **River, Lake and Ground Water Treatment Systems**

Nagpur's UF (NasUF) water treatment package plant is designed to produce high quality drinking water for small towns and villages. NasUF uses hollow fiber Ultrafiltration modules with molecular weight cutoff (MWCO) of 50K Daltons designed to remove contaminants from surface and well water sources. Some of these contaminants are: turbidity, bacteria, viruses, iron & manganese, Natural Organic Matter (NOM), and arsenic.

The hollow fiber membrane filtration mode is an inside-out configuration and has a pore size of 0.01µm. It can handle high turbidity up to 200 NTU without compromising plant production quality. The unit comes with self cleaning filter ahead of the membranes. The treated water exceeds far and beyond EPA and WHO standards for safe drinking water.

NANOTECHNOLOGY FOR WATER PURIFICATION

Nanotechnology offers the ability to control matter at the nanoscale and create materials that have specific properties with a specific function (Roco et al., 1999; European Commission. 2010).

Nanotechnology is...the art and science of manipulating matter at the atomic or molecular scale Nanotechnology is ... The ultimate goal of nanotechnology is to build essentially anything from scratch, atom by atom.

- Size A billionth (10^{-9}) meter.
- Structure how things are put together — arranged or assembled.
- Novel properties Novel and significantly changed physical, chemical, and biological properties the art and science of manipulating matter at the atomic or molecular scale.

Nanotechnology and Nan-engineered materials are being developed rapidly for a large number of applications in all kind of sectors and products, e.g. cosmetics, car tires, building and construction materials, pharmaceuticals etc. Their specific properties related to the small sizes, will provide opportunities to develop new technologies with performance and characteristics that cannot be established with conventional materials and technologies.

Nanotechnology has promising perspectives for drinking water and waste water treatment as well. New and advanced treatment technologies can be developed with very specific targets that are very difficult to achieve with conventional technology. But although the technology is very promising, no actual breakthrough in the water sector has occurred yet. Furthermore, application of nanotechnology in water treatment may be a source for nano-particles itself.

On the other hand, manufacturing and application of nanotechnology and nanomaterials may result in the emission and accumulation of nanoparticles in the environment causing unknown threats for public health and aquatic life. Fate, concentrations and stability of nanoparticles in the environment are in general unknown. Also the removal efficacy of current treatment technology is not known and a topic of great interest.

Because of the promising properties of nanotechnology, but also the disadvantages connected to it, a large research effort is needed. The number of research groups working in the field of nanotechnology is growing. The water sector is however not always aware of the research and development results, because it takes place in different sectors of industry.

Prevention of pollution refers to a reduction in pollution sources and other practices that utilize raw materials, energy, utilities and other resources effectively in order to reduce or eliminate waste generation. Nanotechnology offers many innovative strategies to reduce waste production in various processes such as improving manufacturing processes, reducing hazardous chemicals, reducing greenhouse gas emissions and reducing the use of biodegradable plastics. The discussion below is just a few of many approaches that can be done to reduce environmental pollution. Nanotechnology is actively involved in this sector, both for producing advanced materials that have low pollution levels and improving production efficiency in industrial processes (e.g. nanocatalysts).

- **Nanofiltration**

Nanofiltration is one type of filtration that uses pressure as the driving force. Nanofiltration membranes provide higher thrust or rejection of multivalent ions, pesticides and heavy metals compared with conventional treatment methods. Currently, this technology has become the newest and most leading-edge technology in water treatment and is now available for practical use in your home, business or manufacturing facility. Some reports have been published regarding the performance of nanofiltration membrane (van der Bruggen et al., 2008; Hilal et al., 2004). Depending on the requirement, some manufacturers offer nanofiltration membranes to target different molecules based on their molecular weight. As an example, Dow Filmtec offers a nanofiltration membrane with the capability to remove molecules higher than 90, 200 or 270 g/mol (Mamadou et al., 2009).

Membrane processes are considered key components of advanced water purification and desalination technologies and nanomaterials such as carbon nanotubes, nanoparticles, and dendrimers are contributing to the development of more efficient and cost-effective water filtration processes.

There are two types of nanotechnology membranes that could be effective: nanostructured filters, where either carbon nanotubes or nanocapillary arrays provide the basis for nanofiltration; and nanoreactive membranes, where functionalized nanoparticles aid the filtration process.

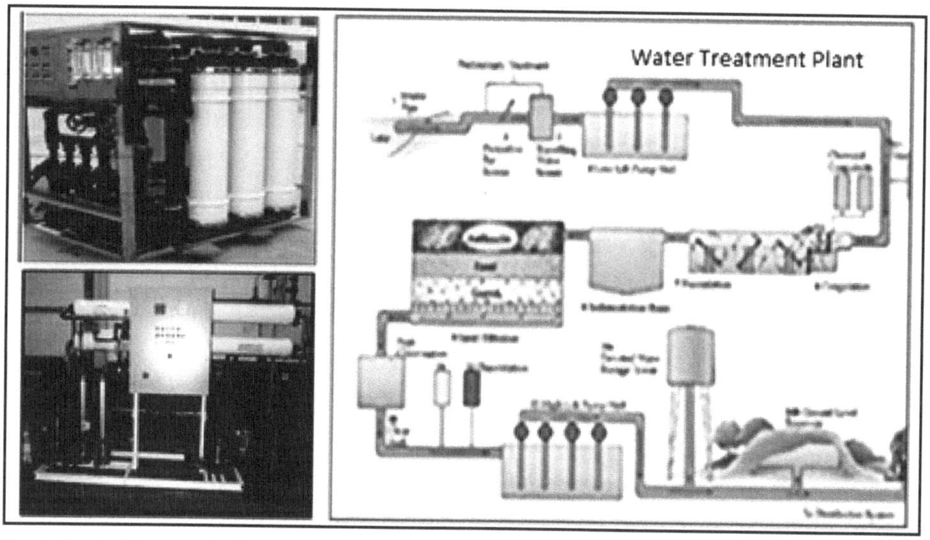

Fig. 6.3: A. Naspure's Reverse Osmosis (RO) Systems; (*Source:* Water and Wastewater Technology Company); B. Water Treatment Plant (*Source:* http://www.naspure.com/index.html)

The researchers also note that advances in macromolecular chemistry such as the synthesis of dendritic polymers have provided opportunities to refine, as well as to develop effective filtration processes for purification of water contaminated by different organic solutes and inorganic anions (Zhang, 2005; Cloete et al., 2010; Kunze et al., 2010; Sharmaa et al., 2009).

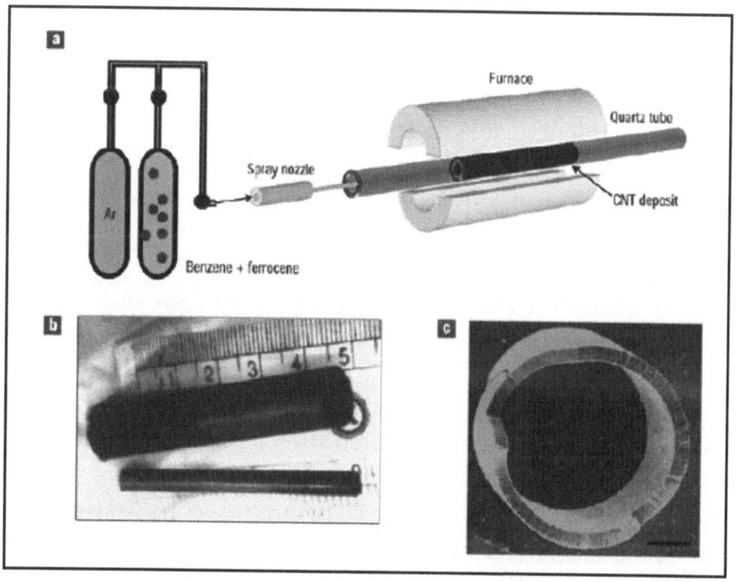

Fig. 6.4: O.N.Srivast et al.,(2004).Nature Materials.3,610-614

- ***Other nanotechnologies for water remediation***

In addition to the examples which have been described above, there are several other examples of nanotechnology applications in water remediation, among others:

- self-assembled monolayers on mesoporous silica (SAMMS);
- dendrimers or dendritic polymers;
- single nanoparticle enzyme (SEN);
- tunable biopolymers;
- nanocrystalline zeolites, etc.

WATER REUSE TECHNOLOGY

(Reclaimed water or recycled water)

Water is given more advanced treatments and is used indirectly for drinking. [Wisely, 2010]

- Reclaimed water for drinking:
- Water sustainability (sustainable landscaping irrigation or groundwater aquifers).

RECLAIMED WATER OR RECYCLED WATER

Is former wastewater (sewage) that is treated to remove solids and certain impurities, and used in sustainable landscaping irrigation or to recharge groundwater aquifers. The purpose of these processes is sustainability and water conservation[2] (Vickers, 2002) rather than discharging the treated water to surface waters such as rivers and oceans. In some cases, recycled water can be used for stream flow augmentation to benefit ecosystems.

The definition of reclaimed water, as defined by Levine and Asaneo, is "The end product of wastewater reclamation that meets water quality requirements for biodegradable materials, suspended matter and pathogens" (Vickers, 2002; Geerts and Raes, 2009). In more recent conventional use, the term refers to water that is not treated as highly in order to offer a way to conserve drinking water. This water is given to uses such as agriculture and sundry industry uses.

Cycled repeatedly through the planetary hydrosphere, all water on earth is recycled water, but the terms "recycled water" or "reclaimed water" typically mean wastewater sent from a home or business through a pipeline system to a treatment facility, where it is treated to a level consistent with its intended use. The water is then routed directly to a recycled water system for uses such as irrigation or industrial cooling.

The recycling and recharging is often done by using the treated wastewater for designated municipal sustainable gardening irrigation applications. In most locations, it is intended to only be used for non potable uses, such as irrigation, dust control, and fire suppression.

There are examples of communities that have safely used recycled water for many years. Los Angeles County's sanitation districts have provided treated wastewater for landscape irrigation in parks and golf courses since 1929.

1. An aquifer is an underground layer of water-bearing permeable rock or unconsolidated materials (gravel, sand, or silt) from which groundwater can be extracted using water well.
2. Water conservation encompasses the policies, strategies and activities to manage fresh water as a sustainable resource, to protect the water environment, and to meet current and future human demand (Defra, 2013).

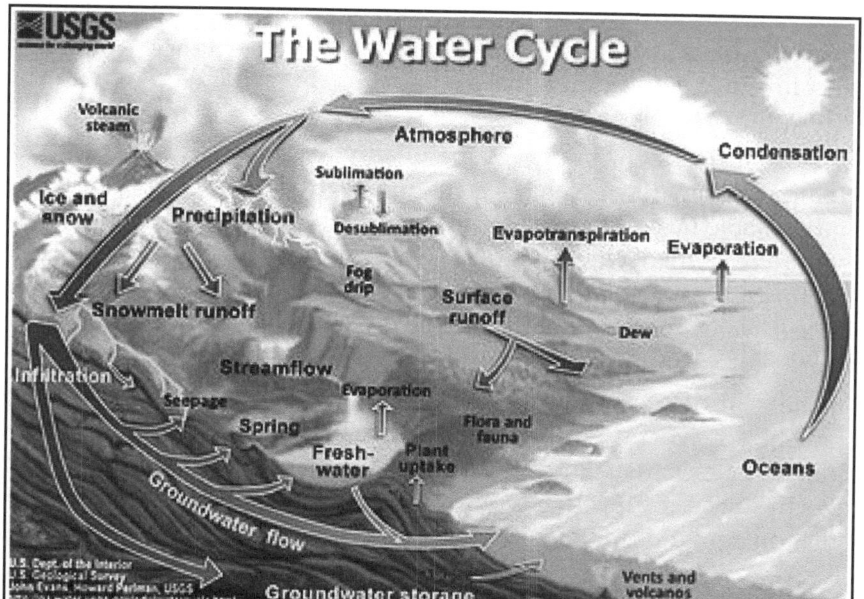

Fig. 6.5: The recycling and recharging is often done by using the treated wastewater for designated municipal sustainable gardening irrigation applications. (*Source:* Pura vida technology http://puravidatechnology.wordpress.com/atmospheric-water-generators.

In other locations throughout the world such as Singapore, water is given more advanced treatments and is used indirectly for drinking.

In spite of quite simple methods that incorporate the principles of water-sensitive urban design (WSUD) for easy recovery of storm water runoff, there remains a common perception that reclaimed water must involve sophisticated and technically complex treatment systems, attempting to recover the most complex and degraded types of sewage. As this effort is supposedly driven by sustainability factors, this type of implementation should inherently be associated with point source solutions, where it is most economical to achieve the expected outcomes. Harvesting of storm water or rainwater can be an extremely simple to comparatively complex, as well as energy and chemical intensive, recovery of more contaminated sewage.

Storm and sanitary sewers were necessarily developed along with the growth of cities. By the 1840s the luxury of indoor plumbing, which mixes human waste with water and flushes it away eliminated the need for cesspools. Odor was considered the big problem in waste disposal and to address it, sewage could be drained to a lagoon, or "settled" and the solids removed, to be disposed of separately. This process is now called "primary treatment" and the settled solids are called "sludge."

At the end of the 19th century, since primary treatment still left odor problems, it was discovered that bad odors could be prevented by introducing oxygen into the decomposing sewage. This was the beginning of the biological aerobic and anaerobic treatments which are fundamental to waste water processes.

Current treatment improves the quality of separated wastewater solids or sludge. The separated water is given further treatment considered adequate for non potable use by local agencies, and discharged into bodies of water, or reused as reclaimed water. In places like Florida, where it is necessary to avoid nutrient overload of sensitive receiving water, reuse of treated or reclaimed water can be more economically feasible than meeting the higher standards for surface water disposal mandated by the Clean Water Act.

The cost of reclaimed water exceeds that of potable water in many regions of the world, where a fresh water supply is plentiful. However, reclaimed water is usually sold to citizens at a cheaper rate to encourage its use. As fresh water supplies become limited from distribution costs, increased population demands, or climate change reducing sources, the cost ratios will evolve also.

Using reclaimed water for non-potable uses saves potable water for drinking, since less potable water will be used for non-potable uses.

It sometimes contains higher levels of nutrients such as nitrogen, phosphorus and oxygen which may somewhat help fertilize garden and agricultural plants when used for irrigation.

The usage of water reclamation decreases the pollution sent to sensitive environments. It can also enhance wetlands, which benefits the wildlife depending on that eco-system. It also helps to stop the chances of drought as recycling of water reduces the use of fresh water supply from underground sources.

DISADVANTAGES

Newer information shows serious public health concerns about pathogens in the water (James, 2005).Many pathogens cannot be detected by currently used tests (Tsai, 2008). Recent literature also does not question the validity of testing for "indicator organisms" instead of pathogens (City of San Diego, 2007) nor do present standards consider interactions of heavy metals and pharmaceuticals which may foster the development of drug resistant pathogens in waters derived from sewage.

In most locations, reclaimed water is not directly mixed with potable (drinking) water for several reasons:

- Utilities providing reclaimed water for non potable uses do not treat the water to drinking water standards.
- Varying amounts of pathogens, pharmaceutical chemicals (e.g., hormones from female hormonal contraception) and other trace chemicals are able to pass through the treatment and filtering process, potentially causing danger to humans. Modern technologies such as reverse osmosis may help to somewhat overcome this problem. An experiment by the University of New South Wales reportedly showed a reverse osmosis system removed ethinylestradiol and paracetamol from the wastewater, even at 1000 times the expected concentration. (Pasco County, 2007).
- Drinking water standards were developed for natural ground water, and are not appropriate for identifying contaminants in reclaimed water. In addition to pathogens, and organic and endocrine disrupting chemicals, a large number of compounds may be present in reclaimed water. They cannot all be tested for, and there is a paucity of toxicity information on many of the compounds (National Research Council, 2012).

INDIRECT POTABLE REUSE

Some municipalities are now investigating Indirect Potable Reuse (IPR) of reclaimed water. For example, reclaimed water may be pumped into (subsurface recharge) or percolated down to (surface recharge) groundwater aquifers, pumped out, treated again, and finally used as drinking water. This technique may also be referred to as *groundwater recharging* (Fig. 6.6). This includes slow processes of further multiple purification steps via the layers of earth/sand (absorption) and microflora in the soil (biodegradation).

- Source water enters the plant and is treated with a biologically aerated filter process to remove ammonia. Air is injected into the base of each treatment cell and the aerated water flows through individual treatment cells containing styrene-based media. The media provide a high specific surface area where micro-organisms attach and act as a filter media for suspended solids removal. This treatment process helps minimize the amount of chemicals needed downstream, and keeps salt levels low in the treated water.

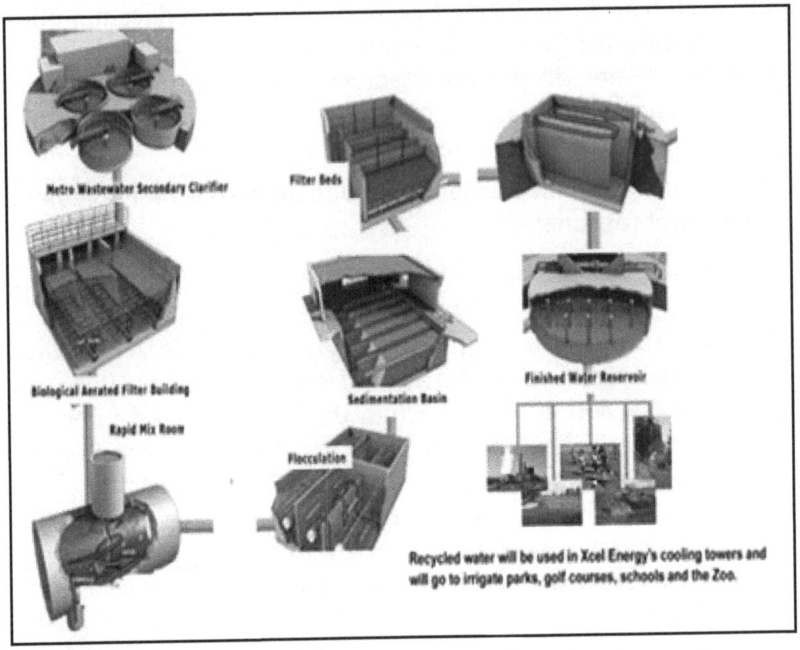

Fig. 6.6: Water Sustainability (Sustainable Landscaping Irrigation or Groundwater Aquifers). http://www.denverwater.org/

- The water is then rapidly mixed with sticky coagulants that can capture suspended solids and nutrients.
- The water is "flocculated," stirred with large, slow-moving paddle wheels. This creates turbulence and increases the contact of solids and coagulant. This allows snowflake-like particles to grow larger and heavier. These large suspended solids then settle out in the sedimentation basin.
- The water then passes through filter beds containing a type of coal called anthracite. This stage traps remaining solids.
- After filtration, the water passes into contact basins where chemicals are added for disinfection and corrosion control before distribution to customers.

As world populations require both more clean water and better ways to dispose of wastewater, the demand for water reclamation will increase. Future success in water reuse will depend on whether this can be done without adverse effects on human health and the environment.

In the United States, reclaimed waste water (Fig. 6.7) is generally treated to secondary level when used for irrigation, but there are questions about the adequacy of that treatment. Some leading scientists in the main water society, AWWA, have long believed that secondary treatment is insufficient to protect people against pathogens, and recommend adding at least membrane filtration, reverse osmosis, ozonation, or other advanced treatments for irrigation water (Scientific American Frontiers, 2014; Middlebrooks, 1982; Tchobanoglous et al., 2003; Jess et al, 2007).

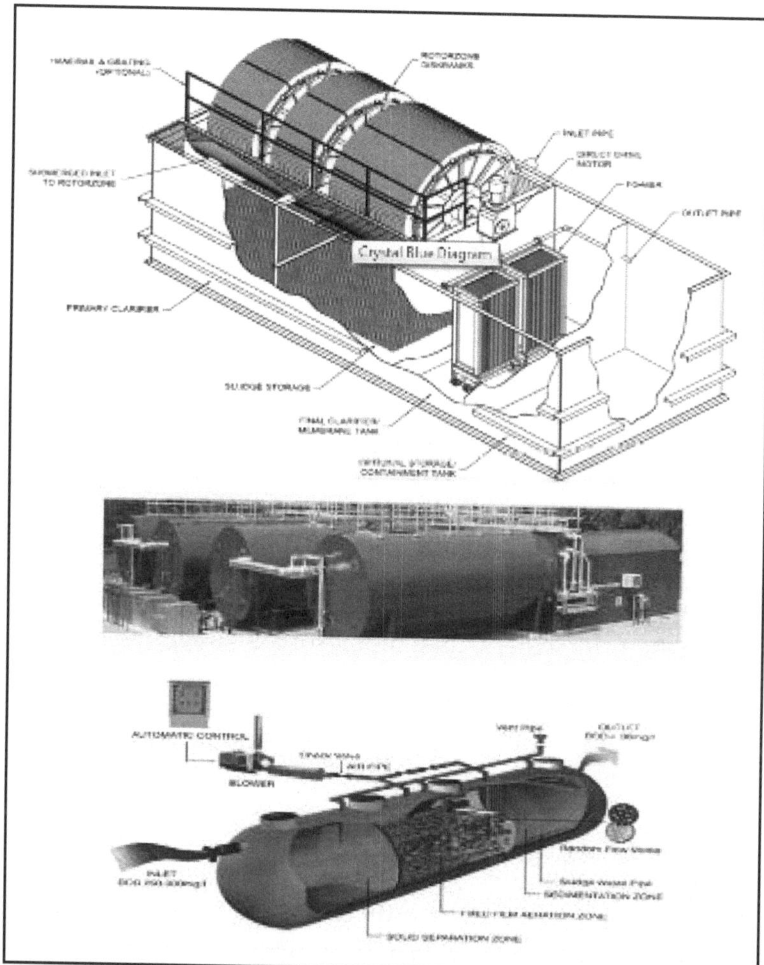

Fig. 6.7: Seprotech water reuse and recycling systems integrate state-of-the-art water technologies with the industry's most advanced filtration, disinfection and membrane components to produce the most environmentally friendly, cost effective and efficient water treatment systems available today. (Source: http://www.seprotech.com).

SEAWATER DESALINATION

One other commonly used option is seawater desalination. Recycling wastewater and desalinating seawater may have many of the same disadvantages, including high costs of water treatment, infrastructure construction, transportation, and waste disposal problems. Although the best option varies from region to region, desalination is often superior economically, as reclaimed water usually requires a dual piping network, often with additional storage tanks, when used for non potable use.

1. Distillation

Distillation is included three types:

- Multi-stage flash distillation
- Multiple-effect distillation
- Vapor-compression

The plant has a series of spaces called stages, each containing a heat exchanger and a condensate collector. The sequence has a cold end and a hot end while intermediate stages have intermediate temperatures. The stages have different pressures corresponding to the boiling points of water at the stage temperatures. After the hot end there is a container called the brine heater.

When the plant is operating in steady state, feed water at the cold inlet temperature flows, or is pumped, through the heat exchangers in the stages and warms up. When it reaches the brine heater it already has nearly the maximum temperature. In the heater, an amount of additional heat is added. After the heater, the water flows through valves back into the stages which have ever lower pressure and temperature. As it flows back through the stages the water is now called brine, to distinguish it from the inlet water. In each stage, as the brine enters, its temperature is above the boiling point at the pressure of the stage, and a small fraction of the brine water boils ("flashes") to steam thereby reducing the temperature until equilibrium is reached. The resulting steam is a little hotter than the feed water in the heat exchanger. The steam cools and condenses against the heat exchanger tubes, thereby heating the feed water as described earlier.

The total evaporation in all the stages is up to approximately 15% of the water flowing through the system, depending on the range of temperatures used. With increasing temperature there are growing difficulties of scale formation and corrosion. 120 °C appears to be a maximum, although scale avoidance may require temperatures below 70 °C.

Vapor compression desalination refers to a distillation process where the evaporation of sea or saline water is obtained by the application of heat delivered by compressed vapor. Since compression of the vapor increases both the pressure and temperature of the vapor, it is possible to use the latent heat rejected during condensation to generate additional vapor. The effect of compressing water vapor can be done by two methods.

2. Ion exchange

Is an exchange of ions between two electrolytes or between an electrolyte solution and a complex. In most cases the term is used to denote the processes of purification, separation, and decontamination of aqueous and other ion-containing solutions with solidpolymeric or mineralic 'ion exchangers'.

Typical ion exchangers are ion exchange resins (functionalized porous or gel polymer), zeolites, montmorillonite, clay, and soil humus. Ion exchangers are either cation exchangers that exchange positively charged ions (cations) or anion exchangers that exchange negatively charged ions (anions). There are also amphoteric exchangers that are able to exchange both cations and anions simultaneously. However, the simultaneous exchange of cations and anions can be more efficiently performed in *mixed beds* that contain a mixture of anion and cation exchange resins, or passing the treated solution through several different ion exchange materials.

3. Membrane processes

- Membrane separation processes operate without heating and is includes: Electrodialysis reversal- Reverse osmosis - Nanofiltration - Membrane distillation -Forward osmosis)
- Membrane separation processes operate without heating and therefore use less energy than conventional thermal separation processes such as distillation, sublimation or crystallization. In waste water treatment, membrane technology is becoming increasingly important. With the help of UF and MF (Ultra/Microfiltration) it is possible to remove particles, colloids and macromolecules, so that waste-water can be disinfected in this way. This is needed if waste-water is discharged into sensitive waters especially those designated for contact water-sports and recreation.
- *Reverse osmosis (RO)* In reverse osmosis, an applied pressure is used to overcome osmotic pressure, a colligative property, that is driven by chemical potential, a thermodynamic parameter. Reverse osmosis can remove many types of molecules and ions from solutions, and is used in both industrial processes and the production of potable water. The result is that the solute is retained on the pressurized side of the membrane and the pure solvent is allowed to pass to the other side. To be "selective", this membrane should not allow large molecules or ions through the pores (holes), but should allow smaller components of the solution (such as the solvent) to pass freely.
- *Nanofiltration* is a relatively recent membrane filtration process used most often with low total dissolved solids water such as surface water and fresh groundwater, with the purpose of softening (polyvalent cation removal) and removal of disinfection by-product precursors such as natural organic matter and synthetic organic matter.
- *Membrane distillation* is a thermally driven separational process in which separation is enabled due to phase change. A hydrophobic membrane

displays a barrier for the liquid phase, letting the vapor phase (e.g. water vapour) pass through the membrane's pores. The driving force of the process is given by a partialvapour pressure difference commonly triggered by a temperature difference.

- *Forward osmosis* is an osmotic process that, like reverse osmosis, uses a semi-permeable membrane to effect separation of water from dissolved solutes. The driving force for this separation is an osmotic pressure gradient, such that a "draw" solution of high concentration (relative to that of the feed solution), is used to induce a net flow of water through the membrane into the draw solution, thus effectively separating the feed water from its solutes. In contrast, the reverse osmosis process uses hydraulic pressure as the driving force for separation, which serves to counteract the osmotic pressure gradient that would otherwise favor water flux from the permeate to the feed. Hence significantly more energy is required for reverse osmosis compared to forward osmosis.

OTHER ALTERNATIVES

In urban areas where climate change has threatened long-term water security and reduced rainfall over catchment areas, using reclaimed water for indirect potable use may be superior to other water supply augmentation methods.

METHODS

1. *Grey water system:* Grey water is wastewater that has been used in sinks, baths, showers, or washing machines, but does not contain sewage and has not been treated at the same levels as recycled water. In a home system, treated or untreated grey water may be used to flush toilets or for irrigation. Some systems now exist which directly use grey water from a sink to flush a toilet (Grey Water, 2007; Treehugger, 2007).
2. *Rain water harvesting system:* Although there are concerns about the quality of rainwater in urban areas, due to air pollution and acid rain, many systems exist now to use untreated rainwater for non potable uses or treated rainwater for direct potable use. Urban design systems which incorporate rainwater harvesting and reduce runoff are known as Water Sensitive Urban Design (WSUD) in Australia, Low Impact Development (LID) in the United States and Sustainable urban drainage systems (SUDS) in the United Kingdom. There are also concerns about rainwater harvesting systems reducing the amount of run-off entering natural bodies of water.
3. *Atmospheric Water Generator* (*AWG*)

The AWG (Fig. 6.8) is able to produce drinking water from the air. It is important to remember in this context that the atmosphere contains 10 times more water than all rivers of the world together and that this water is distributed across all regions.

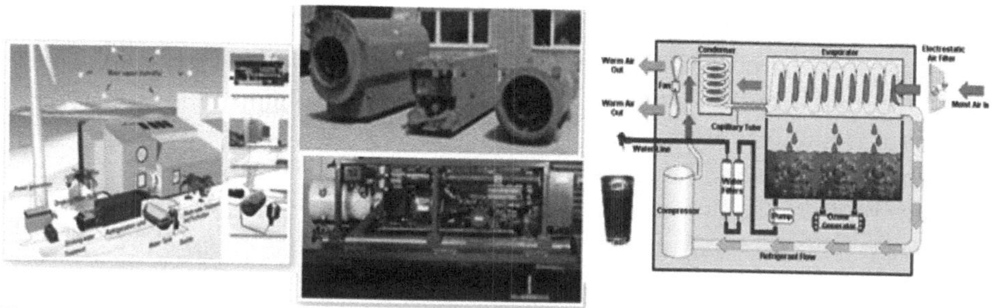

Fig. 6.8: The machines employed suck in large volumes of air, cool it down to dew point and collect the resulting condensation water, which is then filtered and mineralized. A single machine can generate up to 10,000 gallons of water per day, thus providing the water supply for entire villages. *Source:* http://en.wikipedia.org/wiki/Atmospheric_water_generator

The basic technology used for AWG originally came from the mining sector and utilizes the humidity borne in the air to produce drinking water by means of condensation. While the systems used in mining were primarily designed for cooling the air, they simply produced condensation water as a by-product. We use the process in reverse in order to produce drinking water. So here, water is the main product. The machines employed suck in large volumes of air, cool it down to dew point and collect the resulting condensation water, which is then filtered and mineralized. Through this process, pure drinking water is obtained that meets the quality standards of the WHO. In regions with high temperatures and high humidity levels, a single machine can generate up to 10,000 gallons of water per day, thus providing the water supply for entire villages.

The water production process:

- Utilization of the atmosphere as a water reservoir.
- Production of water through the use of very high-efficiency refrigeration technology to condense the humidity in the air.
- Multiple use of the water so produced through the utilization of water treatment technology – water recycling.

4. Water Remediation

Remediation of contaminated water – the process of removing, reducing or neutralizing water contaminants that threaten human health and/or ecosystem. Many areas, especially in developing countries, are seriously contaminated or damaged with consequent impoverishment of natural resources and serious effects on human health. Remediation of contaminated water – the process of removing, reducing or neutralizing water contaminants that threaten human health and/or ecosystem productivity and integrity – is a field of technology that has attracted much interest recently.

Nanoscale zero-valent iron: a new technology for groundwater remediation

In general, remediation technologies can be grouped into categories using thermal, physico-chemical (Fig. 6.9) or biological methods. The various techniques usually work well when applied to a specific type of water pollution, though no readily available treatments were discovered that could clean all types of pollutants. Due to the complex nature of many polluted waters, it is frequently necessary to apply several techniques to soil from a particular location to reduce the concentrations of pollutants to acceptable levels.

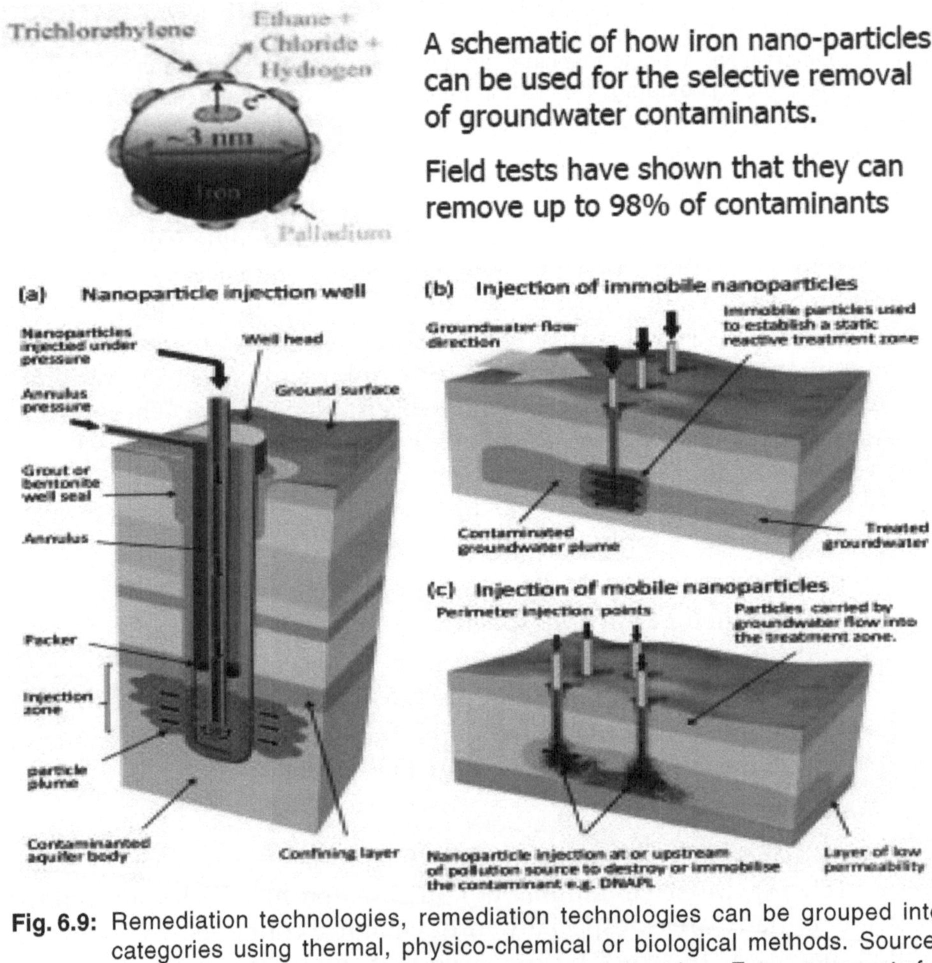

Fig. 6.9: Remediation technologies, remediation technologies can be grouped into categories using thermal, physico-chemical or biological methods. Source: Crane, R A, Scott, T B. (2012) Nanoscale zero-valent iron: Future prospects for an emerging water treatment technology. J Haz.Mat. 211, 112-125.

B-Bioremediation (Green Technology)

Green technologies for water treatment plant. The technologies developed by us include bio-filtration in pretreatment to remove organic matter and ammonia, high-purity PACl coagulant to enhance coagulation efficiency, anti-fouling membrane filtration to recover spent filter backwash water, operational performance and evaluation enhancement (OPEE) programme to advance the management for water treatment plant, environmentally friendly technology for sludge reduction and reclamation, and smart control system.

Some species of bacteria and algae has been utilized to purify industrial effluents (extract metals from their surrounding). Biotechnological approaches are recommended, where metal extracting forms (mainly algae) can be grown in ponds, where factory effluents (rich in heavy metals) are discharged. The microbes will extract the heavy metals and sequester them inside their cell-membranes. The metal can be subsequently recovered from these microbes. This subject is described as *phytoremediation* (Fig. 6.10).

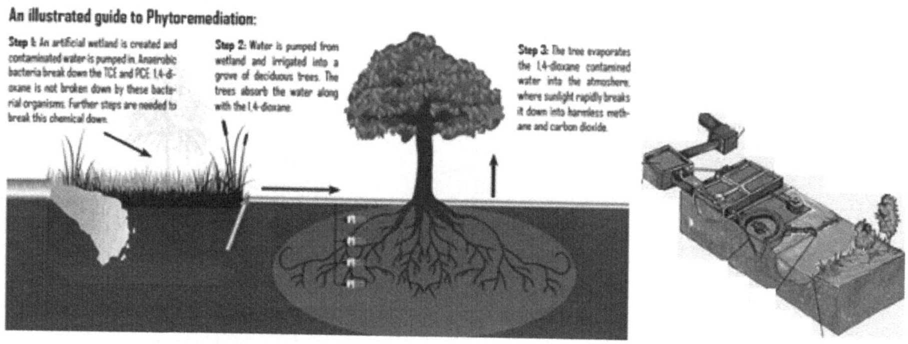

Fig. 6.10: An illustrated phytoremediation

Uses

- Treatment of waste water and Industrial effluents
- Drinking and process water
- Removal of Heavy metals, PCBs and Dioxins from contaminated water ecosystems by the use of aquatic plants (Phytofiltration) and their products (Powders, Granules, Sediments and Combinatorial Mixtures of different aquatic plants).

Proprieties

- the cost of the phytoremediation is lower than that of traditional processes both *in situ* and *ex situ;*
- can be employed in areas that are inaccessible without excavation;
- the plants can be easily monitored;
- the possibility of the recovery and re-use of valuable metals (by companies specializing in "phyto mining");
- it is potentially "the least harmful" method because it uses naturally occurring organisms and preserves the environment in a more natural state.

Nereda (Fig. 6.11) is an innovative state-of-the-art biological wastewater treatment technology that purifies water using the unique features of 'aerobic granular biomasses. Contrary to conventional processes, the purifying bacteria concentrate naturally in compact granules, with superb settling properties.

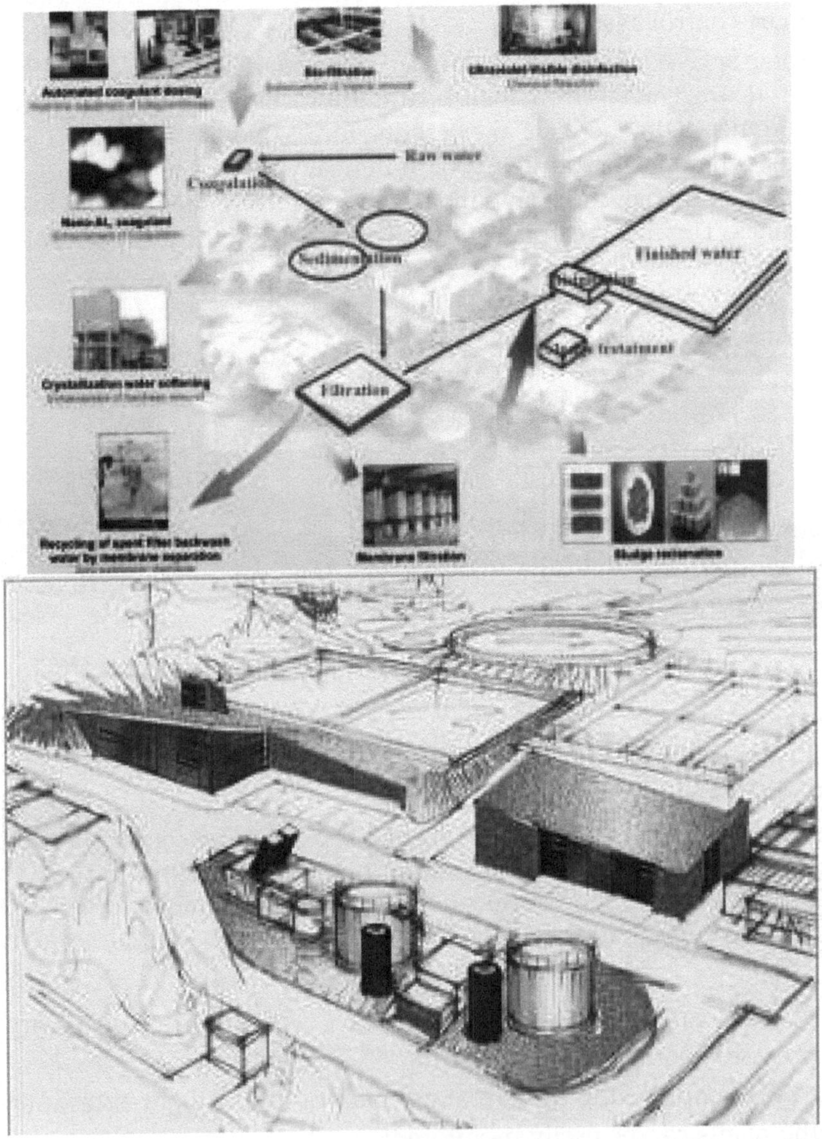

Fig. 6.11: Aerobic granular biomass: Nereda is an innovative state-of-the-art biological wastewater treatment technology (Source: Nereda technology www.dhv/ nereda.com).

As a result of the large variety of biological processes that simultaneously take place in the granular biomass, Nereda is capable of producing excellent effluent quality. Even when not particularly targeted, extensive biological phosphorus and nitrogen reduction is an intrinsic attribute of this technology, resulting generally in chemical-free operation.

CONCLUSION

Over large parts of the world, humans have inadequate access to potable water and use sources contaminated with diseases.Nanotechnology offers many innovative strategies to reduce waste production in various processes. Nanotechnology has promising perspectives for drinking water and waste water treatment as well.New and advanced treatment technologies can be developed with very specific targets that are very difficult to achieve with conventional technology. The AWG is able to produce drinking water from the air. It is important to remember in this context that the atmosphere contains 10 times more water than all rivers of the world together and that this water is distributed across all regions.

REFERENCES

Anzecc/Armcanz (2014) Australian Guidelines for Water Quality Monitoring and Reporting. http://www.ea.gov.au/water/quality/nwqms/#monitor

City of San Diego Rules and Regulations for Reclaimed Water. City of San Diego. 31 January 2007.

Cloete, T. E., de Kwaadsteniet, M., Botes, M. and Lopez-Romero, J. M. (2010). Nanotechnology in Water Treatment Applications, Norfolk: Caister Academic Press.

Crane, R A, Scott, T B. (2012) Nanoscale zero-valent iron: Future Prospects for an Emerging Water Treatment Technology. J Haz.Mat. 211, 112-125.

Defra, (2013) "Water Conservation" defra.gov.uk. 2013. Retrieved January 24.

Dziuban EJ, Liang JL, Craun GF, Hill V, Yu PA, et al (2006). "Surveillance for Waterborne Disease and Outbreaks Associated with Recreational Water — United States, 2003-2004". MMWR Surveill Summ. 55 (12): 1-30.

European Commission.(2010). Communicating Nanotechnology. Why, to Whom, Saying what and how? Available at http://cordis.europa.eu/nanotechnology.

Geerts, S.; Raes, D. (2009). "Deficit Irrigation as an on-farm Strategy to Maximize Crop Water Productivity in Dry Areas". Agric. Water Manage 96 (9): 1275-1284.

Grey Water SydneyWater.com.au 31 January 2007.

Hilal, N., Al-Zouhi, Darwish, H.A., Muhammad, A.W. and Arabi, M.A. (2004). A Comprehensive Review of Nanofiltration Membranes: Treatment, Pretreatment, Modelling, and Atomic Force Microscopy. Desalination, 170: 281-308.

James D. Oliver, (2005), The Viable but Nonculturable State in Bacteria, J. of Microbiology pp. 93-100.

Jarroll EL Jr., Bingham AK, Meyer EA (1980). "Inability of an Iodination Method to Destroy Completely Giardia Cysts in Cold Water". Western Journal of Medicine 132 (6): 567-9.

Jess C. Brown and Andrew Salveson,(2007), Emerging Disinfection Technologies Florida Resources Journal, July 6.

Kahn FH, Visscher BR (1975). "Water Disinfection in the Wilderness — a Simple, Effective Method of Iodination". Western Journal of Medicine 122 (5): 450-3.

Koski TA, Stuart LS, Ortenzio LF (1966). "Comparison of Chlorine, Bromine, and Iodine as Disinfectants for Swimming Pool Water". Applied Microbiology 14 (2): 276-9.

Kunze, C., Schulz, R., Teunchens, L. and Velzen, L. V. (2010). Environmental Remediation of Radioactively Contaminated Sites, Environmental Radiation Survey and Site Execution Manual (EURSSEM.

Last, James, ed. (2001). A Dictionary of Epidemiology. New York: Oxford University Press. p. 185. ISBN 978-0-19-514169-6. OCLC 207797812.

Mamadou, D., Duncan, J.S., Savage, N., Street, A. and Sustich, R.C. (2009). Nanotechnology Applications for Clean Water, Norwich, NY: William Andrew Inc.

Middlebrooks, E.J. (1982). Wastewater Stabilization Lagoon Design, Performance and Upgrading. McMillan Publishing.

Nwachuku N, Gerba CP, Oswald A, Mashadi FD (2005). "Comparative Inactivation of Adenovirus Serotypes by UV Light Disinfection". Appl Environ Microbiol. 71 (9): 5633-6. doi: 10.1128/AEM.71.9.5633-5636.2005. PMC 1214670.

Nwachcuku N, Gerba CP (2004). "Emerging Waterborne Pathogens: Can We Kill them All?". Current Opinion in Biotechnology 15 (3): 175-80. doi:10.1016/j.copbio.2004.04.010.

Parrish, Ryan (2014). "WHO Focuses on Vector-borne Diseases for World Health Day 2014". Vaccine News Daily (Chicago, Illinois). Retrieved 7 April, 2014.

Petrini, B. (2006). "Mycobacterium Marinum: Ubiquitous Agent of Waterborne Granulomatous Skin Infections". Eur J Clin Microbiol Infect Dis. 25 (10): 609-13. doi:10.1007/s10096-006-0201-4

Purlain, Ted (2012). "Lancet Addresses Emerging Infectious Vector-borne Diseases". Vaccine News Daily (Chicago, Illinois). Retrieved 7 April, 2014.

Purple Rain Education Programme. Pasco County, Florida. 31 January 2007.

Roberts, Larry S.; John, Janovy; Gerald D., Schmidt (2008). Foundations of Parasitology. McGraw Hill. ISBN 978-0-07-302827-9. OCLC 226356765.

Roco, M. C., Williams, S. and Alivisatos, P. (1999). Nanotechnology Research Directions: Vision for Nanotechnology in the Next Decade, Washington, DC: IWGN Workshop Report, U.S. National Science and Technology Council.

Santa Cruz (2012). "Emerging Vector-borne Diseases Create New Public Health Challenges". Science Daily (Rockville, Maryland). Retrieved 7 April,University of California.

Scientific American Frontiers (2014).

Sharmaa, Y.C., Srivastava, V., Singh, V.K., Kaul, S.N. and Weng, C.H. (2009). Nano-adsorbents for the Removal of Metallic Pollutants from Water and Wastewater. Environ. Technol., 30: 583-609.

Tchobanoglous, G., Burton, F.L., and Stensel, H.D. (2003). Wastewater Engineering (Treatment Disposal Reuse)/Metcalf & Eddy, Inc. (4th ed.). McGraw-Hill Book Company.

The Health and Environment Linkages Initiative (HELI). "Vector-borne Disease". Geneva, Switzerland: World Health Organization. Retrieved 7 April, 2014.

Tsai, Kan-Jen (2008). "Bacterial Heavy Metal Resistance". Osaka Biology. Retrieved 2008-05-11.

Van der Bruggen, B., Manttari, M. and Nystrom, M. (2008). Drawbacks of Applying Nanofiltration and how to Avoid them: A Review. Separat. Purificat. Technol., 63: 251-263.

Vickers, Amy (2002). Water Use and Conservation. Amherst, MA: water plows Press. p. 434.

Water Reuse: Potential for Expanding the Nation's Water Supply Through Reuse of Municipal Wastewater. National Research Council. 2012.

Water Saver Technologies Aqus Uses Sink Greywater for Toilet. Treehugger.com. October 7, 2006. Retrieved May 22, 2007.

"Water - Use It Wisely."(2010) U.S. Multi-city Public Outreach Programme. Park & Co., Phoenix, AZ. Accessed 2010-02-02.

WordNet Search 3.1. Vector". Princeton University. Retrieved 7 April, 2014.

Zemlyn S, Wilson WW, Hellweg PA (1981). "A Caution on Iodine Water Purification". Western Journal of Medicine 135 (2): 166-7.

Zhang, W. (2005). "Nanotechnology for Water Purification and Waste Treatment". In Frontiers in Nanotechnology, Washington, DC: U.S. EPA Millennium Lecture Series.

Pages: 122-139

FISH HABITAT AND AQUACULTURE
Edited by: Dr. Sanjay Kumar Gupta; Dr. Pawan Kumar 'Bharti'
ISBN: 978-93-5056-744-9
Edition: 2015
Published by: Discovery Publishing House Pvt. Ltd., New Delhi (India)

7

An Account on the Morphometric and Meristic Traits of *Bagarius yarrelli* (sykes) from the Eco-habitat of River Brahmaputra with a Note on its Conservation Prospect

Bhaskar J. Saud

ABSTRACT

The South East Asian fish *Bagarius yarrelli* is considered to be the single most widely distributed largest cat fish attaining 2 m in length. *B. yarrelli* often called as giant devil catfish is the largest member of the sisorid family. In the present study, 200 specimens were collected from the Brahmaputra River to investigate the morphometric and meristic variation among the populations. For this a total of 18 morphometric traits and 11 meristic traits were studied. The morphometric characters persuade with 17 parameters when individually compared with standard length exhibit significant correlation among them. Rampant fishing on fingerlings and the adults of the species causes a drastic decline in the population of *B. yarrelli* in the Brahmaputra River. The threats and the conservation prospects of the species are discussed in the chapter.

Key words: *Bagarius yarrelli,* Brahmaputra River, Conservation, Morphometric, Meristic.

INTRODUCTION

Bagarius yarrelli (Sykes, 1841) is the giant species of the genus *Bagarius* as well as the largest member of the sisoridae family. It is one of the largest cat fish of Asia locally known as Baghar/ Baghari in lower Assam and Gorua in Upper Assam and Goonch in English. It is the largest fish of the Brahmaputra River system growing up to the standard length of more than 6 feet and weighting up to 200 kg. It is a bottom dwelling fish with highly voracious feeding habit. Owing to its voracious feeding habit, it is often called as Devil Fish. Being exclusively carnivorous it feeds mainly on living prey fish. Of the two species found in India, *Bagarius yarrelli* (Sykes, 1841) differs from its closer species *Bagarius bagarius* (Hamilton) in the position of pelvic fin and adipose origin relative to the dorsal fin and anal fin respectively. It is also found in the Indus and Ganges drainages, Xe Bangfai basin in Laos, and Indonesia (Roberts, 1983; Ng & Kottelat, 2000). In India *Bagarius yarrelli* distributed in Krishna, Godavary, Ganges, Brahmaputra and Irrawaddy river (Roberts, 1983; Kottelat, 1989; Talwar & Jingran, 1991; Rainboth, 1996; Jayaram, 1999, 2006; Karmakar, 2000; Kottelat, 2001). Mamnur Rashid *et al.*, 1997; Sheikh *et al.* 1997 and Karmakar, 2000, have reported it from the Brahmaputra drainage.

It is one of the important catfish with immense economic value in particular to the lower Brahmaputra valley. But due to overexploitation and other anthropogenic causes the population status of the fish is worn-out from its natural habitats and categorized under the sections of *"vulnerable"* (NBFGR, CAMP report, 1998). In this present investigation a study on the morphometric study and conservation prospect of *Bagarius yarrelli* from the Brahmaputra basin has been carried out.

MATERIALS AND METHODS

Study Area

The present investigation has been carried out in the Brahmaputra River basin. The unique river system of the world finds its origin in the Chema Yungdung glacier of Tibet and flow through the region furnishing huge ichthyofaunal diversity to the state Assam, the second largest province of North East India, which is a global hotspot of fish faunal diversity. For the comprehensive brevity of the studies maneuvered in the present investigation, major fish markets and the landing stations were selected for specimen collection. The river Brahmaputra originates in the Chema Yundung glacier of Tibet. From its origin in southwestern Tibet as the Yarlung Tsangpo River, it traverses a total distance of 2880 km. which comprises an easterly course of 1625 in Tibet, a south and westerly course of 918 km in India and a course of 337 km in Bangladesh. In India the Brahmaputra flows through the state of Arunachal Pradesh for 278 km. mostly across the Himalayas, where it is called Dihang or Siang River. The Dihang emerges onto the plains at Passighat near Kobo in Assam, which at 52 km. down stream from the Pasighat, it is joined by two large rivers Lohit and Dibang and from this point the river is known as Brahmaputra. The Brahmaputra River flows for about 670 km. through the state of Assam along the Assam valley. And within Assam valley the Brahmaputra receives 103 tributaries (including sub tributaries), 65 on the north bank and 38 on the south bank.

Fig. 7.1: Satellite Imaginary of River Brahmaputra

MORPHOMETRIC STUDY

Morphometric and meristic characters have often been used in species classification studies by statistical techniques. The measurement like the Standard Length (SL), Body Depth (BD), Head Length (HL), Head Width (HW), Eye Diameter (ED), Snout Length (SnL), Interorbital Distance (IRW), Pre dorsal Length (PDL), Post dorsal Length (PoDL), Dorsal fin Length (DFL), Pectoral fin Length (PFL), Pelvic fin Length (PlFL), Anal fin Length (AFL), Adipose fin Length (AdFL), Length of dorsal fin base (LDB), Length of adipose fin base (LAB), and Length of anal fin base (LanB)[Plate- I] has studied following the methods described by Lowe-Me Connell (1971) and Talwar and Jhingran (1991) and expressed in terms of percentage of the Standard length of the fish. The correlations among the different characteristics have been calculated by using the formula after Karl-Pearson (1857-1936).

The following meristic counts have been made according to the method given by Lowe-Me Connell (1971).

Number of rays in the dorsal fin.

Number of rays in the Pectoral fin.

Number of rays in the Pelvic fin.

Number of rays in the Anal fin.

Number of rays in the Caudal fin.

RESULTS AND OBSERVATION

Morphometric count of Bagarius yarrelli

The result observed from the measurement of *Bagarius .yarrelli* from the studied areas have been represented in (Table 7.1). Two hundred (200) numbers of samples are examined to record the morphometric detail for taxonomic conclusion as purported below:

- **Standard length**: The mean value of standard length is found to be 63.96 and ranges from 9.2 to 203.2
- **Body Depth**: The mean value of body depth is found to be 10.82 and ranges from 1.7 to 34.36. The body depths represent about 16.92 % of the standard length of the fish (Table 7.1). The coefficient of correlation (r) is found 0.982 at 1% level between the standard length and body depth (Table 7.2).
- **Head length**: The mean value of Head length is found to be 19.78 and ranges from 3.1 to 62.87 and which represent about 30.92 % of the standard length (Table 7.1). The correlation coefficient (r) between the standard length and head length has been recorded as 0.964 at 1% level (Table 7.2).
- **Head width**: The mean value of Head depth is found to be 14.77 and ranges from 2.5 to 46.71 and which represent about 23.1% of the standard length (Table 7.1). The correlation coefficient (r) between the standard length and head width has been recorded as 0.962 at 1% level (Table 7.2).
- **Eye Diameter**: The mean value of eye diameter is found to be 2.02 and ranges from 0.4 to 6.12 and which represent about 3.16% of the standard length (Table 7.1). The correlation coefficient (r) between the standard length and eye diameter has been recorded as 0.876 at 1% level (Table 7.2).
- **Snout length**: The mean value of Snout length is found to be 8.93 and ranges from1.3 to 28.4 and which represent about 13.96% of the standard length (Table 7.1). The correlation coefficient (r) between the standard length and snout length has been recorded as 0.982 at 1% level (Table 7.2).
- **Inter-orbital distance**: The mean value of Inter-orbital distance is found to be 6.2 and ranges from 0.9 to 19.72 and which represent about 9.7% of the standard length (Table 7.1). The correlation coefficient (r) between the standard length and Inter-orbital distance has been recorded as 0.961 at 1% level (Table 7.2).

Table 7.1: Variation of the Morphometric characters of *Bagarius yarrelli* and Their Relationship (in percentage) with the Standard Length (SL) of the Fish Collected from Natural Habitat

Parameters	ME Mean (cm)	RANGE (cm)	% of Standard Length
Standard length	63.96	9.2 - 203.2	1
Body depth	10.82	1.7 - 34.36	16.92
Head length	19.78	3.1 - 62.87	30.92
Head width	14.77	2.5 - 46.71	23.1
Eye diameter	2.022	0.4 - 6.42	3.16
Snout length	8.93	1.3 - 28.4	13.96
Inter orbital width	6.2	0.9 - 19.72	9.7
Pre dorsal length	23.89	3.4 - 75.72	37.35
Post dorsal length	31.98	6.1 - 101.6	50
Dorsal fin length	17.4	2.5 - 55.28	27.2
Pectoral fin length	22.85	3 - 72.61	35.72
Pelvic fin length	11.14	1.6 - 35.4	17.42
Anal fin length	11	1.1 - 24.2	17.2
Adipose fin length	7.24	1.5 - 34.96	11.32
Length of dorsal fin base	7.61	1.1 - 24.2	11.9
Length of adipose fin base	7.41	1.2 - 28.09	11.58
Length of anal fin base	7.41	1.2 - 28.09	11.58

Table 7.2: Correlation Between Standard Length and Other Morphometric Character of *Bagarius yarrelli*

	SL	BD	HD	HW	ED	SnL	IRW	PDL	PoDL	DFL	PFL	PIFL	AFL	AdFL	LDB	LAB	LAnB
SL	1	0.9824	0.9645	0.9624	0.8766	0.9820	0.9611	0.9798	0.9967	0.9755	0.9886	0.9807	0.9794	0.9955	0.9955	0.9879	0.9834
BD	0.9824	1	0.9863	0.9730	0.8922	0.9965	0.9890	0.9925	0.9937	0.9879	0.9731	0.9882	0.9858	0.9884	0.9884	0.9921	0.9703
HD	0.9645	0.9863	1	0.9789	0.9076	0.9888	0.9889	0.9919	0.9877	0.9918	0.9756	0.9873	0.9867	0.9760	0.9760	0.9814	0.9374
HW	0.9624	0.9730	0.9789	1	0.9122	0.9687	0.9586	0.9733	0.9678	0.9717	0.9705	0.9772	0.9790	0.9717	0.9717	0.9658	0.9653
ED	0.8766	0.8922	0.9076	0.9122	1	0.8808	0.8496	O.9078	0.8781	0.9287	0.9014	0.9180	0.8779	0.8895	0.8895	0.8933	0.8708
SnL	0.9820	0.9965	0.9888	0.9687	0.8808	1	0.9912	0.9968	0.9857	0.9883	0.9773	0.9859	0.9889	0.9884	0.9884	0.9966	0.9631
IRW	0.9611	0.9890	0.9889	0.9586	0.8496	0.9912	1	0.9832	0.9776	0.9758	0.9563	0.9722	0.9797	0.9693	0.9693	0.9785	0.9331
PDL	0.9798	0.9925	0.9919	0.9733	0.9078	0.9968	0.9832	1	0.9867	0.9956	0.9849	0.9963	0.9910	0.9896	0.9896	0.9956	0.9606
PoDL	0.9967	0.9937	0.9877	0.9678	0.8781	0.9857	0.9776	0.9867	1	0.9902	0.9762	0.9891	0.9865	0.9936	0.9936	0.9781	0.9602
DFL	0.9755	0.9879	0.9918	0.9717	0.9287	0.9883	0.9758	0.9956	0.9902	1	0.9868	0.9972	0.9886	0.9877	0.9877	0.9863	0.9523
PFL	0.9886	0.9731	0.9756	0.9705	0.9014	0.9773	0.9563	0.9849	0.9762	0.9868	1	0.9911	0.9891	0.9939	0.9939	0.9816	0.9658
PIFL	0.9807	0.9882	0.9873	O.9772	0.9180	0.9859	0.9722	0.9963	0.9891	0.9972	0.9911	1	0.9941	0.9934	0.9934	0.9887	0.9667
AFL	0.9794	0.9858	0.9867	0.9790	0.8779	0.9889	0.9797	0.9910	0.9865	0.9886	0.9891	0.9941	1	0.9923	0.9923	0.9828	0.9644
AdFL	0.9955	0.9884	0.9760	0.9717	0.8895	0.9884	0.9693	0.9896	0.9936	0.9877	0.9939	0.9934	0.9923	1	1	0.9901	0.9820
LDB	0.9955	0.9884	0.9760	0.9717	0.8895	0.9884	0.9693	0.9896	0.9936	0.9877	0.9939	0.9934	0.9923	1	1	0.9901	0.9820
LAB	0.9879	0.9921	0.9814	0.9658	0.8933	0.9966	0.9785	0.9956	0.9781	0.9863	0.9816	0.9887	0.9828	0.9901	0.9901	1	0.9706
LAnB	0.9834	0.9703	0.9374	0.9653	0.8708	0.9631	0.9331	0.9606	0.9602	0.9523	0.9658	0.9667	0.9644	0.9820	0.9820	0.9706	1

Standard Length **(SL)**, Body Depth **(BD)**, Head Length **(HL)**, Head Width **(HW)**, Eye Diameter **(ED)**, Snout Length **(SnL)**, Interorbital Distance **(IRW)**, Pre dorsal Length **(PDL)**, Post dorsal Length **(PoDL)**, Dorsal fin Length **(DFL)**, Pectoral fin Length **(PFL)**, Pelvic fin Length **(PlFL)**, Anal fin Length **(AFL)**, Adipose fin Length **(AdFL)**, Length of dorsal fin base **(LDB)**, Length of adipose fin base **(LAB)**, and Length of anal fin base **(LanB)**.

- **Pre dorsal length**: The mean value of Pre dorsal length is found to be 23.89 and ranges from 3.4 to 75.72 and which represent about 37.35 % of the standard length (Table 7.1). The correlation coefficient (r) between the standard length and Pre dorsal length has been recorded as 0.979 at 1% level (Table 7.2).
- **Post dorsal length**: The mean value of Post dorsal length is found to be 31.98 and ranges from 6.1 to 101.6 and which represent about 50.00% of the standard length (Table 7.1). The correlation coefficient (r) between the standard length and Post dorsal length has been recorded as 0.996 at 1% level (Table 7.2).
- **Dorsal fin length**: The mean value of dorsal fin length is found to be 17.4 and ranges from 2.5 to 55.28 and which represent about 27.2% of the standard length (Table 7.1). The correlation coefficient (r) between the standard length and dorsal fin length has been recorded as 0.975 at 1% level (Table 7.2).
- **Pectoral fin length**: The mean value of Pectoral fin length is found to 22.85 and ranges from 3 to 72.61 and which represent about 35.72% of the standard length (Table 7.1). The correlation coefficient (r) between the standard length and Pectoral fin length has been recorded as 0.988 at 1% level (Table 7.2).
- **Pelvic fin length**: The mean value of Pelvic fin length is found to be 11.14 and ranges from 1.6 to 35.40 and which represent about 17.42% of the standard length (Table 7.1). The correlation coefficient (r) between the standard length and Pelvic fin length has been recorded as 0.980 at 1% level (Table 7.2).
- **Anal fin length**: The mean value of anal fin length is found to be 11 and ranges from 1.5 to 34.96 and which represent about 17.2 % of the standard length (Table 7.1). The correlation coefficient (r) between the standard length and anal fin length has been recorded as 0.979 at 1% level (Table 7.2).
- **Adipose fin length**: The mean value of adipose fin length is found to be 7.24 and ranges from 1.2 to 23 and which represent about 30.92% of the standard length (Table 7.1). The correlation coefficient (r) between the standard length and adipose fin length has been recorded as 0.995 at 1% level (Table 7.2).
- **Length of dorsal fin base**: The mean value of dorsal fin base is found to be 7.61 and ranges from 1.1 to 24.20 and which represent about 11.32% of the standard length (Table 7.1). The correlation coefficient (r) between the standard length and length of dorsal fin base has been recorded as 0.995 at 1% level (Table 7.2).

- **Length of adipose fin base**: The mean value of adipose fin base is found to be 7.41 and ranges from 1.2 to 28.09 and which represent about 11.9% of the standard length (Table 7.1). The correlation coefficient (r) between the standard length and length of adipose fin base has been recorded as 0. 987 at 1% level (Table 7.2).
- **Length of anal fin base**: The mean value of dorsal fin base is found to be 7.41 and ranges from 1.2 to 28.09 and which represent about 11.58% of the standard length (Table 7.1). The correlation coefficient (r) between the standard length and length of dorsal fin base has been recorded as 0.983 at 1% level (Table 7.2).

MERISTIC COUNTS

Meristic characters are illustrated by the number of rays in dorsal fin, pectoral fin, pelvic fin, anal fin and caudal fin of the studied fish (Figures 7.1-7.6). The following meristic counts were made according to the method given by Lowe Meconell (1971).

Number of Dorsal fin ray: The mean number of dorsal fin ray is found to be D I 7

Number of pectoral fin ray: The mean number of dorsal fin ray is found to be P I 12

Number of Pelvic fin ray: The mean number of dorsal fin ray is found to be V I 5

Number of Anal fin ray: The mean number of dorsal fin ray is found to be A II 12

Number of Caudal fin ray: The mean number of caudal fin ray is found to be C 18

Fin Formula: D i/ 7; P i/ 12; V i/ 5; A ii/ 12; C 18

Bagarius yarrelli has a broad and moderately depressed head with broad inferior mouth. Maxillary barbells are large in size. Fins are large in size with filamentous extensions in dorsal, pectoral and caudal fin. Dorsal fin with a non serrated spine and seven (7) rays; pectoral fin with a non serrated spine and twelve (12) rays; pelvic fin with a non serrated rays and five (5) serrated rays; anal fin with two non serrated and twelve (12) serrated rays and caudal fin rays 19 as recorded following the method given by Lowe Meconell (1971) almost in conformity with Roberts (1983) Talwar & Jingran (1991) and Jayaram (2006). The morphometric characters persuade with 17 parameters when individually compared with standard length exhibit clear indication to confirm the species as *Bagarius yarrelli*. The statistical correlation with significant results (Table 7.2) in this respect confirmed authentic base of morphometric relationship with the species characters.

PLATE - I

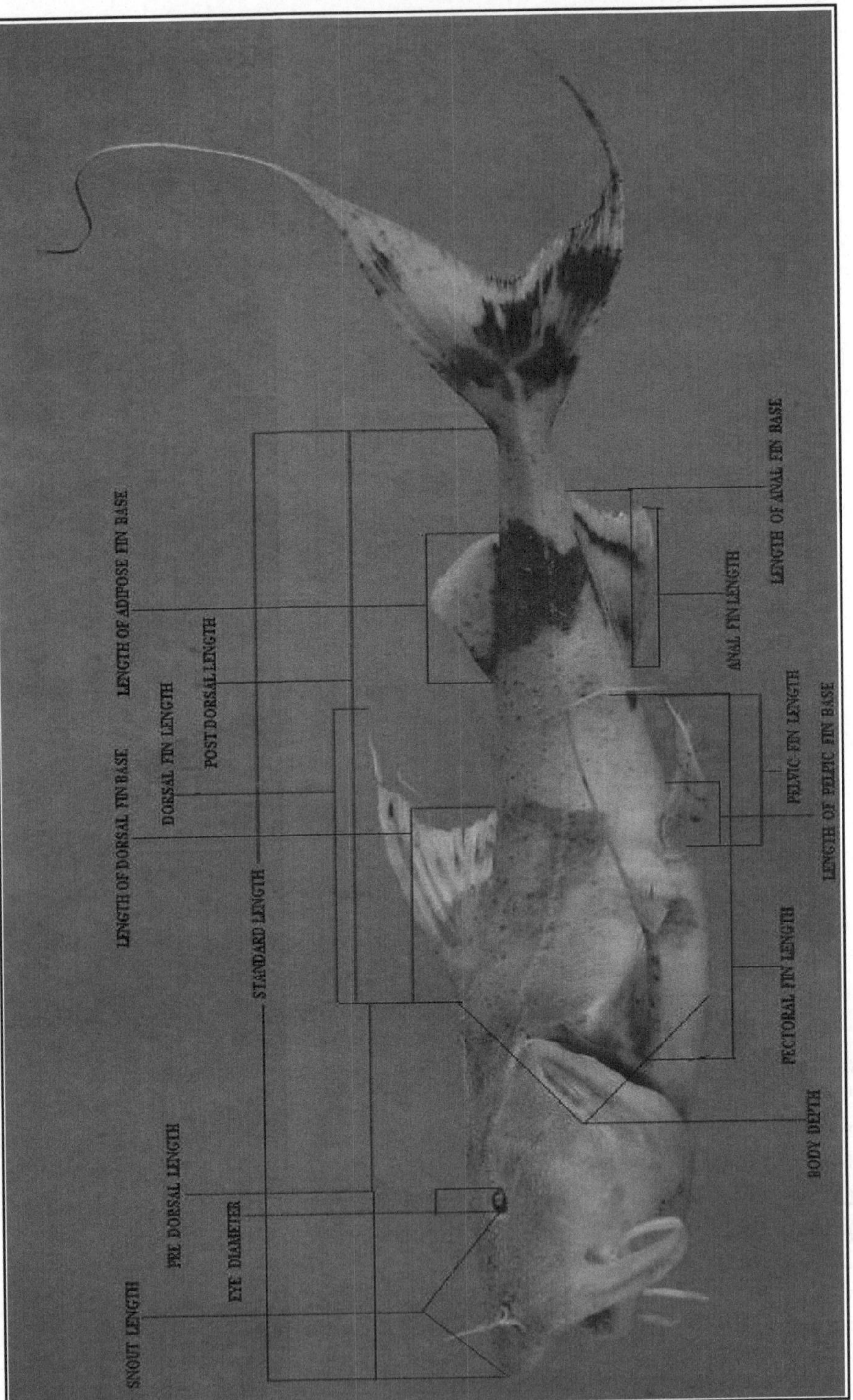
LENGTH OF DORSAL FIN BASE
LENGTH OF ADIPOSE FIN BASE
DORSAL FIN LENGTH
POST DORSAL LENGTH
STANDARD LENGTH
SNOUT LENGTH
PRE DORSAL LENGTH
EYE DIAMETER
ANAL FIN LENGTH
LENGTH OF ANAL FIN BASE
PELVIC-FIN LENGTH
LENGTH OF PELPIC FIN BASE
PECTORAL FIN LENGTH
BODY DEPTH

PLATE - II

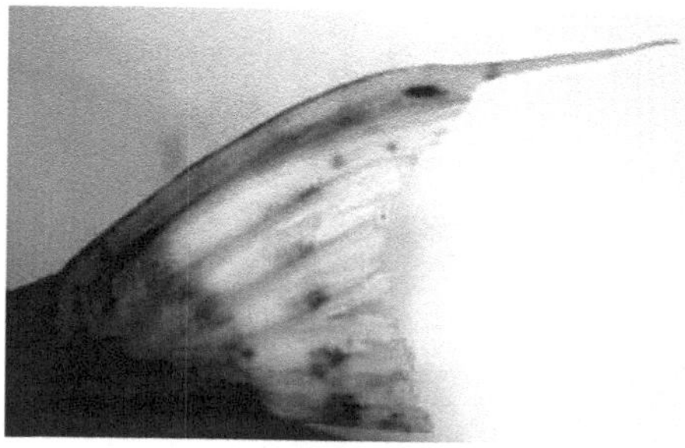

Fig. 7.1: Dorsal Fin of *Bagarius yarrelli*

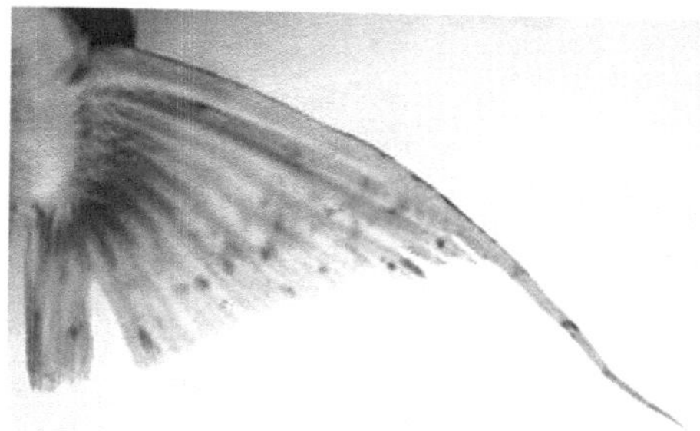

Fig. 7.2: Pectoral fin of *Bagarius yarrelli*

Fig. 7.3: Pelvic fin of *Bagarius yarrelli*

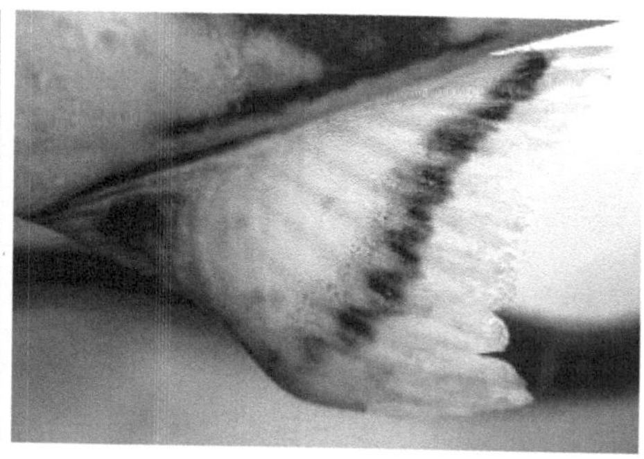

Fig. 7.4: Anal fin of *Bagarius yarrelli*

Fig. 7.5: Caudal fin of *Bagarius yarrelli*

Fig. 7.6: Adipose fin of *Bagarius yarrelli*

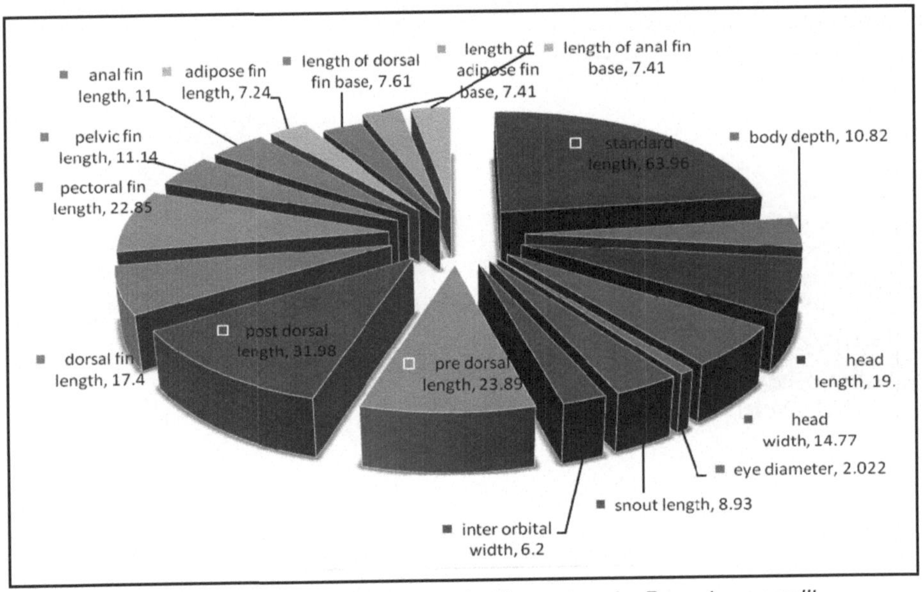

Fig. 7.7: Variation of Morphometric Characters in *Bagarius yarrelli*

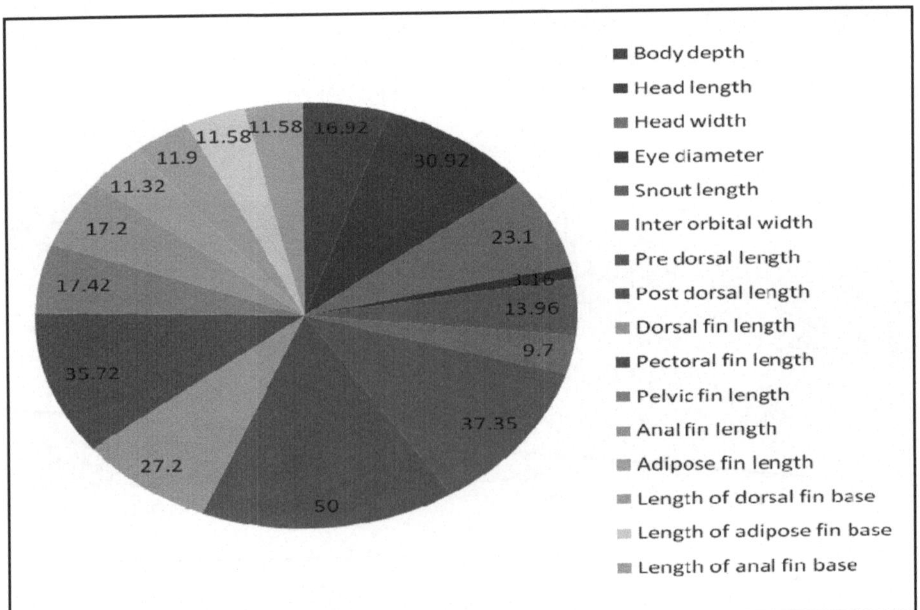

Fig. 7.8: Variation of Morphometric Characters of *Bagarius yarrelli* and Their Relationship (in%) with Standard Length of the Fish

PLATE - III

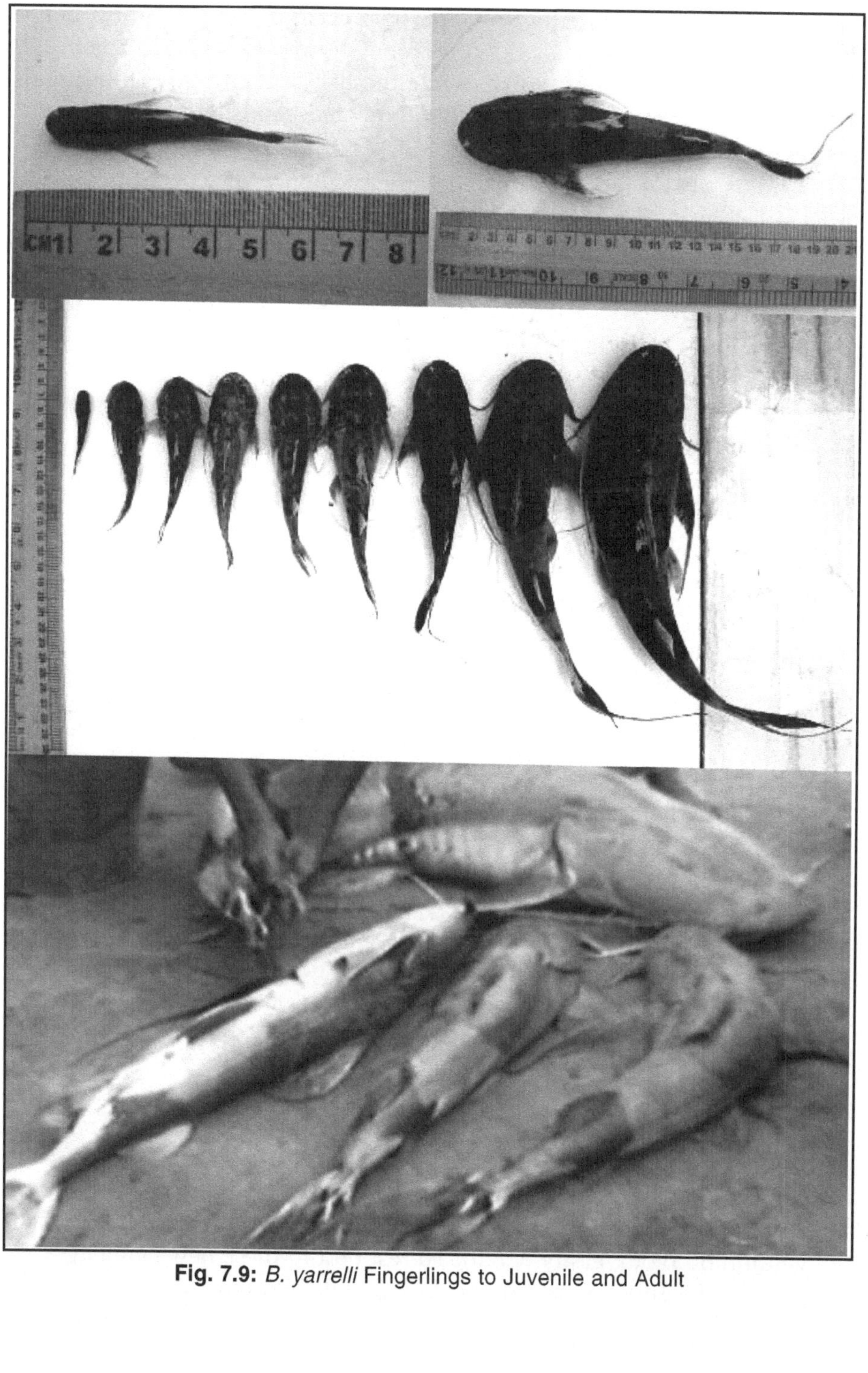

Fig. 7.9: *B. yarrelli* Fingerlings to Juvenile and Adult

The colour of the fish is olivaceous to rich tan or brown color with three darkly pigmented bands or blotches on the body. However the color varies with the habitat (Dutta 1974). In the present investigation it is noticed that fishes caught from fast flowing zone showed olivaceous body color with faded bands without blotch, while the fish catching from the sluggish zones are brown in color with darkly pigmented bands and with numerous blotches.

Gudger (1945) reported that the largest goonch of "5 ft in fork length and 136 lbs" was caught by hook and line in Yammuna near Okhla in 1975. Hora (1939) also stated that it can grow up to 6 ft and to weight of over 250 lbs. In the present study also a specimen of length 203.2 cm weighting ca 145 kg is recorded from Goalpara fish market. This indicates that the River Brahamaputra is a productive sheet of environment for the favourable growth of *B. yarrellii* which is resulted from such a high body weight and length. This proves that the fish is the largest in size among all the fishes of the River Brahmaputra.

During the course of present investigation an abnormal specimen of *B. yarrelli* has found. The specimen is found with teratological abnormalities in vertebral column. In the specimen the tail is deflected upwards almost from the origin of the adipose fin which twisted up making an arc (figure 7.10). The abnormality could not perhaps jeoperdise the normal function of the fish.

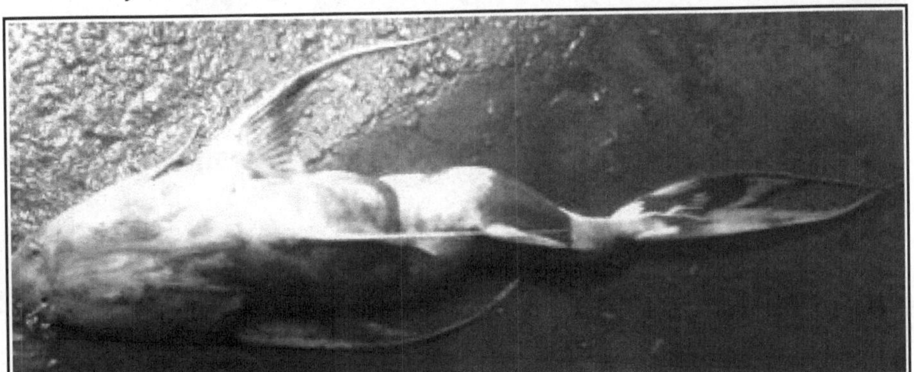

Fig. 7.10: *Bagarius yarrelli*, Showing Teratological Abnormalities in Vertebral Column

THREATS AND CONSERVATION PROSPECT OF *B. YARRELLI*

The word conservation is widely used today in the context of Nature and Natural resources. Conservation means sustained use of natural resources so that they are available to the future generation so that humanity do survive with quality life. In recent years the international community has also become sensitive to conservation of natural resources, which is evident from the Convention on Biodiversity (CBD). To respond to these new challenges and developments, India enacted the Biological Diversity Act (BDA) 2002,

Fisheries and aquaculture have a promising role to play in social development by providing nutritional security for the Indian population and contribution to the economic advancement of farmers and fishery workers. But the natural population of many fish species have experienced drastic reduction in number, largely due to the effect of the overexploitation, habitat alteration, overharvesting, construction of dams etc. In this regard India's Conservation and Management Plan (CAMP 1998) has identified 327 threatened freshwater fish in India and categorized as critically endangered, endangered, vulnerable, low-risk-near threatened, low-risk least concern, data deficient and extinct/extinct from wild. The present population of the *B. yarrelli* also shows a drastic decline in the Brahmaputra River. In this present investigation the conservation prospect of this giant fish has also been studied.

CONSERVATION STATUS

India's Conservation and Management Plan (CAMP 1998) categorized *Bagarius yarrelli* under the sections of *"vulnerable"*

DECLINE AND THREATS

B. yarrelli has undergone a widespread decline in range and abundance throughout much of the stretches of the Brahmaputra River system in recent decades. The reasons for this decline are not clearly understood, as interactions between threatening processes are extremely complex. However such a decline is often associated with its habitat modification (stream channelization), increased turbidity and siltation, changes in flow regimes, industrial and domestic pollutants, pesticides, and construction of impoundments etc. In this study some important factors responsible for dwindling population of the species in the Brahmaputra River are identified during the study periods, which are discussed here under.

1. **Changes to flow regimes**

   It has been argued time and again that the natural flow regime plays a critical role in sustaining native biodiversity and ecosystem integrity in river. The natural flow regime defines the river ecosystems. *Bagarius yarrelli* prefer fast running water for their survival and the alteration of this condition may be detrimental to their biological activity like breeding and spawning etc. Due to heavy siltation and erosion in the region causes the siltation in the river for which the water current slows down causing alteration of the habitat and ecology for the fishes like *Bagarius yarrelli* living in the fast flowing water.

2. **Loss of habitat**

   Humans become successful competitor for water with fish and other organisms. It is observed that *Bagarius yarrelli* is a bottom dwelling fish and need certain depth for its nesting. But increased bank erosion decreases the river depth and thus causing habitat degradation for the fish. Another major threat to the habitat degradation of Brahmaputra River is from the noisy engine boats (locally called *Bhut Bhuttis*) which scurry across the river. The oil mix water from the engine boats pollutes the river water contributing the habitat degradation of the fish. Pesticides used indiscriminately in the fringed agriculture fields of the river islands (*chars*) also contribute pollution in the river periphery.

3. **Destructive harvesting methods**

   Excessive fishing pressure is now a major threat to the aquatic biodiversity. Use of fine meshed net for catching smallest sized fish etc. causing serious depletion of fish species from its natural habitat. The use of Masuri jal in fishing of fingerlings of the species is one of the reasons for its drastic decline.

4. **Juvenile killing**

   Wanton killing of juveniles and gravid fishes in the river is another important cause of depletion of the fish from the region. The enforcement of fishery Act is not effectively followed which by order of the Department of Fisheries, Government of Assam ban fishing of juvenile and gravid fishes in the River during 15 th April to 1st July. During this period *Bagarius* fishing is found to be done intensively in the prospective spawning zone.

CONSERVATION STRATEGY

In general, aquatic conservation strategies should support sustainable development by protecting biological resources in ways that will preserve habitat and ecosystems. So the anthropogenic activities such as deforestation along the river bank sides which causes erosion of river, excessive use of motor boats and overexploitation of fish resources should be minimized to restore the habitat of *Bagarius yarrelli.* The natural flow pattern and discharge regimes of the river should kept in monitored and work for restitution of the same should be done to ensure the restoration of the habitat of the fish.

The destructive harvesting of the fish should be checked by ensuring that there should not be any use of mosquito net during and after the breeding period of the fish. And this can be ensuring through proper enforcement of the Fishery Act of 1897 (modified in 1956) in the studied area. Large numbers of fingerlings are used to kill during the months of May to July by the use of mosquito nets which should be prevented as a conservation measure. Yadav and Chandra (1994) have also suggested the same for conservation of fishery resources in North Eastern Region of India. However the conservation measure to the fishery resources in the region is largely been slow and inadequate, which is a general opinion for other workers also working in this region (Biswas *et al.*, 2001; Sarkar *et al.*, 2008).

From the study of the habitat of *Bagarius,* it is found to be unique to the specific river character and therefore, initiation of cultural conservation is not at all a ready solution. Present study, therefore, emphasize the river resource conservation of *Bagarius yarrelli* through community-based management that will encourage resource conservation and at the same time promote equity in resource access. Therefore, through this investigation, effort has been made to encourage use of management interventions that will consistent with this natural ecological process considering following methods:

1. Management activities should be planned and executed with community participation through a Local Implementation Committee. The Committee must represent traditional fishers, landless laborers, farmers, local leaders and professionals, etc. The elected local government administrator serves as adviser to the Committee.
2. Management activities should include participatory planning with villages around the ecosystem to identify problems and work out possible solutions, particularly conservation measures with the least potential for adverse impacts on the existing social relations and on the local environment.
3. Possible management interventions should identified through a series of open community consultation meetings and participatory appraisals supplemented by preliminary surveys.
4. Biological monitoring may be made to investigate fishery potential and productivity of the water resources with the help of biologist.
5. Restriction of harmful fishing gears for a limited period and to establish small fish sanctuaries which the community volunteered to protect.
6. Limited motor boating should be permitted for transportation, which is a common phenomenon of studied area of *Bagarius*.
7. To reduce the conflict among the stakeholders, some tasks need to be included; fisheries co-management need to be developed based on the real situation in the field; - family fishing gear need to be redefined based the specific location; information and documents relating to fishing lot management and fisheries community management need to be public informed.
8. With the low of conscience of the society, the awareness building need to be strengthened for all level including policies makers, fish folk.
9. Improve the capacity of the research and extension work on the fisheries. The research results need to be updated and taken into considerations and actions.

Alternative livelihood option for the fishermen community involved in *Bagarius* fishing needs to be worked out and implemented which can not only reduce the pressure on the capture fishery as a whole but also help conservation of *B. yarrelli* in the River. At least during the banned season the fishers should given short time income generating livelihood option so that they can keep themselves away from fishing the gravid fishes like *B. yarrelli*.

CONCLUSION

Many species of freshwater fishes are acutely threatened by overfishing and loss of habitat. Large and long-lived riverine species, which often migrate over long distances to complete their life cycle, are particularly at risk. The giant devil catfish *B. yarrelli* is now believed to deplete drastically from its natural habitat. The species has been listed in vulnerable category. Its precarious status is likely to be the result of excessive harvesting over the past few decades, and to a lesser extent habitat degradation. Again, significant incidental harvest of juveniles continues to be a problem. There is currently no overall conservation and recovery strategy for this giant fish. It is a flagship species for the aquatic biodiversity conservation in the River Brahmaputra and a combination of reduction in harvest, reduction in fingerlings/juvenile killing and conservation/restoration of critical habitat will only reduced the threats to the species.

REFERENCES

Biswas S.P., A. Baruah and S. Boruah. (2001): Conservation Status of Fish Resources in the Brahmaputra Basin. *Tropical Zoology*. 2 & 3: 125-131.

CAMP (1998). Conservation Assessment and Management Plan for Freshwater Fishes of India. Zoo Out reach Organization and NBFGR, Lucknow, pp: 156.

Dutta (1974). Observation of Some Biometric Features of Leiognathus Species (cav) *J. Indian fish. Soc.*

Gudger, L. (1937). An Albino of Tarpon, *Tarpon atlanticus*, the Only Known Specimen. American Museum Novitates, 944: 1-4.

Hora S.L. (1939). The Game Fishes of Indian. Part VI. The Goonch, *Bagarius bagarius* (Hamilton). *J. Bombay Nat. Hist. Soc.* 40: 583-593.

Jayaram, K.C. (1999). *The Fresh Water Fishes of the Indian Region*. Narendra Publishing House, Delhi, pp: 551, pls. 1-18.

Jayaram, K.C. (2006). *Cat Fishes of India*. Narendra Publishing House, Delhi, 383 pp., pls. 166-205.

Karmakar, A.K. (2000) Fish Communities and Their Distribution in Himalayan Drainage System. *Records of the Zoological Survey of India*, 98, 25-37.

Kottelat, M. (1989). Zoogeography of the Fishes from Indochinese Inland Waters with an Annotated Checklist. *Bulletin Zoologisch Museum, University van Amsterdam*, 12, 1-55.

Kottelat, M. (2001a). *Fishes of Laos*. WHT Publications Ltd., Colombo, Sri Lanka, pp: 198.

Kottelat, M. (2001b). *Freshwater Fishes of Northern Vietnam. A Preliminary Check-list of the Fishes Known or Expected to Occur in Northern Vietnam with Comments on Systematics and Nomenclature.* Environment and Social Development Unit, East Asia and Pacific Region. The World Bank. pp: 123.

Lowe – Mc connel, R. H. (1971). *Identification of Fresh Water Fishes.* In Methods for Assessment of Fish Production in Feswaters. Blackwel Scientific Publications. Oxford and Edinburgh, pp. 45-81.

M.S. Sheikh, J. Kalita, and A. Dutta. (1997). The Status of the Giant Freshwater Catfish *Bgarius bagarius* (Ham) in the Brahmaptra River. *Tiger paper*. 24(3): 22-25.

Mamnur Rashid, M., Aminul Haque, A.K.M. & Rahman, A.K.A. (1997). A Checklist of Ichthyofauna of the River Dharla of Fulbari (Kurigram). *Bangladesh Journal of Animal Science*, 26, 133-140.

Ng, H.H. & Kottelat, M. (2000). Descriptions of Three New Species of Catfishes (Teleostei: Akysidae and Sisoridae) from Laos and Vietnam. *Journal of South Asian Natural History*, 5: 7-15.

Pandey, A.K., G.S. Sandhu, (1992). *Encylopedia of Fishes and Fisheries of India*, pp. 581-582, Vol. No. 7.

Roberts, Tyson R. (1983). "Revision of the South and Southeast Asian Sisorid Catfish Genus *Bagarius*, with Description of a New Species from the Mekong". *Copeia* (2): 435-445.

Rainboth, W.J. (1996). *Fishes of the Cambodian Mekong. FAO Species Identification Field Guide for Fishery Purposes*. FAO, Rome, pp: 265.

Sarkar U.K, A.K. Pathak, W.S. Lakra, (2008). Conservation of Freshwater Fish Resources of India: New Approaches, Assessment and Challenges. Biodiversity and Conservation. 17 (10), 2495-2511.

Talwar, K and V.G. Jhingran (1998). Inland Fishes (Vol. 1 & 2). Narendra Publishing House. 2nd Edition.

Talwar, P.K. & Jhingran, A.G. (1991). *Inland Fishes of India and Adjacent Countries. In 2 Vols*. Oxford & IBH Publishing Co., NewDelhi, Bombay, Calcutta, pp: 1158.

Yadava, Y.S. and Chandra, R. (1994). Some Threatened Carps and Cat Fishes of Brahmaputra River System. pp. 45-55. *In* P.V. Dehadrai, P. Das and S.R. Verma (eds). Threatened Fishes of India, Nature Conservators, Muzaffarnagar.

Pages: 140-159

FISH HABITAT AND AQUACULTURE
Edited by: Dr. Sanjay Kumar Gupta; Dr. Pawan Kumar 'Bharti'
ISBN: 978-93-5056-744-9
Edition: 2015
Published by: Discovery Publishing House Pvt. Ltd., New Delhi (India)

8

Aquaculture Development and Sustainable Environmental Management Towards Food Security

Sagar C. Mandal

ABSTRACT

Aquaculture is widely considered an important component for enhancing food security, income, foreign exchange earnings and employment to the rural population in developing countries. There is a need to measure the potential contribution of aquaculture towards improving food security. Over one billion people worldwide rely on fish as their primary source of animal protein. Average annual fish consumption in the world is 16.1 kg per capita. In the last 30 years, animal protein consumption per capita in developing countries has more than doubled, as a direct result of technology advancement in aquaculture. About 10.7 million people involved in aquaculture with the majority from developing countries, accounting for about 96% of the global total and come from extensive to semi-intensive aquaculture systems mainly of fish in ponds, integrated farming and stocking of fish into natural or impounded water bodies. Fish contributes to national food self-sufficiency through direct consumption and through trade and exports. However, development of aquaculture has generated debate over the social and environmental costs and benefits. Application of biotechnology in aquaculture represents a wide range of opportunities to increase the growth rate in farmed species, improve nutritional value of aqua feeds, improve fish health management, restore and protect environments. The sustainable approach to the development, management and regulation of aquaculture can ensure environment and aquaculture industry long-term economic and social benefits and a step ahead towards food security.

Key words: Sustainable, Fish, Devlepment, Security, Aquaculture.

INTRODUCTION

Aquaculture is the farming of aquatic organisms, including fish, molluscs, crustaceans and aquatic plants, is often cited as one of the means of efficiently increasing food production. Fish provides a good source of protein and essential micronutrients and thus plays an important role in the prevention of many human diseases (Williams & Poh-Sze, 2003). About nine million people are employed in the aquaculture industry, which provides them with supplementary income during lean seasons (FAO, 2003). Aquaculture could increase the availability of low-cost fish in local markets bringing poor households above poverty threshold levels relatively quickly (Edwards, 1999). Larger scale commercial aquaculture, practiced in many developing countries, can enhance the production for domestic and export markets bringing much needed foreign exchange, revenue and employment, thereby contributing to food security (Subasinghe, 2003).

Aquaculture is widely considered an important component for enhancing food security, national income, foreign exchange earnings and employment to the rural population in many developing countries. However, little information is available concerning the direct and indirect impacts of aquaculture on food security and poverty alleviation in most developing countries. Food insecurity remains one of the most visible dimensions of poverty and is generally the first sign of extreme destitution. "Food security", defined by FAO as "a condition when all people, at all times, have physical and economic access to sufficient, safe and nutritious food to meet their dietary needs and food preferences for an active and healthy life", concerns not only food production and distribution but also has social, economic and institutional dimensions. Although aquaculture could theoretically bring numerous benefits to the quality of life of millions throughout the world, until the effects of this technology can be measured and quantified, the true benefits cannot be fully understood. There is a need for a direct, simple and rigorous method to measure the potential contribution of aquaculture towards improving food security. Food security exists when all people, at all times, have physical, social and economic access to sufficient, safe and nutritious food that meets their dietary needs and food preferences for an active and healthy life (SPFS, 2003).

POVERTY AND FOOD SECURITY

Fish is a rich food for the poor. This is mainly for two reasons. Firstly, fish is nutritionally rich food for human (Huong & Cuong, 2012). The presence of essential nutrients such as iodine, vitamin B12, vitamin D, essential fatty acids EPA and DHA, high quality protein and the very rich source in calcium, iron, zinc and vitamin A. Secondly, fish is used in many developing countries as a primary source of animal protein. According to the FAO (2012), it reveals that fish accounted for 17% of the global population's intake of animal protein and 6.5% of all protein consumed during the year 2009. Globally, fish provides about 3.0 billion people with almost 20 percent of their average per capita intake of animal protein and 4.3 billion people with about 15% of such protein. According to the FAO (2012), over one billion people worldwide rely on fish as their primary source of animal protein. Average annual fish consumption in the world is 16.1 kg per capita. In South-East Asia most major species of fish produced are primarily for local consumption. In the last 30 years, animal protein consumption per capita in developing countries has more than doubled, as a direct result of technological advancement in aquaculture.

It has been reported by the FAO (2014) that total aquaculture production in 2012 was over 66 million tonnes. A significant trend in much of developing Asia is the growth in commercial and small farm aquaculture, spurred by increasing demand. The Asian region contributes over 88 per cent of global production, while China remains the world's largest producer in the sector with 41 million tonnes produced in (2012).

The connection between poverty and food insecurity is important. Poverty is considered as one of the major causes of food insecurity. So, poverty eradication is essential to improve access to food by the people (FAO, 2003). According to the World Bank, poverty is multidimensional phenomenon, encompassing inability to satisfy basic needs, lack of control over resources, lack of education and skills, poor health, malnutrition, lack of shelter, poor access to water and sanitation, vulnerability to shocks, violence and crime, lack of political freedom and voice. It is estimated that about one-fifth of the world's population is currently living in extreme economic poverty; defined as living on less than US$1 per day.

The most destructive problems facing by the world's poor people are hunger and malnutrition. The FAO State of Food Insecurity Report 2002 estimates that 799 million people in 98 developing nations are not getting enough food to lead normal, healthy and active lives. Food demand and in particular the demand for fish, has continued to rise, and it is forecasted that expanding populations and changing eating habits will make a doubling of food output imperative in the next 30 years. This demand mainly has to be met from local food production systems. Aquaculture contributes to poverty alleviation as it provides employment to millions of people. It also generates income and as prices for most food commodities fall, fish prices are expected to rise reflecting the imbalance between demand and supply.

CONTRIBUTION OF AQUACULTURE TO RURAL DEVELOPMENT

Rural development can be explained as the process of sustained growth of the rural economy and improvement of well-being of rural people, but it is particularly the development of the agricultural and allied sector, which is widely believed to provide the main impetus not only for reducing poverty and hunger but also for ensuring food security for all. In the context of the rural poor, aquaculture often complements catches from traditional fisheries. Often, the capture or culture of aquatic species forms the basis of food security, enabling the use of livestock or cultured fish as a source of income generation. Aquaculture becomes an attractive and important component of rural livelihoods in situations where increasing population pressures, environmental degradation or loss of access limit catches from wild fisheries (IIRR *et al.*, 2001).

Various types of aquaculture form an important component within agricultural and farming systems development. These can contribute to the alleviation of food insecurity, malnutrition and poverty through the provision of food of high nutritional value, income and employment generation, decreased risk of monoculture production failure, improved access to water, enhanced aquatic resource management and increased farm sustainability (FAO, 2000; Prein & Ahmed, 2000).

Large and small-scale fish-farming activities are remarkably diverse and locally specific, making their characterization a challenge. Employment at farm level includes people operating hatcheries, nurseries, grow-out production facilities and part time and occasional labours hired to work for aquaculture production. Employment at other links along aquaculture value chains include people working as input suppliers, middle traders and domestic fish distributors, processors and exporters and vendors. In the case of the small scale operators, overall, like their fisheries counterparts most of these operators are characterized by low capital investments, low equipment and inputs, and low productivity. They are often a family based activity, where part of the production may be retained for household-consumption. About 70-80% of aquaculture ventures are considered small scale (De Silva & Davy 2009; Subasinghe *et al*, 2012).

The number of people employed in aquaculture varies from country to country, but recent data suggests that previous global estimates are a considerable under-estimate. It was indicated that there were about 10.7 million people involved in aquaculture in 2008 with the majority from developing countries, accounting for about 96% of the global total (FAO/ WHO, 2011). A more recent estimate derived from case studies suggests that the number of people employed in global aquaculture would be close to 11.89 million full time equivalent jobs in these selected country case studies only. These case studies represent however just below 20% of the global aquaculture production. Extrapolation to the global production level suggests that total employment in global aquaculture value chains could be about 38.4 million full time persons (Phillips *et al.*, 2013).

AQUACULTURE PRODUCTION INTENSITY, RISKS AND BENEFITS

There are different types of aquaculture systems are being used by different fish growers in the world. These systems are divided into extensive, semi-intensive, intensive and super intensive type of farming based on inputs and other management practices followed. More is the intensification in the farming practices; more will be the production from unit area of the water body. However, the major production of world aquaculture products comes from extensive to semi-intensive aquaculture systems (Halwart, 2005). The common system are farming of fish in ponds, however, integrated farming such as integrated rice-cum-fish farming or the stocking of fish into natural or impounded water bodies are also com-mon. It is very difficult to estimate the contribution of these types of aquaculture production since small-scale and dis-persed production data do not appear in official statistics and the produce is mainly consumed or traded locally. Few examples of aquaculture activities that have significant positive impacts on the rural poor are fry rearing and the development of nursing networks, the integration of fish farming with rice crops in floodplains and the more remote areas particularly in Asia, sustaining and restoring aquatic biodiversity through simple management technique. In coastal areas, the farming of mud crabs, oysters, mussels, cockles, shrimps, fish and seaweeds provides employment for the rural poor by engagement as labour and for collection of seed and feed for fish and shell fishes (Halwart, 2005).

It is obvious that intensive aquaculture systems yield more production from a given unit, which is achieved through the use of advanced technology and a higher degree of management. Intensive inland and coastal cage aquaculture of high-value fishes like salmonids has been encouraged and supported to develop remote rural areas in Europe and South America (Halwart, 2005). Similar systems have emerged in Asia and Australia for warm-water carnivorous fish such as groupers, yellowtail, snappers and sea bass. The benefits of aquaculture in rural development relate to health and nutrition, employment, income and farm sustainability. It creates own enterprise employment, including for women and children and provides income through sale of what can be a relatively high value product.

Other benefits of aquaculture include an increased availability of fish in local rural and urban markets and concomitant reduction in household expenditure through sparing consumption of other income generating farm products. Aquaculture can also offer benefits from the utilization of common resources, particularly for the landless, through cage culture, culture of molluscs and seaweeds, and enhanced fisheries in communal water bodies. An important, though often overlooked benefit which is particularly relevant for integrated aquaculture systems is their contribution to increased farm efficiency and sustainability.

Agricultural by-products such as manure from livestock and crop residues can serve as fertilizer and feed inputs for small-scale and commercial aquaculture. Fish farming in rice fields contributes to integrated pest management and integrated management of vectors of human medical importance. Ponds become important as on-farm water reservoirs for irrigation and livestock in areas where there are seasonal water shortages. So, considering all these benefits it is not surprising that aquaculture produc-tion has grown rapidly since the 1970s and has been the fastest growing food production sector in many countries for nearly two decades and the sector exhibiting an overall growth rate of over 11 percent per year since 1984. By 2002, the produc-tion of all cultured aquatic organisms had reached 51.4 million tons. More than 260 fish, crustacean, and mollusc species representing the most important animals used in aquaculture world-wide have been listed. Although not all aquatic organisms may be suitable for culture, the variety of cultured species is still increas-ing. China produces major share of the total world aquaculture production including freshwater fishes, followed by molluscs and aquatic plants (Halwart, 2005).

AQUACULTURE AND ENVIRONMENT

Aquaculture is an important economic activity in many countries and offers opportunities to contribute to poverty alleviation, employment, community development, reduction of exploitation of natural resources and food security in tropical and subtropical regions. The development of aquaculture has, however, generated debate over the social and environmental costs and benefits. Viewed alternatively as a solution to overfishing or as a massive threat to marine and freshwater environments, aquaculture has come to the forefront of debates about the long-term viability of global food production systems. World Wildlife Fund is working to reconcile the opportunities that aquaculture provides with the risks it poses to society and the environment.

Aquaculture often referred to as fish farming includes the production of more than 400 species of aquatic organisms including marine and freshwater fish, crustaceans and seaweeds.

Aquaculture is the fastest growing food production system in the world. From 1993 to 2003, aquaculture production more than doubled, reaching an estimated 54 million metric tons (mmt). It accounts for more than 30 percent of commercial fish and shellfish production every year. It is estimated that by 2020, aquaculture will produce more than 68 mmt (excluding aquatic plants), accounting for about 40 percent of global seafood production. Countries like China, Chile, Madagascar, produce fish, shellfish, and/or sea plants by aquaculture. Like agriculture, aquaculture is practiced in both developed and developing countries. The growth of aquaculture has been spurred by an ever-increasing demand for seafood and the limited supply of wild fish. For more than 30 years, per capita seafood consumption has increased and the world population has grown, with the boom in aquaculture a response to the increasing demand. Aquaculture has been heralded for its potential to meet the increases in seafood demand, and to take pressure off wild fisheries. However, aquaculture can have serious impacts on the environment. Wastes from fish farms can pollute adjacent waters and harm fish and other wildlife. Chemicals such as antibiotics can be released into the environment from aquaculture ponds. Escaped farmed species can compete with wild ones for food and shelter, transfer disease and introduce nonnative DNA into the wild gene pool. In addition to polluting habitat, aquaculture can have direct negative impacts on wild populations of fish, birds, and mammals such as seals and sea lions. The young of farmed species produced in marine and freshwater environments are susceptible to predation by birds and other wild animals, prompting farmers to use lethal methods to control predation. Small wild fish, like anchovies, are caught to produce fishmeal and fish oil; the primary ingredients in feed given to shrimp, salmon, and other carnivorous species. Fish caught to make fish feed now represent a third of the global fish harvest. As aquaculture grows, so does the pressure on these wild fisheries.

The impacts of aquaculture production vary by species, based on the species' unique characteristics and how they interact with their environments. But the impacts also vary by location: in rivers or lakes, inland, along the coastline, in the oceans, on the seafloor. For example, clams, scallops, oysters and mussels filter nutrients and particulates from the water whether they are raised suspended from ropes and rafts or grown on the ocean floor. But harvesting shellfish from the seabed frequently requires dredges that disrupt and destroy natural habitat, making suspended culture the better choice from the environmental perspective.

Sustainable aquaculture production on environment friendly depends on the correct combination of farming systems such as health management, feeds and improved germplasm (Browdy *et al.*, 2012). As aquaculture is still a relatively new industry, its recent development has entailed major changes in land and water body use. The ecological conversions to introduce aquaculture have often disturbed existing uses and users, and some have been ecologically damaging. The conversion of large areas of land and wetlands to fish and shrimp farms, and of coastal, lake and river habitat to cage, raft and stake culture has had major environmental impacts such as loss of biodiversity, introduction of alien species, pathogens and parasites, pollution from farm and farm chemical wastes, increases in soil and ground water salinity and the loss of ecosystem functions (Barraclough and Finger-Stick, 1996; EJF, 2002). It was estimated that aquaculture have led to the additional destruction of 10% of mangrove areas, over and above destruction from other land uses (World Bank, 2006) and had detrimental consequences on the food security of the people. Most of the aquaculturists are now more confident that the era of severe environmental problems is behind and that aquaculture is on the road of sustainability (EC. 1999; Costa-Pierce et al. 2012). Now, aquaculture has become a more accepted form of fish production as more people in the developing countries have become more dependent on aquaculture fish for their livelihood and source of animal protein.

Choice of production technique or technology also determines environmental impacts, as is the case with a range of species produced in man-made ponds, including tilapia, shrimp, trout, and catfish. If the ponds are drained at harvest, nutrients are released into the environment and large volumes of water are required to refill the ponds. But when the species are harvested using nets, water and nutrients remain in the ponds for many production cycles. With today's better, and still improving, technology, many fish can be raised in recirculating systems that require very little water exchange, reducing the amount of discharged nutrient-rich effluents. Even within salmon aquaculture that uses open net-pen technology, the management practices of different farms can produce different environmental impacts. Variables that determine environmental impacts include where net pens are built, the strength of ocean currents at different locations, the producer's efficiency of feed use, decisions on chemical and antibiotic treatments, and maintenance of pens to prevent escapes.

WAYS TO INCREASE THE ROLE OF AQUACULTURE IN RURAL DEVELOPMENT

(a) Aquaculture intensification and expansion

Through intensification in the farming systems, diversification or expansion of area under aquaculture production, the current trend of increasing production can be maintained. The expansion of land-based culture systems in inland areas has the greatest potential because aquaculture can be integrated with agriculture on current agricultural land in smallholder and commercial farming systems. The great potential lies in the integration of aquaculture and irrigation systems and aquaculture can also make use of land that is unsuitable for agriculture such as swamps or saline areas introducing suitable candidate species.

A wide diversity of inland and coastal aquatic resources exists, which can provide opportunity for the integration of aquaculture for the development in the rural areas. This will require proper planning and institutional coordination which are often difficult to achieve and can cause considerable expenditure. The difficulties and expenditures relate to the often cumbersome structures of bureaucrats and procedures of government agencies; the complexity of the scientific, technical and economic issues involved; and large numbers of informed decisions need to be taken. Increasing production through intensified management practices require an increased level of feeds and fertilizers, that are derived from farm made or procured from market, or a combination of both. Infrastructure development reduces costs and increases availability of feed and fertilizers and also allows farmers to intensify their production level. Since this requires increased investment in the production system, other enabling features include the development of markets and access to finance. Many of the technical aspects of aquaculture are relatively well developed, however there is a knowledge gap between what is known globally and what is available to farmers. Weak extension systems and lack of local examples of intensified aquaculture also limit farmer's ability and willingness to take more risk.

Application of biotechnology in aquaculture represents a wide range of opportunities to increase the growth rate in farmed species, improve nutritional value of aqua feeds, improve fish health management, restore and protect environments, extend the range of aquatic species and to improve the management and conservation of wild stocks. Improved breeding capabilities, larval nutrition and advances in genetic technologies now permit a wide range of genetic manipulations to be performed on aquatic species. Modern biotechnologies are usually developed for farming systems with high inputs of feed, labour, and husbandry. Many biotechnologies could also be directed at low-input systems, farming systems in marginal areas or to meet other needs specific to a given rural community, however the requirement for recouping development costs of many forms of biotechnology generally puts this approach to aquaculture out of reach of most aquafarmers. Furthermore, the application of biotechnologies often also requires a certain level of capacity and resources. Small hatchery operations increase the local supply of fingerlings and can enable farmers to enter aquaculture as an activity. These small hatcheries are essential for the development of rural aquaculture but often have limited pond areas or water availability, hence may be unable to maintain the genetic quality of their broodstock and over a period of time lose genetic quality and performance. In this situation the intervention of government hatcheries or of a larger scale com-mercial hatchery is required. In each case, consideration must be given to the specific stage of rural development in a given area, extension programmes and how to integrate such activities within prevailing livelihood strategies.

The introduction of exotic species is another strategy used to increase value from farming systems in rural areas, for example, tilapia production is much higher in Asia than in its native Africa. Introduced species often are genetically improved or domesticated species, to some extent. It is imperative; however, that environmental risk assessment and other applicable regulations are followed since introductions may pose a risk to the environment and the local biodiversity. Aquaculture's potential for contributing to global food production is far from being fully realized. Many recent international gatherings recognized the role that aquaculture can play in national economic development, global food supply and achievement of food security, and declared that the sector has the potential to continue to contribute even more to peoples' livelihoods.

Land-based culture systems in inland areas have the greatest potential because aquaculture can be integrated with the existing agricultural practice of small-scale farming households. Coastal aquaculture also contributes to rural development by alleviating poverty and enabling livelihood diversification of subsistence fisher folk. Social, economic and institutional issues have been recognized to be the most important constraints to greater contributions by aquaculture to rural development. To attain its full potential, the aquaculture sector will require new approaches in the coming decades. These will undoubtedly vary in different regions and countries, and the challenge is to develop approaches that are realistic and achievable within each social, economic, environmental and political circumstance. In an era of globalization and trade liberalization, such approaches should not only focus on increasing production, they should also focus on producing a product that is affordable, acceptable and accessible to all sectors of society.

(b) Integration of aquaculture into national development

Aquaculture needs to become part of national development plans, developed in consultation with stakeholders and ensuring feedback mechanisms allowing the poor to influence development. Aquaculture planning also needs to be integrated with water resource management planning for inland areas and coastal management planning in coastal areas as well as into other economic and food security interventions for rural areas. This may be done through the establishment of a multi-sectoral coordinating process both at sectoral policy formulation level and at the extension service level.

Furthermore, aquaculture should be pursued as an integral component of community development, contributing to sustainable livelihoods, promoting human development and enhancing social wellbeing of poorer sectors. Aquaculture policies and regulations should promote practical and economically viable farming and management practices that are environmentally sustainable and socially acceptable. Aquaculture development should complement wild fisheries to the extent possible. Aquaculture has an important role to play with regard to the conservation and sustainable use of endangered fish as the culture of valuable native fish species can take pressure from wild populations.

(c) Public-private sector partnership and regional cooperation

Public–private partnerships in aquaculture and the establishment of aquaculture networks have shown to be able to contribute considerably to the sectoral development. Although the establishment of such partnerships and networks may be a time consuming, costly and difficult task, they make it possible to address constraints and opportunities in a manner what otherwise would not have been allowed. Cooperation between governments, NGOs and civil society further provides opportunities for awareness raising, targeting and creating dialogues between the various stakeholders. Regional cooperation between aquaculture farmers, producers and marketing associations, research institutes and governments is essential. South-South Cooperation between Asian countries and those in Africa and Latin America is a useful tool to disseminate these experiences. A supportive institutional environment involving public and private sectors is required for aquaculture to contribute to improved livelihoods. The rural poor need to be provided, at least initially, with public sector support, while commercial aquaculture requires less intervention. In the longer term, aquaculture has to function on a self-financing basis within the private sector.

Necessary action includes to focus limited public resources on strategic government infrastructure and flexible and efficient extension services that meet producers' needs, to promote and facilitate the private sector production of feed and seed, to encourage credit for medium- and large-scale producers, to facilitate the formation of farmers' associations and encourage community production, and to encourage investment in building the institutional capacity and knowledge base concerning sustainable aquaculture practices to manage the sector.

(d) Information, awareness raising and capacity building

There is a need for assessing and documenting information on experiences and application of good practices, and for raising awareness and advocating products and benefits derived from aquaculture. Information exchange and transfer through collaboration and coordination between national and regional aquaculture institutions and agencies should be promoted. Experiences from traditional and other aquaculture systems that have proven to be sustainable and the lessons learnt should be promoted and disseminated as part of strategies for an effective transfer of aquaculture knowhow into areas and regions where it has no tradition. Capacity building should be based on a participatory farmer focused and needs-based approach.

ROLE OF AQUACULTURE

1. Nutritional benefits

Over one billion people worldwide rely on fish as their primary source of animal protein (Lehane, 2013). Around the world, average annual fish consumption is 16.1 kg per capita. In South-East Asia most major species of fish produced are primarily for local consumption, with Thailand and Vietnam deriving over a third of their fish production from aquaculture. In the last 30 years, animal protein consumption per capita in developing countries has more than doubled, as a direct result of technology advancement in aquaculture. Those living in poverty and in lower socio-economic households are unable to access sufficient nutritional food to ensure their health and wellbeing. Often the food produced or purchased consists of cereals or low-cost staple ingredients; budgets are unable to stretch to include meat or fruit and vegetables. Fish, particularly produced through aquaculture, is commonly cheaper than other animal meat. It also contains much higher protein levels, as well as other important minerals and vitamins. As a means of providing greater nutrition for many poorer households, increased availability of fish can mean better health and a more diverse diet.

Fish contributes to national food self-sufficiency through direct consumption and through trade and exports. In traditional fish eating countries in Asia and Oceania, per capita consumption are mostly above 25 kg. In some island countries in the Pacific the per capita consumption are above 50 kg per year or even as high as 190 kg as is the case in Maldives. The extreme importance of fish to food security and nutrition may be illustrated by assessments on the situation in Africa. FAO estimates that fish provides 22 percent of the protein intake in sub-Saharan Africa. This share, however, can exceed 50 percent in the poorest countries (especially where other sources of animal protein are scarce or expensive). In West African coastal countries, for instance, where fish has been a central element in local economies for many centuries, the proportion of dietary protein that comes from fish is extremely high: 47 percent in Senegal, 62 percent in Gambia and 63 percent in Sierra Leone and Ghana.

Indirectly, commercial aquaculture leads to increased food security by providing opportunities for employment and income generation for local communities. More than 500 million people in developing states reportedly depend on fisheries and aquaculture for their livelihood. As a majority of aquaculture production occurs in developing states, a rise in income leads to an increase in food purchasing power and, more importantly, diversification. The consumption of non-staple foods, including fish and vegetables, has a positive correlation with income growth, supporting food security and greater nutritional content in diets.

In general terms, aquaculture can benefit the livelihoods of the poor either through an improved food supply and/or through employment and increased income. However, at present little or no hard statistical information exists concerning the scale and extent of rural or small-scale aquaculture development within most developing countries, nor concerning the impact of these and the more commercial-scale farming activities and assistance projects on food security and poverty alleviation. Despite the lack of information concerning the role of rural aquaculture, there is one sure benefit of consuming fish, and that is the nutritional and health benefit to be gained from its valuable nutritional content. Food fish has a nutrient profile superior to all terrestrial meats. It is an excellent source of high quality animal protein and highly digestible energy, as well as an extremely rich source of omega-3 polyunsaturated fatty acids (PUFAs), fat soluble vitamins (A, D and E), water soluble vitamins (B complex), and minerals (calcium, phosphorus, iron, iodine and selenium). In fact, if there is a single food that could be used to address all of the different aspects of world malnutrition, it is fish - the staple animal protein source of traditional fishers.

2. Small farm aquaculture

In rural populations, aquaculture, in addition to increasing food production, is often undertaken as a secondary source of income. In developing states the role of fish farming has increased exponentially, with many agricultural farmers discovering that the integration of aquaculture into their production systems leads to increased land and yield productivity. While the benefits of aquaculture are widely discussed, it is important to note quantitative data highlighting this contribution is limited, with few objective evaluations available. Despite arguments to the contrary, it is still too early to determine the exact impact of aquaculture on food security and poverty alleviation. There is, however, great potential for aquaculture to support income security and nutritional diversity, as part of an integrated approach.

As poverty is often worst among rural communities, aquaculture presents an opportunity to diversify income and protect against market fluctuations in the prices of agricultural products. This integrated system of using agricultural land to raise fish, increases potential yield rates per annum. Diversification also increases overall land productivity, by utilising farm by-products as aquaculture feed and the water from aquaculture sites as a means of irrigating crops.There are considerable constraints on aquaculture, particularly when intensive production is the key income generator for a farmer. Poorly developed infrastructure and limited access to transportation or urban centers, can challenge its effectiveness. Where transportation is difficult, communication services are basic and access to markets is limited, it is challenging for a farmer to generate an income through aquaculture.

Access to financial and social assistance is also a driving factor in successful aquaculture production. Because they are vulnerable to price volatilities, small-farm holders rely on access to capital for farm development and financial and social assistance to provide a safety net. Intensive aquaculture is a particularly high risk enterprise, as a failed harvest leaves no alternative income stream. Small loans and credits to purchase fish feed, chemicals and seeds are often required to begin a production cycle. In Vietnam, collectors and traders are of particular importance, as they often provide loans in advance and take payment at harvest time.

Another limitation is access to markets, particularly in urban centers. Prices for fish are highest in urban centers and the ability of farmers to access and sale fish in these markets can greatly influence potential income generation. Many farmers rely on local markets to sell produce; however, with fish production increasing, an over-supply of fish can lower market value and decrease potential income benefits. Middlemen and traders are often engaged to sell fish further afield, where prices for fish are higher. Farmers without access to urban markets are limited to selling fish at a set price to these middlemen, who then sell them at a higher price to urban buyers. Governing bodies need to prioritise access to markets for local farmers, to increase profit margins.

3. Commercial aquaculture

According to the FAO, commercial aquaculture refers to "fish farming operations whose goal is to maximize profits, where profits are defined as revenues minus costs". The global fish trade is currently estimated at US$56 billion, surpassing most traditional agricultural exports. Economists at the World Fish Research Centre and the International Food Policy Research Institute (IFPRI), estimate that the total world production of food-fish will increase by over 40 per cent by 2020. Internationally, approximately 40 per cent of the world's fish supply is traded, as compared with 10 per cent of the meat supply.

The economic impact of commercial aquaculture is significant, with large commercial aquaculture farms providing business profits, employment, taxes and generating further investment in the industry. Commercial aquaculture has the potential to stimulate economic growth and create jobs, assisting in poverty alleviation as it does so. As many as thirty-five million people are directly employed in the fisheries sector worldwide, 20 per cent of them in the aquaculture industry; indirectly the industry supports several times this number.

It is suggested that commercial aquaculture can contribute significantly to food security, providing employment and income generation to those in developing countries. Furthermore it provides a reliable supply of affordable aquatic food products with greater access to markets across the developing and developed world. The linkage of the commercial aquaculture sector to local economies is twofold; both directly and indirectly it supports other sectors through the purchase and sale of goods and services. It can also link through investment in infrastructure development, human resources and foreign exchange, all of which support economic growth.

SUSTAINABILITY AND AQUACULTURE

The term "sustainability" or also "sustainable development", often used as nothing more than a catch-phrase, has much more to offer. Sustainable development is defined as one that "meets the needs of the present without compromising the ability of the future generations to meet their own needs" (WCED, 1987). For sustainability, "the environment should be protected in such a condition and to such a degree that environmental capacities i.e. the ability of environment to perform its various functions, are maintained over time, at least at levels sufficient to avoid future catastrophe, and at most at levels which give future generations the opportunity to enjoy an equal measure of environmental consumption" (Therivel *et al.*, 1992). The Rio Declaration (UNCED, 1992) is the most important global document in recent times on sustainable development and human survival.

The Rio Declaration adds that "the major objective of sustainable agriculture and rural development is to increase food production in a sustainable way." UNCED (1992) recognizes the multi-sectoral use of water resources for domestic consumption, sanitation, agriculture, industry, urban development, hydropower generation, inland fisheries, transportation, recreation, and other activities. It emphasizes the protection of the quality and supply of freshwater resources through application of the integrated approach to the use, development, and management of water resources.

The concept of sustainable aquaculture involves three interrelated aspects: production technology, social and economic aspects, and environmental aspects (ADB-NACA, 1994; AIT, 1994). Aquaculture technology must be sufficiently productive to make it an attractive option to alternative and possibly competing uses of resources. Maximum biological yields may not be the most appropriate goal, but rather those commensurate with the resources of a particular farmer. Sustainable aquaculture systems make environmentally sound use of resources. Such systems must not divert or replace resources that may be used in a more productive way for other purposes and must not degrade the environment that the livelihood of future generations is jeopardized. In short, sustainable aquaculture systems must be productive, socially relevant, profitable, and environmentally compatible (AIT, 1994).

Sustainable development is a concept to guarantee a livable environment for all people in the long term, encompassing three main fundamental components of sustainable development: preservation of a functional environment, economic welfare and social equity. Similarly, in the field of aquaculture, aiming for sustainability requires not only the achievement of environmental objectives, but also to provide clear economic advantages for aquaculture farmers in the long term. The sustainable development meets the needs of the present without compromising the ability of future generations to meet their own needs. Such sustainable development in the field of agriculture, forestry, fisheries sectors conserves land, water, plant and animal resources, is environmentally non-degrading, technically appropriate, economically viable and socially acceptable. Sustainable development is based on long-term considerations, being an integrative and is not a regional approach. It is usually presented in three aspects such as ecological, economic and social sustainability in broader perspective.

Aquaculture is facing the challenge of sustainable development as with all other food production and also industrial practices. Aquaculture has grown consistently over the last half century from the production of less than 1 million tonnes of product in the 1950s to 66 million tonnes in 2012. Whereas capture fishery production is static and has even been decreasing for years, aquaculture continues to grow more rapidly than any other animal food-producing sector. Aquaculture will continue to play a large and increasing part in the world's fish production to meet the globally rising demand for fishery products. It is therefore essential to continuously pursue methods and means to make production practices in aquaculture more sustainable, efficient and cost-effective by, for instance, improving human capacity, resource use and environmental management. The use of the Best Management Practices (BMPs) approach to address some of the aquaculture sector limitations and in particular the impacts that uncontrolled development of fish-farming may have on the environment have been relatively successful in reducing the risk of these environmental impacts (Hishamunda *et al.*, 2012). Best Management Practices often lack the necessary awareness, organizational capacity and marketing skills to participate in these BMPs programmes, small-scale producers may end up excluded from these schemes (Bush *et al.*, 2013).

APPLICATION OF SUSTAINABLE PRINCIPLES TO AQUACULTURE

(a) Improving ecological sustainability

Water, nutrients, the area used for the farm, and energy are the most important topics related to the ecological sustainability of aquaculture farms. Regarding water, both the amount needed and the quality are important aspects. One important goal in all systems is to reduce the amount of freshwater needed to relieve the natural ecosystems. The best management practice naturally depends on the type of aquaculture. Traditional carp ponds, for example, need water only for replacing the evaporation and seepage; the outflow is limited to the harvest. Recirculation aquaculture systems, like the

Danish model trout farms, are another example of how to substantially reduce the amount of water needed. An efficient use of the required nutrients is also essential for environmental sustainability. Reducing feed losses by an advanced feeding regime and the selection of appropriate feeds is the first step. The use of periphyton, as in the Hungarian case study, is one possibility. The use of different fish species in the same ponds, a polyculture, may raise the nutrient efficiency because of the different ecological niches of the fish species, which are used. Regarding the use of energy, this is a particularly major topic in recirculation aquaculture systems. It is possible and important to reduce the amount of energy by increasing the energy efficiency, e.g. through the use of more efficient pumps. With regard to energy use, the aim is to produce at least the same amount of fish with less energy or more fish with the same amount of energy.

(b) Improving economical sustainability

An aquaculture is economically sustainable and viable, if the farm is profitable, the farm revenue is reliable and the farm system and products are accepted by the consumer. In many cases, improving environmental sustainability can be connected to the optimization of economic sustainability. For instance, a more efficient use of feed and nutrients or the reduction of the use of freshwater is not only positive for the environment, it can also reduce costs. Depending on national laws, reducing wastewater contributes also to the lowering of production costs. A more local or regional distribution of products will decrease the transport costs, which are partly energy costs. The diversification of the aquaculture can buffer market fluctuations. Polyculture or the additional productions of renewable resources, garden plants or fish fry are examples applied in the Sustain Aqua case studies. Production of traceable high quality products can both increase realized prices and consumer confidence. Fully endorsing sustainability can be a valuable argument to increase consumer acceptance. However, all these aspects need to be evaluated very individually, because the availability of all resources needed for an aquaculture (water, land, nutrients, energy) vary greatly between the different countries and regions. In the vicinity of a big city, for instance, a highly intensive recirculation system might be very much sustainable, especially if it can be heated by waste heat; whereas in rural areas, it might be economically much more sustainable to run a large extensive carp pond, as land and water is relatively cheap and available. There is no doubt that fishers living in remote areas face extremely severe living conditions, several empirical studies suggest that in other circumstance fishers can also be relatively well-off, thanks to the cash they derived from their fishing activities (Neiland & Béné, 2004; Béné *et al.*, 2009).

(c) Improving social sustainability

The issue of social sustainability is also very complex. It includes employment opportunities in the sector, the conditions of employment on the aquaculture farm (hygiene, safety, training), but also the general public in connection with e.g. recreation, health and nutritional issues. Important aspects are also the attractiveness of aquaculture to the younger generation or in which way an aquaculture system preserves culture and traditions. Social sustainability was not a primary focus of sustainable aquaculture, which concentrated more on technical solutions to directly increase economic and environmental sustainability, but if achieved support social sustainability.

Many a time, "gender" and "gender and development" focus mainly on women. It should be remembered that men's conditions and behaviour are also critical in social and gender relations and that men can also suffer from food and nutrition insecurity. The gender in a fisheries context evokes typically themes of the gendered divisions of fisheries labour, women's roles in productive and reproductive spheres, women's agency in the sector and women in fisheries and aquaculture institutions (Harper *et al.*, 2013). Deeper analyses are emerging, revealing the dynamics of gender issues of significance to food security and nutrition, such as the importance of the intersections between gender and social factors such as culture, economic class, religion and social status and the gendered impacts of the massive sectoral change such as modernization, mechanization, market concentration and labour cost reduces.

CONCLUSION

The small-scale aquaculture farms exhibited tremendous growth in the past decade. The high demand and high price of the product will support for aquaculture development within the general agricultural settings and help both producers and domestic consumers. A need to focus on the policy measures and regulatory framework for the use and access to resources such as land and water is necessary as they affect the competitiveness of small-scale and resource-poor farmers. To address the food security and poverty alleviation the policies should provide increased institutional and infrastructure support for diversification of production and trade and integration of production systems and development of backward and forward linkages by resource-poor households. Aquaculture is supplying a significant proportion of the fish and shellfish consumed and is now a global industry. However, it can exacerbate the impact of human activities on our already stressed coastal and inland aquatic and wetland zones. A sustainable approach to the development, management and regulation of aquaculture can ensure that both the environment and industry provide long-term economic and social benefits. If managed understandingly, aquaculture can become a sustainable industry supplementing the food supply from capture fisheries and a step ahead towards food security.

REFERENCES

ADB-NACA (1994). Regional Study and Workshop on Aquaculture Sustainability and the Environment. RET A 5534, 11 pp. + annexes. Asian Development Bank and Network of Aquaculture Centres in Asia-Pacific, Bangkok.

AIT (1994). Partners in Development: the Promotion of Sustainable Aquaculture. Asian Institute of Technology, Bangkok, 98 pp.

Barraclough, S. and Finger-Stick, A. (1996). Some Ecological and Social Implications of Commercial Shrimp Farming in Asia. Discussion Paper No. 74, Geneva: United Nation Research Institute for Social Development (UNRISD), 62 p.

Béné, C., Belal, E., Baba, M. O., Ovie, S., Raji, A., Malasha, I., Njaya, F., Na Andi, M., Russell, A. and Neiland, A. (2009). Power Struggle, Dispute and Alliance Over Local Resources: Analyzing 'Democratic' Decentralization of Natural Resource Through the Lenses of Africa Inland Fisheries. *World Development* 37(12): 1935-1950.

Browdy, C.L., Hulata, G., Liu, Z., Allan, G.L., Sommerville, C., Passos de Andrade, T., Pereira, R., Yarish, C., Shpigel, M., Chopin, T., Robinson, S., Avnimelech, Y. and Lovatelli, A. (2012). Novel and Emerging Technologies: Can They Contribute to Improving Aquaculture Sustainability. *In*: R.P. Subasinghe, J.R. Arthur, D.M. Bartley, S.S. De Silva, M. Halwart, N. Hishamunda, C.V. Mohan and P. Sorgeloos (eds). Farming the Waters for People and Food. Proceedings of the Global Conference on Aquaculture 2010, Phuket, Thailand. 22-25 September 2010. pp. 149-191. FAO, Rome and NACA, Bangkok.

Bush, S.R., Belton, B., Hall, D., Vandergeest, P., Murray, F.J., Ponte, S., Oosterveer, P., Islam, M.S., Mol, A.P., Hatanaka, M., Kruijssen, F., Ha, T.T., Little, D.C. and Kusumawati, R. (2013). Certify Sustainable Aquaculture. *Science* 341: 1067-1068.

De Silva, S. and Davy, F.B. (2009). Success Stories in Asian Aquaculture. Springer, 214 pp.

EC (1999). Shrimp Culture-Impact of Tropical Shrimp Aquaculture on the Environment in Asia and the Pacific/Mangroves, Shrimp and the Development of Coastal Areas in Central America. EC Fisheries Cooperation Bulletin 12(4), European Commission.

EJF (2002). Risky Business: Vietnamese Shrimp Aquaculture – Impacts and Improvements. London: Environmental Justice Foundation, 34 p.

Edwards, P. (1999). Aquaculture and Poverty: Past, Present and Future Prospects of Impact. SIFAR, Rome.

FAO (2000). Small Ponds Make a Big Difference. Integrating Fish with Crop and Livestock Farming. Food and Agriculture Organization of the United Nations, Rome, Italy, 30 pp.

FAO (2003). The Role of Aquaculture in Improving Food Security and Nutrition. Committee on World Food Security, Food and Agriculture Organization of the United Nations, Rome.

FAO/WHO. (2011). Report of the Joint FAO/WHO Expert Consultation on the Risks and Benefits of Fish Consumption, Rome, 25-29 January 2010. FAO Fisheries and Aquaculture Report No. 978. Rome, FAO. 50 p.

FAO (2012). The State of World Fisheries and Aquaculture 2012, Rome, Food and Agriculture Organization of the United Nations, 230 pp.

FAO (2014). The State of World Fisheries and Aquaculture 2014. Rome. 223 pp.

Halwart, M. (2005). The Role of Aquaculture in Rural Development. Agriculture & Rural Development 2/2005, Fish Resources. Food and Agriculture Organization of the United Nations (FAO), Rome, Italy, pp. 41-44.

Harper, S., Zeller, D., Hauzer M., Pauly, D. and Sumaila, U.R. (2013). Women and Fisheries: Contribution to Food Security and Local Economies. *Marine Policy* 39: 56-63.

Hishamunda, N., Ridler, N., Bueno, P., Satia, B., Kuemlangan, B., Percy, D., Gooley, G., Brugere, C. and Sen, S. (2012). Improving Aquaculture Governance: What is the Status and Options. In: R.P. Subasinghe, J.R. Arthur, D.M. Bartley, S.S. De Silva, M. Halwart, N. Hishamunda, C.V. Mohan and P. Sorgeloos, (eds). Farming the Waters for People and Food. Proceedings of the Global Conference on Aquaculture 2010, Phuket, Thailand. 22-25 September 2010. pp. 233-264. FAO, Rome and NACA, Bangkok.

Huong, N.V. and Cuong, T.H. (2012). Freshwater Aquaculture's Contribution to Food Security in Vietnam: A Case Study of Freshwater Tilapia Aquaculture in Hai Duong Province. *J. ISSAAS* 18(1): 6-17.

IIRR, IDRC, FAO, NACA and ICLARM (2001). Utilizing Different Aquatic Resources for Livelihoods in Asia: A Resource Book. International Institute of Rural Reconstruction, International Development Research Centre, Food and Agriculture Organization of the United Nations, Network of Aquaculture Centers in Asia-Pacific, and International Center for Living Aquatic Resources Management, 416 pp.

Lehane, S. (2013). Fish for the Future: Aquaculture and Food Security (Strategic Analysis paper). Future Directions International Pty Ltd., 80 Birdwood Parade, Dalkeith WA 6009, Australia, pp. 8.

Neiland, A.E. and Béné, C. (eds.) (2004). Poverty and Small-Scale Fisheries in West Africa. Published by Kluwer Academic Publishers for the Food and Agriculture Organization, 254 p.

Phillips, M., Nhuong, T.V. and Subasinghe, R. (2013). Aquaculture Big Numbers. Working Paper. Version #12 June 2012. WorldFish and FAO.

Prein, M. and M. Ahmed, 2000. Integration of Aquaculture into Smallholder Farming Systems for Improved Food Security and Household Nutrition. Food Nutr. Bull. 21: 466-471.

SPFS. (2003). The Special Programme for Food Security of the United Nations. FAO, Rome.

Subasinghe, R., Ahmad, I., Kassam, L., Krishnan, S., Nyandat, B., Padiyar, A., Phillips, M., Reantaso, M., Weimin, M. and Yamamoto, K. (2012). Protecting Small-scale Farmers: A Reality within a Globalized Economy. *In*: R.P. Subasinghe, J.R. Arthur, D.M. Bartley, S.S. De Silva, M. Halwart, N. Hishamunda, C.V. Mohan & P. Sorgeloos (eds). Farming the Waters for People and Food. Proceedings of the Global Conference on Aquaculture 2010, Phuket, Thailand. 22-25 September 2010. pp. 705-717. FAO, Rome and NACA, Bangkok.

Subasinghe, R.P. (2003). An Outlook for Aquaculture Development: Major Issues, Opportunities and Challenges. Review of the State of World Aquaculture. FAO, Rome.

Therivel, R, Wilson, E., Thomson, S., Heany, D. and Pritchard, D. (1992). Strategic Environmental Assessment. Earthscan Publications Ltd., London, 181 pp.

WCED. (1987). Our Common Future. World Commission on Environment and Development, Oxford University Press, Oxford, 400 pp.

Williams, M. J. and Poh-Sze, C. (2003). Fisheries Production in Asia: Its Role in Food Security and Nutrition. IX Asian Congress of Nutrition, New Delhi, India.

World Bank (2006). Aquaculture: Changing the Face of the Waters Meeting the Promise and Challenge of Sustainable Aquaculture. World Bank, Agriculture and Rural Development, 138 pp.

Pages: 160-183

FISH HABITAT AND AQUACULTURE
Edited by: Dr. Sanjay Kumar Gupta; Dr. Pawan Kumar 'Bharti'
ISBN: 978-93-5056-744-9
Edition: 2015
Published by: Discovery Publishing House Pvt. Ltd., New Delhi (India)

9

Probable Candidate Species of Exotic Fish for Promotion of Diversified Aquaculture in India

Madhumita Mukherjee, Ashim Kumar Borah

ABSTRACT

Aquaculture is one of the main reasons for introduction of alien species in to aquatic ecosystems. As much as 17% of the global aquaculture production is contributed by introduced species (Bartley & Casal, 1998). Over the last few years, the aquaculture entrepreneurs/farmers have been demanding importation of new fish strains and varieties in view of competition in the Indian fish market. The fisheries sector occupies a very important place in the socio-economic development in India. It has been recognized as a powerful income and employment generator as it stimulates growth of a number of subsidiary industries and is a source of cheap and nutritious food besides being a huge earner. Today while framing policy for fisheries & aquaculture the ground truth is often ignored which sometimes make the policy unacceptable to the stake holders. For instance the culture of *Clarias gariepinus* (Thailand magur) and *Piaractus brachypomus* (Pacu) is one such case. Being motivated with higher fish production *vis-à-vis* higher income entailing lower risk large number of population of rural areas have entered in the venture of production of seed and table size of these exotic fish. Successful breeding and seed production of Pacu, *Piaractus brachypomus* locally names as Rupchanda (In Bengal) was done in captivity. Brooders were collected and raised in brooders tank up to the age of 4 years with sufficient feed and water quality management. Male and female fish were injected with pituitary extraction @ 2 mg/Kg body weight in case of male and @ 12 mg/Kg body weight in case of female. In case of female only an initial dose of hormone was administered @ 2 mg/Kg body weight 6 hour before the final dose. After 6-7 hours striping was done for fertilization and the fertilized eggs were release in the circular hatchery for hatching. After 2 days, hatchlings were removed from hatchery to the nursery. General study among the farmers in the locality of Naihati, West Bengal revealed that this sp. not only grows well up to 1.5 kg in one year with a survival rate approximate 90% but also prove itself as a compatible species in a composite fish culture pond.

Further, a case study in Malda district of West Bengal showed that people from different profession right from rickshaw puller to Silk pupae producer are also engaged with either production or trading of this species. Another study made in the Tafatchar village and some others villages like Dighirpar, Raghabpur and Choura at Bashirhat-I block, North 24 parganas district revealed that the respondents have acquired many electronic/luxury materials after adoption of the culture of exotic catfish (*Clarias gariepinus*).While analyzing the Socio-psychological aspects it revealed that most the people have become resource- rich from the status of landless labourer or resource- poor category involving them on the same. Scientific studies on the impact of *Piaractus brachypomus* and *C. gariepinus* species on biodiversity and socio-economic aspects and their potential invasiveness (capacity to survive, propagate and establish in wild) are imperative. Most importantly, it is the source of livelihoods for a large section of the economically backward population of the state. In terms of governance, fisheries are considered as a state subject and as such the primary responsibility for their development rests with the State Governments. Modern scientific technologies to enrich the farmers' knowledge need be moved towards an ecological sustainable future. The possible threats and environmental risks of such culture of exotic fishes required to deal through policy decisions that introduction of exotic fish species will require planning and scientific research to determine optimal conditions for aquaculture under stringent guidelines.

INTRODUCTION

Piaractus brachypomus (Pacu), a native fish of South America has been clandestinely introduced recently as an alien species mainly into West Bengal, India via Bangladesh. Pacu were probably introduced in India in 2003 or 2004 and leading hatchery owners soon started culture in captivity to raise brood stock for commercial breeding programmes. It is observed that the tendency of breeding Pacu and raising it's seed is more among the fish farmers of West Bengal. Besides breeding individual species, the fish breeders are also interested in conducting hybridization programmes between Indian major carps, and exotic species as they are largely unaware about the genetic consequences of such activities. A few leading farmers of West Bengal has already standardized the captive breeding and culture techniques of this fish.

Clarias gariepinus (Thailand magur) is also one of the most important commercial freshwater fishes in Africa. Global capture has more than doubled in the past 50 years, from 17,500 tons in 1955 to 46789 tons in 2005, highlighting the increasing importance of the species in recent years. By contrast, production of Clarias *gariepinus* in aquaculture has only expanded since the 1980s, with a sharp increase in global production since 2000. Features of the species that make it desirable for introduction into fisheries include a high growth rate and resistance to handling and stress. *Clarias gariepinus* has good organoleptic qualities and is one of the most suitable species for aquaculture in Africa. The species is marketed live, fresh and frozen; eaten broiled, fried and baked. *C .gariepinus* of about 70-80 gms to confuse the buyers and exploit higher price. *C. gariepinus* is being cultured in West Bengal by a huge number of farmers.

These are very fast growing species which can withstand adverse water conditions; however it has been banned by the policy framers citing ecological disaster. But the hard truth is that farmers all over the country are culturing the species successfully in different suitable places and they are getting a ready market for sale. So mere banning has become a force as nobody is really observing the ban. The reason is quite understandable, this fish grows fast, provide good nutritional supplement, it does not require costly management procedure and it has its own market thereby giving an additional income to the farmers of India.

Under such circumstances, it will be prudent to legalize the culture of these species as because the ban has miserably failed. The legalization of course should be done under scientific supervision and the culture could be promoted in arid zones like Bankura, Purulia, Birbhum of West Bengal, Rajasthan and other parts of the country, where seasonal water bodies can be used for this culture. A strict vigilance is to be kept so that this species does not get access to any natural water systems. The legalization (under such restriction) will be a wise decision in this time of food scarcity, unemployment and resource scarcity. The culture of this hardy species will be away to utilize the seasonal derelict water bodies which otherwise could not have been used for pisciculture, moreover value addition projects can enhance the market spectrum of the species.

Therefore instead of treating this fish as an ecological nuisance let us try to formulate a policy to turn this species to our advantage. As it is often said 'When you get a lemon it makes sense to prepare a lemonade'

HABITAT AND BIOLOGY OF PACU

- Pacu fish is a very large freshwater fish that can grow to monstrous sizes in excess of 2 feet and weighing more than 50 pounds.
- Pacu fish do not have very distinct stages of life in their life cycle. They grow continuously throughout their entire lives without major changes to their generally appearance.
- The size of a Pacu fish is limited by its tank dimension. However, it will still grow to at least half the tank size before its growth gets stunted.
- Pacu fish feed on vegetable matter in the wild, but will also scavenge on carcasses and take bites of the fins of other fishes if resented with the opportunity.
- The juveniles of Pacu fish all have red bellies because this mimicry of Piranha helps them avoid potential predators when they are young.
- Diversification of aquaculture is essential for the betterment of fish farmers in the present day situation. Keeping this view in mind Pacu, *Piaractus brachypomus* may be an important candidate species for mass production in aquaculture pond. It grows very fast and attains a weight of 1.5 kg in a year. It is a very tasty fish and hardy fish in nature. It can tolerate acidity and can also be farmed in neutral water condition. More over it can tolerate salinity as high as 10 ppt and dissolved oxygen as low as 0.5 ppm. (Datta and Nandeesha, 2006).
- Pacu, locally called Rupchanda is basically native of Amazon and Orinoco river system of South America. This fish is also known as red pomfret belongs to the family Serrasalmidae. This fish is a close relative to Piranha as the family is same. But they are completely different species with distinct differences. They differ in feeding habit and behavior. Rupchanda is basically a vegetarian fish but they can eat almost any food.

BROODER MANAGEMENT OF PACU

Pacu, *Piaractus brachypomus* has a narrow plate shaped dark grey body, black upper body and back, and a small mouth with blunt teeth. Pacu possesses 31-34 gill rakers and about 85-94 lateral line scales on the gill arch (Datta and Nandeesha, 2006). Pacu can attend 20 kg in size. For breeding purpose brooders were collected locally and were raised in the composite fish culture tank along with *Cyprinus carpio.* The size of the tank is 0.5 hactor with a depth of 5 feet on an average.

Fig. 9.1: Pacu Brooder Management Tank Provided Aeration

Regular feeding was done @ 6% of the body weight of Pacu. Feed were provided at the evening time just after sunset. Daily feeding was done and at the same time and place. Boiled peas along with fish meal and ground nut oil cake were used as supplementary feed. Aeration was provided by means of pump. As the *Cyprinus carpio* is a good fish for bottom racking these fishes were liberated to utilize the excess feed provided to Pacu and for racking the bottom for better pond management. Regular water quality (Table 9.1) was maintained by means of water exchange in a certain interval, aeration etc. were done to accelerate the gonadal maturity of the brood fish as well as to maintain the hygienic condition of pond. Brood fish were getting maturity for breeding after 3-4 years. For male 3.5 kg and for female 5 kg respectively is ideal weight for breeding.

Table 9.1: Some Basic Water Quality Parameter in the Brooders Tank

Tank	Temp (°C)	pH (ppm)	DO (ppm)	NH_4N (ppm)	Alkalinity (ppm)	Hardness
Brooders tank	29±1	7.5-8.0	6-6.5	–	130±12	112±5
Breeding tank	31±1	7.7-7.9	6.2-6.5	–	125±12	119±5

During breeding season sex can be easily identified by some external feature of the brood fish. Comparatively swollen belly with round reddish vent, female brood fish can be easily differentiate from male having pointed vent with depressed belly. Mature male oozed milt with slight pressure at the belly. Fecundity is less in Pacu mainly due to its flat morphological feature. Average fecundity is 35000 – 40000/Kg body weight.

Fig. 9.2: A 5 kg. Female Pacu Brooder Ready for Breeding

BREEDING PROCEDURE

Brood fish were collected from brooders tank one day before of breeding and kept separately sex wise in hapa. No feed were provided during this period. Sex ratio was maintained for breeding as 1:1. Pituitary gland extraction was used for hypophysation. Initial dose of hormone was administered @ 2 mg per kg body weight in female. No male were injected at the time of initial injection to female. After 6 hours, final dose were injected @ 12 mg per Kg body weight in female and 2 mg per Kg body weight in case of male. After injecting the hormone both the male and female fish were kept in a breeding pool for courtship. Injected fish may also be kept in cement cisterns, with induced fish producing a characteristic vibrating sound on the walls of the cistern. After 6-7 hours of final dose administration striping were done for fertilization.

The eggs are stripped out in trays and the milt and eggs mixed with a feather and the addition of water. The ratio of males: females for stripping are usually 1:1 or 1.5:1 depending on the maturity and density of the milt.

Fig. 9.3: Pacu Brooder

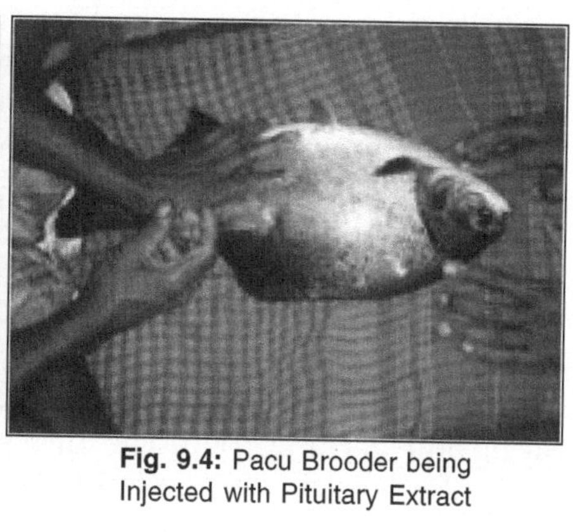

Fig. 9.4: Pacu Brooder being Injected with Pituitary Extract

Fertilized, water harden eggs are comparatively small in size. Eggs are slightly sticky in nature. To remove the stickiness we are using "multani mati" (available in grocery). Fertilized eggs were then transferred to the hatching pool with gentle water circulation.

Environmental factors play an important role with regard to both the dose of inducing hormone required and stripping. When the temperature is high, i.e.34-35°C, then the requirement of both the dose of inducing hormone and stripping is less. Again, for better fertilisation a congenial environment is needed. The fertilised eggs are transferred successfully into two hatching jars in 48 hours and in between the hatchlings are kept in Hapa. As the yolk is absorbed the hatchlings become longer. From the 3rd day onwards the hatchling are ready for sale.

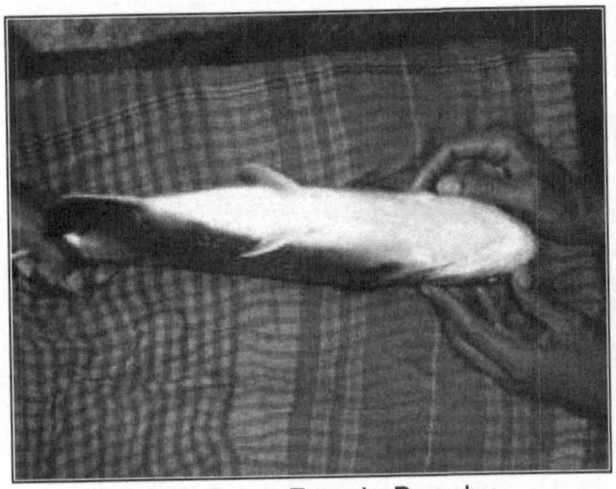

Fig. 9.5: Pacu: Female Brooder

Fig. 9.6: Pacu: Male Brooder

After 20-22 hours of fertilization, hatchlings were come out from egg case. Hatchlings were kept here for two days. During this period closed observation and monitoring must be there for water quality management. Desire water quality was managed by regular cleaning of inner hapa as the egg shells are entangled by the centrifugal force of the circular water movement. Water for hatchery management were used from the source of overhead tank where mixing of water from fish tank and from submersible pump were done continuously. Then the spawn were shifted to the previously prepared nursery tank and stocked @ 2 lakh/Bigha.(1 ha=7.5Bigha Aeration was provided in the nursery.

Nursery Management: During Nursery management, the spawn or hatchlings are stocked in the nursery pond, prepared beforehand, at the rate of 1,50,000 individuals/ha. The spawn are fed with artificially prepared feed made from groundnut oilcake, rice polish, soyabean dust and also on zooplankton. Generally, 2 kg of feed/ha is given daily for Induced breeding of pacu in captivity with pituitary extract. Within 8-10 days the spawn develop into fry, which are transferred to rearing ponds. A 3 ha pond is ideal for rearing and stocking pond. The ideal stocking density in rearing pond should be usually around 1, 00,000 individuals/ha.

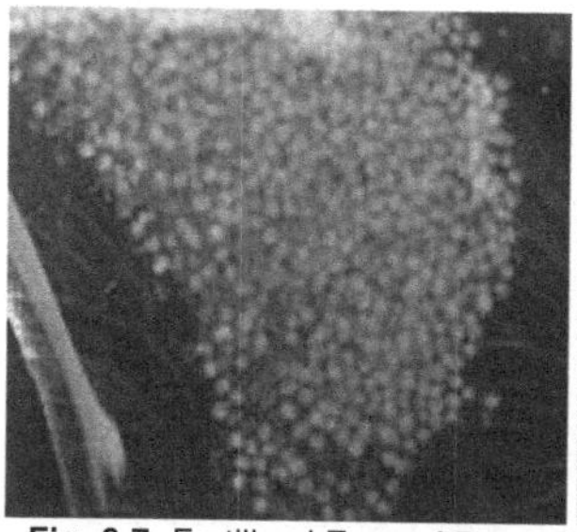

Fig. 9.7: Fertilized Eggs of Pacu

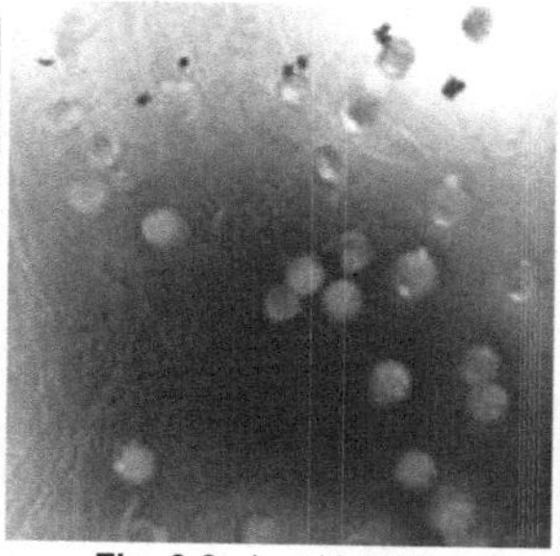

Fig. 9.8: Just Hatching

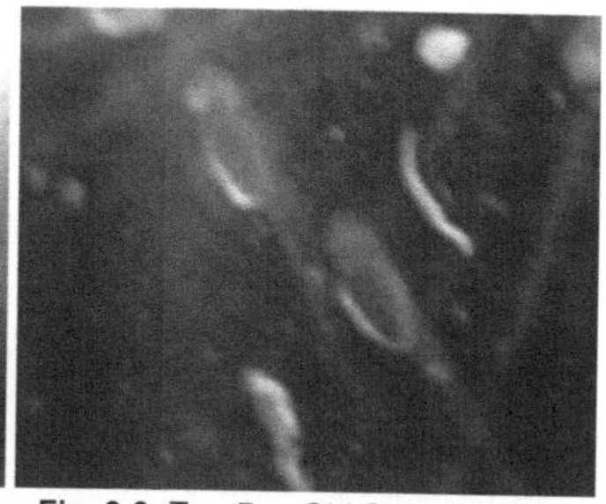

Fig. 9.9: Two Day Old Spawn of Pacu

Fig. 9.10: Pacu Fingerling Ready for Stocking

Fig. 9.11: Pacu Fingerling also Used as Ornamental Fish

In rearing pond, the fry are fed with artificial food at the rate of 5kg/ha/day made from groundnut oil cake, sunflower oilcake and fish meal, and also with boiled rice and Canadian peas.

Stocking density: They are normally stocked at the ratio of 1 pacu: 3 Indian major carps when poly culture is undertaken. It attains maturity at 3 + years in age with a stocking density of 2,000 - 2,500 individuals/ha. Some farmers reported that poly culture gives better result than monoculture.

In order to achieve higher table fish production, apart from traditional pisciculture with six species some more new species might be introduced with higher growth rate, better taste and standard food value which not only supplement the fish production quantitatively but enhance the earnings from a certain unit area of water body. Keeping this view in mind as well as the acceptability as table fish and availability of fish seed intensive culture of Pacu (*Piaractus sp*), a column feeder along with surface feeder like Catla *(Catla catla)* and bottom feeder like *Cypinus carpio* and/or Mrigal *(Cirrhinus mrigala)* might be introduced.

Keeping this view in mind as well as the acceptability as table fish and availability of fish seed intensive culture of Pacu (*Piaractus sp*), a column feeder along with surface feeder like Catla *(Catla catla)* and bottom feeder like *Cypinus carpio* and/or Mrigal *(Cirrhinus mrigala)* might be introduced.

CULTURE PROCEDURE

Stocking Density: 10,000 nos /ha (Pacu - 80%; Catla- 15% & Mrigal/ Cyprinus Carp - 5%)

Culture period: 8 months

As the seeds to be liberated are of advanced fingerling, application of Mahua oil cake might be avoided and to remove the existing fish stock (before undertaking the intensive culture practice) repeated netting to be made. Cleaning of aquatic weeds to be done. Then lime to be applied @ 300 kg/ha 7-10 days before stocking. Depth of the water to be maintained at least 2 meters. Regular feeding with Ground nut oil cake, boiled whole pea and fish meal at a ratio of 2:2:1 @ 5 - 10% of total body weight.

Periodical netting at an interval of 10 - 15 days and monthly application of lime 80 - 100 kg per hecter to be done. Culture of Pacu may be started in me month of February from pond preparation. Fish should be liberated during March. Harvest of production may be done during the month of October. It has been found mat within this eight month culture individual Pacu fish gain the weight of 1000 to 1200 gm if, supplementary feeding and regular monitoring of pond environment are done. So from the economic point of view 8 month culture period of Pacu along with Catla and Mrigal/Cyprinus is best.

Apart from culture as table fish, Pacu has very high market demand as ornamental fish because it's beautiful look and presence in aquarium during juvenile stage. Study revealed that there is very rare occurrence of disease among Pacu. Though due to close resemblance with piranha, Pacu is not advocated for culture in many countries due to fear of unwanted entry of the deadly Piranha fish in open as well as closed system, Govt. of Malaysia lifting the ban on culture of the fish (Modh-Zaini *et al*, 1991).

For rapid promotion of culture of Pacu, standardization of seed production and larvae rearing technique is essential. So breeding technique in captivity with hypophysation was successfully done by the Deptt. of Fisheries Govt. of West Bengal.

HABITAT AND BIOLOGY OF THAILAND MAGUR (C. GARIEPINUS)

- *Clarias gariepiunus* lives in a variety of freshwater environments, including still waters, such as lakes, ponds and pools. It is prominent in rivers, rapids and around dams, and may be found at depths of 4-80 m.
- The species has the ability to adapt to extreme environmental conditions and can live in a pH range of 6.5-8.0. It is also able to live in very turbid waters and can tolerate temperatures of 8-35°C, although its optimal temperature for growth is 28-30°C (Teugels 1986). The presence of an accessory breathing organ enables this species to breathe air when very active or under very dry conditions.

- The species is mainly a benthic feeder, but occasionally forages in surface waters. Clarias is omnivorous and preys on a wide variety of animals, including fish, birds, frogs, snails, crabs and shrimps. It also feeds on detritus, plant material and small aquatic invertebrates, and can filter-feed on plankton. There is, therefore, an issue of predation on indigenous fish populations (Vitule et al. 2006). *C. gariepiunus* can live in very poorly oxygenated waters, and if the gills collapse or become clogged it has the ability to secrete mucus to keep the skin moist. It is also capable of burrowing into the sediments of drying water bodies (Skelton 1993). Spawning takes place during the rainy season (July to December) in flooded deltas.

CASE STUDIES OF CULTURE IN WEST BENGAL

(a) North 24 Parganas District

A study was made in the Tafatchar village at Bashirhat-I block, North 24 parganas and some others villages like Dighirpar, Raghabpur and Choura at the same block. The study conducted during 2008-09.

1. The farmers residing in periurban areas of North 24 Parganas have shown a remarkable achievement in introducing and cultivating catfishes with their own technology with simple inputs to get an optimum profit.
2. Locally available feed ingredients and kitchen wastes were used as feed for culturing the catfishes.
3. The farmers of Tafatchar, North 24 Parganas, West Bengal utilized the cheaply available slaughterhouse wastes to feed catfishes. They used to feed approximately a 75-100 kg of waste to feed 10,000 fingerlings of 2-3 months in age, gradually increasing as the biomass grows. According to a recent estimate the amount of slaughterhouse wastes produced annually in India is 2,100,000 tons, most of which is produced in the cities where waste disposal has already become an issue. African catfish, being an omnivorous fish, feeds on these wastes and converts them efficiently into flesh.
4. It's FCR recorded from 0.90 to 1.1
5. The production from these firms varies between 40-60 tonnes/ha/3-4 months.
6. Round the year from this village on a 15-20 tonnes of fish are transported to Assam, Nagaland, Delhi, Haryana, Punjab etc (Fig. 9.14-9.15).
7. Considering the above statistics, production of *C. gariepinus* from that village alone comes to 7300 tones/year.
8. Wholesale price for the above was stated to be Rs. 40/- per kg against the cost of production of Rs. 23/- kg
9. Ornamental Magur are being cultured by the fish farmers in some parts of West Bengal. This Magur is having a very good demand in ornamental fish industries.

Fig. 9.12: Adult catfish i.e. *Clarias* gariepinus

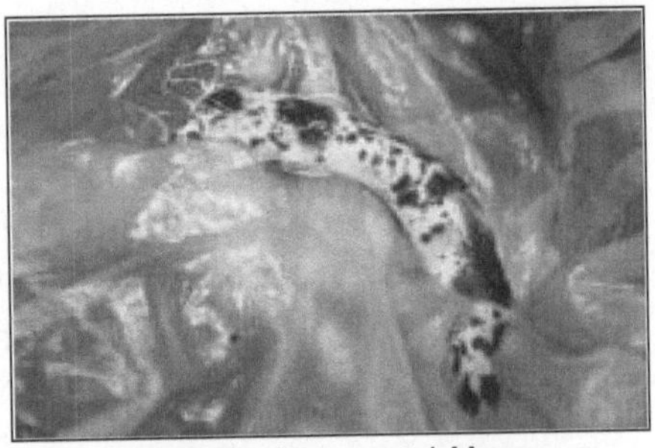

Fig. 9.13: Ornamental Magur

Fig. 9.14

Fig. 9.15

Fig. 9.14-9.15: Prawn head and floating material supplied as feed for *C. gariepinus*

Fig. 9.16

Fig. 9.17

Fig. 9.16-9.17: A hall from culture pond of *C. gariepinus*

Fig. 9.18: Magur Seeds

Fig. 9.19

Fig. 9.20

Fig. 9.19-9.20: Pond preparation for culturing of *C. gariepinus*

(b) Malda District

Exotic magur, *Clarias gariepinus*, though it is a ban species, day by day culture of this fish species become popular in some parts of Malda District. Due to various reasons it becomes the main fish crop in this locality and people mostly depended on culture of this fish to maintain their family. Now a day more or less 10000 people are attached with this "industry" directly or indirectly only in Kaliachak –I Block according to local source. Right from producer to exporter, from Vanwala to Silk pupae producer are engaged with this profession. It is reported among 15 Block of Malda District this fish culture practiced by farmers mainly in three blocks, *i.e.* Kaliachak-1, Kaliachal-II, & Kaliachak-III and very few area in English Bazar block. Among these areas extensive culture is going on Kaliachak-I Block. It may be noted here that among exotic magur farmers, 90% farmers come from Muslim community.

(i) Culture in Kaliachak-I Block

Clarias gariepinus culture in the locality of Kaliachak – I Block started 10-12 years back. Sk. Mustak Ali, Vill: P.O. –Barasujapur, P.S. Kaliachak, fish farmer started this culture collecting seeds from Naihati, N-24-Pgs in an experiment basis. After that it is spreading to the farmers as it very easy task to culture them to earn money. Initially the main profession of this area was business with Mango and sericulture. Day by day people are changing their profession and shifted to lucrative exotic magur culture. 80% farmers become converted to Gariepinus farmer and earn their bread & butter from this so called ban species. Survey report stated that more or less 400 farmers in Kaliachak – I Block are engaged with this profession and approximately 3000-3200 bigha water area comes under this exotic magur culture (local people call "China magur culture"). There are 14 Gram Panchayat in this block, farmers mainly from 4 blocks are engaged with this culture which may be represented as follows.

Sl. No.	Name of Gram Panchayat	Name of Village	Approximate No. of Farmers	Approximate Water Area (Bigha)
1.	Bamangram-Masimpur	1. Bamangram 2. Masimpur 3. Harugram 4. paharpur	200	1500
2.	Sujapur	1. Bara Sujapur 2. Choto Sujapur 3. Najirpur 4. Madhugram 5. Chamagram 6. Balupur	100	800
3.	Gayeshbari	1. Bakharpur 2. Chashpara 3. Gayesbari 4. Kalapahar	50	400
4.	Jalalpur	1. Sherpur 2. Sahidpur 3. Baluachara 4. Phatankhali 5. Selimpur 6. Sabdanagar	50	300

CULTURE PRACTICE

Most of the culture ponds located outside the residential area (that's why local people do not have any objection to the farmers). Size of the ponds varied from 0.5-5 bigha. Some farmers excavated new ponds also in the fallow low lying area. Farmers also used local ponds where no other fish production is possible. Farmers collected seed from Naihati and Basirhat. Seeds, for liberation directly to the culture tanks, are of two types: i) 50-60 g. (local name 'Chalai') and ii) 100 no of seeds /kg (local name 'pin'). Generally there are three crops in a year. There is no need of conventional pond preparation. Farmers use only use lime @ 50-60 per bigha before water filling and also spread lime @ 40-50 Kg per bigha in one month interval. Stocking density is very high. 5- 6 quintal per bigha. Stocking size varied from 50-60 g. or 100 no of seed per Kg. Culture is totally depends on supplementary feed. Feeding rate is also very high. The main food are i) silk moth pupae (locally called "Risha" – a by product of local sericulture cottage industry. ii) Fish waste (collected from local fish market. iii) chicken waste, iv) waste from local hotel (mixed food of rice, curry and kitchen waste). Presently farmers also used very expensive pelleted food (C.P. food – Rs. 28/Kg.).

Fig. 9.21: Palleted C.P. food

Fig. 9.22: Silk Pupae- "Risha"- Main Food for Exotic Magur

When farmers use the seed of 50-60 g the culture period extend for 4 month and when they used the seed of 100 no of seed per Kg., culture period continue for 6-7 month. Generally during summer culture period is less than winter. When the fish are getting wt of 500-600 g per individual, farmers started harvesting. Production rate 3000-3500 kg/Bigha. i.c. 22500-26250 kg per Hactor. Presently selling rate is Rs. 65/Kg at Arat. As the culture of this fish is become so popular in respect of earning and less risk factor, lease rend of pond in locality is become so high i.e up to Rs. 90000/- per Bigha for three years.

Fig. 9.23: This Fallow Pond also used for Magur Culture

Fig. 9.24: A Typical Exotic Magur Culture Pond

Fig. 9.25: Food are being Supplying to the Fish

Fig. 9.26: Farmers of Exotic Magur at the Culture Site

LOCAL MARKET/"ARAT"

Local people do not prefer to consume this fish so far and fishes are exported in different area through 'Aratdat'. Farmers have very good contact and relation to the Aratdar. There are seven "Arat", exclusively for exotic magur.

Fig. 9.27: Aratdar- Md Anarul Hauque

Fig. 2.28: Fishes are being Loaded

MARKETING SYSTEM

Aratdar help the farmers by providing seeds, feed and some time giving culture technology. It is not necessary that producer bound to sell fish to the aratdar from where they have taken seed, feed as loan. Present market rate @Rs. 65 per Kg. There are no middle man between the producer and the aratdar. After assembling fish in the arat, fishes are stored in big cemented tank or in nos of big Aluminium hundies.

Fig. 9.29: Fishes are Stocked in Cemented Tank

Fig. 9.30: Fishes are Stocked in Aluminium Hundies

Fishes are loaded in mini 407 No. trucks (25-30 quintal fishes are loaded at a time) and exported to different state mainly in Bihar (Purnia, Madhepura, Jamboni, Katihar etc.), Nepal (Birat nagar, Lahan, Katmandu etc.) and some parts of Nagaland. In the peak period Aratdar exported average 6-7 tons of fish per day. Md. Anarul Hauque, an aratdar stated that they are getting Rs. 1 per kg Fish as gross profit and Rs. 0.1 per Kg. as net profit.

CONSTRAIN OF EXOTIC MAGUR CULTURE IN THE LOCALITY

Farmers are facing some problem in respect of exotic magur culture as:

1. "Matha fata rog": a common disease when skull of fish becomes broken and fishes ultimately died.

2. Lack of technical knowledge of culture practice (some time heavy mortality occurred due to over feeding).
3. Farmers have to depend on Naihati or Basirhat for seed.
4. High rate of lease rent.

(b) Culture in Kaliachak – II Block

Out of 10 Gram Panchayat farmers from three G.P. are practicing exotic magur culture in Kaliachak – II Block. More or less 100 farmers are engaged in exotic magur culture. Approximate culture area 500-550 Bigha. Name of Gram Panchayat and Village where the exotic magur culture is going on are as follows:

Sl. No.	Name of Gram Panchayat	Name of Village
1.	Uttar Laxmipur	1. Nichutala 2. Sukarditola 3. Palutola 4. Bhakattola 5. Chamatola 6. Kahala
2.	Gangaprasad	1. Amlitola 2. Gangaprasad 3. Satangapara
3.	Mothabari	1. Munsitola

Case study of a Farmer Culturing Exotic Magur, *Clarias gariepinus*

Md. Abdur Rauf, Vill+Po. Bamangram, PS- Kaliachak, Malda District, age 45 years culturing this magur for last 6 years. He has taken lease two ponds covering area 2 Bigha with an exorbitant lease rent – Rs. 90000/- per Bigha for three years. He is doing 2 cycle per year: during summer – 5 months (Baishakh – Bhadra) and during winter 6 month culture (kartic – Chaitra).

Fig. 9.31: Md. Abdur Rauf, a farmer

Fig. 9.32: Harvested *Clarias gariepinus*

He is preparing pond with total dewatering the pond and before filling water applying lime @ 50-60 Kg/bigha. Stocked fish @ 5 quintal per bigha of 50-60 g. size per individual seed. Feeding is done mainly with "Risha" and fish waste along with hotel waster and chicken waste. Average harvest quantity 30 quintal/ Bigha. He is presently selling fish @ Rs. 65 per Kg. After deducting all the investing cost he is earning approximate Rs. 60000-70000 per bigha per year. He is happy with this culture and trying to increase his culture area in near future.

DISCUSSION

After survey and interact with the local people it is felt that this fish culture may be promoted among the rural farmers by giving them proper technology and guidance. People in the locality may be made aware how to culture this fish in a controlled manner without hampering the ecological balance. Farmers are very much keen to have proper culture technology and seed production and also low cost feed production. Most importantly, it is the source of livelihoods for a large section of the economically backward population of the state. Strict imposition of ban of culture of this species is practically very difficult for the rural people who already achieved the remarkable profit through this culture of fish.

At the same time it is being cultured in most of the neighboring countries like Bangladesh. Thus, scientific and controlled cultured methods may be applied in order to make income generation of the rural people as well as nutritional supply and maintaining the ecological balance. Culture of the Exotic Thailand magur, *Clarias gariepinus* may be implemented in seasonal water bodies/arid zones especially in the Districts of Birbhum, Purulia and Bankura of West Bengal and other arid zones of the country where water exist only for a period of 5-6 months. However cautions must be exercised so that they do not get access into the natural water bodies which might upset the ecological balance of the endemic species. Necessary policy decision coupled with application of scientific culture methods in controlled environment may provide a new dimension for the income generation, socio-economic up-liftment as well as protecting ecological balance.

IMPACTS OF INTRODUCTION OF PACU & THAILAND MAGUR

- In order to achieve higher table fish production, apart from traditional pisciculture with six species, some more new species might be introduced with higher growth rate, better taste and standard food value which not only supplement the fish production quantitatively but enhance the earnings from a certain unit area of water body without hampering the ecological balance.
- Commercialization of any new economically viable fish for aquaculture needs some study, time and experiences. General study among the farmers in the locality of Naihati, West Bengal revealed that this sp. not

only grows well up to 1.5 kg in one year with a survival rate approximate 90% but also prove itself as a compatible species in a composite fish culture pond.

- In case of culture of Pacu, along with *Cyprinus* gives better result in economic point of view.
- As it already gain a good market, widespread farming of Pacu is essential as a potential candidate species in aqua farming. So, Pacu farming may be recommended as a new member for commercial aquaculture practice.
- Being motivated with higher fish production *vis-à-vis* higher income entailing lower risk large number of population of rural areas have entered in the venture of production of seed and table size exotic fishes especially *Clarias gariepinus*.
- The landless labours of the area have accepted the profession whole heartedly. Thus, socio-economic conditions of the farmers have got uplifted.
- A study was made in the Tafatchar village at Bashirhat-I block, North 24 parganas and some others villages like Dighirpar, Raghabpur and Choura at the same block. The study conducted during 2008-09 with the help of pretested structured schedule. The extension functionaries of the State Government staff and the member of Tafatchar Hybrid Mastya Jibi Samity were engaged for collection the data. The data was collected with the help of statistical package. It revealed that the respondents have acquired many luxury materials after adoption of the culture of exotic catfish. Most of them belongs to schedule cast and Muslims of the fishers community (44% and 24.60% respectively). While analyzing the Socio- psychological aspects it reveals that most the people have become resource- rich from the status of landless labourer or resource- poor category involving them on the same.
- The seed and table size exotic fish producers informed that at no circumstances they are going to stop these activities despite of the ban imposed by the Government.
- Thus, it will be a Herculean task to restrain them from this hazardous occupation since it has become the livelihood for them.

A FEW PROBABLE CANDIDATE SPECIES FOR AQUACULTURE IN INDIA

1. *Puntius Javanicus* (Tawes): As per the report of FAO, this species was introduced in India during 1972 for aquaculture purposes. This species is commonly known as Java Puthi in India. It is extensively cultured in the state like West Bengal, Assam etc. It attains max length of 40.5 cm. It can be regarded as good candidate species for commercial aquaculture and can be used as best alternative to remove aquatic weed in place of *Ctenopharyngodon idella*.

Fig. 9.33: Java Puthi

2. *Myxocyprinus asiaticus* (Chinese Sucker): This High Fin Shark, treated as both food and aquarium fish is a native species of China. It is mostly seen in aquarium shops of India and also in neighbouring countries like Bangladesh. It attains maximum length of 30 cm. This fish is a bottom dweller and omnivorous in nature but also prefers vegetations. This Chinese high-fin banded shark looks fare best when fed plenty of vegetable matter (Galib, 2010). They accept algae wafers and never turn up their noses at live or frozen foods. They also enjoy flakes, pellets, and food sticks (Aqualandpetplus, 2009). Few farmers from Naihati, West Bengal are culturing this species in their farm pond. Hence, from Indian desk, our scientist may standardize the breeding & culture technique for commercial aquaculture. No artificial breeding is recorded till date.

Fig. 9.34: Chinese High Fin Branded Shark

3. *Jade perch:* The Barcoo grunter (*Scortum barcoo*) is a native fish of the Lake Eyre and Bulloo-Bancannia catchments. It is a relatively new aquaculture species and is marketed under the name jade perch. In Queensland, Australia the aquaculturist's farm jade perch in either tanks or ponds. Successful jade perch farming involves carefully managing stocking rates, water quality and diet. Industry suggests that production of 5-10t per hectare is attainable in well-managed ponds. It is an omnivorous species and can grow upto 450-800g in 4-7months. The minimum temperature required for culture is above 20°C and it contains high omega-3-fattyacid. It is suitable for culture in moderate subtropical to Tropical temperature.

Fig. 9.35: Jade perch

CONCLUSION

Considering the positive impact in introducing of new species of exotic fishes in Indian waters and aquatic biodiversity, the above said exotic fish varieties should be cleared and legalized by the National Committee on introduction of Aquatic species in Indian Waters, New Delhi with scientific supervision and monitoring. The committee represented by the Fisheries Development Commissioner, DAHD&F, Ministry of Agriculture, Govt. of India and Experts may study the relevance of introduction of these species on Indian aquatic environment.

It is reported that in Bangladesh, consumption of these fish makes a significant contribution to the nutrition of poor people. This indicates nutritive value of catfish as good as any other quality animal protein. The fat content is also less so, it can become a part of nearly anyone's diet. The local production of these cat- fishes has caused a drastic reduction of market price from Rs. 120 to Rs 40. This is mainly due to reduced transport cost, which in turn helps poor people to get quality protein at an affordable price.

The countries like Thailand, Vietnam, Bangladesh & China (Ali, M.L., 1999, 2007, DoF, 2005, Diana, J.S., S.L. Kohler, and D.R. Ottey, 1988, Lin, C.K. and J.S. Diana, 1995) are widely culturing Thailand magur and making profitable value added products. Therefore mere banning the same in India will be a competitive disadvantage from our farmers.

Further, the Giant barb or Siamese giant carp (*Catlocarpio siamensis*), the largest carp species of the world, originates from the South East Asian Countries like Thailand, Cambodia and Vietnam is famous for it's delicacy. This species is critically endangered but not yet IUCN red listed. Research is being carried out by the scientist of South East Asian Countries like Thailand, Cambodia and Vietnam etc. and effort has been made for breeding, propagation and it's culture through introducing in pond culture system to save the Giant barb. The maximum length reported is around 3 m, but more commonly about 1-2 m and 70-120 kg. Among the countries in the South East Asian region, only Thailand has been successful in artificial breeding.

Class : Teleostomi
Order : Cypriniformes
Family : Cyprinidae
Genus : *Catlocarpio*
Species: *siamensis*
Common names:
English : Siamese giant carp

Fig. 9.36

Super Tilapia or GIFT Tilapia (Genetical Improvement of farmed Tilapia) developed through selective breeding of several strains of Nile Tilapia by the scientist of World Fish Centre (formerly ICLARM) is widely cultured at present in various countries such as Israel, China, Taiwan, Vietnam, Philippines, Thailand, Indonesia, Malaysia and also in Bangladesh & Srilanka because, it grows faster, survives better than the original fish, more disease resistant than carps, and there is no serious environmental hazards reported and high potential of export of tilapia in fillet form these countries to US, Europe and Japan. Hence, in the coming days there is a great possibility of introducing mono sex Nile Tilapia/GIFT (Super Tilapia) in commercial aquaculture of India.

The induced breeding techniques of riverine catfish *Rita rita*, commercially important cat fish species of Bangladesh have already been established by using carp pituitary gland (PG) extract. In India, the Department of Fisheries, Govt. of West Bengal undertook a project called

"Effect of Climate change on Aquaculture" and collected quality brooders of riverine catfish *Rita rita* from river Ganga and distributed among farmers for it's maintenance and to carry out breeding trial. One such farmer Shri. Dhiman Pal of Naihat,North 24 Pargana District, West Bengal is maintaining this species in his culture pond to carry out breeding trial.

Fig. 9.37: *Rita rita* Collected from River Ganga

Fig. 9.38: Dr. Madhumita Mukherjee, ED (T) is seen Along with Farmer Shri. Dhiman Pal of Naihati, in his Farm

The over exploitation, modification of freshwater habitats by damming rivers, siltation in river bed has changed the ecology of the breeding ground and it has lead to decrease the population of fish species like Indian shad (*Hilsa ilisha*), the carps (*Labeo calbasu*), the Devil Catfish (*Bagarius bagarius*) *Rita rita* etc. from the Ganga river system. Dubey (1994) also categorized *Rita* spp. among the declining indigenous fauna of India. The induced breeding techniques of riverine catfish *Rita rita,* commercially important cat fish species of Bangladesh have already been established using carp pituitary gland (PG) extract.

One of the probable mitigating measures that can be taken against the extinction of these fish species is to initiate domestication and breeding programme where by mass production of quality seeds can be ensured.

Further, we should adopt some of the conservation measures for these endangered catfish include, In-situ conservation, establishment of fish sanctuaries, habitat restoration, stock transfer, (Obtaining sufficient number of fertilized eggs and introduction of the hatched larvae into a new environment), ex situ conservation (cryopreservation of sperms, eggs or embryos) etc.

REFERENCES

Alikunhi, K,H. and Sukumaran, K.K., 1964. Preliminary Observations on Chinese Carps in India. *Proc. Indian Acad. Sci., 60* (3): 171-88.

Aqualandpetplus. 2009. How to Keep Your New Chinese High-Fin Branded Shark Aqualand info on Myxocyprinus Asiaticus, Retrieved on December 16, 2009. http://aqualandpetsplus.com/Sharks,%20Banded%20Chinese.htm.

Biology and Culture Potential of Pacu in India Published by M. Lakshmana Kumar and Others in October, 2011 edition of Aquatech.

Bunting, S.W., Kundu, N. and Mukherjee, M. .2002. Situation Analysis: Production Systems and Natural Resource Management in PU Kolkata. Sterling, UK: Institute of Aquaculture, University of Sterling

Cambray J.A. (2003) The Need for Research and Monitoring on the Impacts of Tanslocated Sharptooth Catfish, Clarias Gariepinus, in South Africa. African Journal of Aquatic Science 28 191-195.

(Clariidae). Annales Musee Royal de l's Afrique Centrale 247, 1-199.

Data. M.K. and M.C. Nandeesha (2006). Pacu (*Piaractus brachypomus*) an Acid Water Loving Exotic Finfish, Enters Indian Aquaculture Scene. Fishing Chimes 26(9): 10-12.

DoF, 2005. Fisheries Resource Information of Bangladesh, Souvenir of National Fish Fortnight, 2005.

Diana, J.S., S.L. Kohler, and D.R. Ottey, 1988. A Yield Model for Walking Catfish Production in Aquaculture Systems. Aquaculture, 71: 23-35.

Diwedi, S.N., Bhaumik, Utpal, Paria, T. and Saha, S.K.,2003. Status of Exotic Catfishes and Its Impact in Aquaculture Sector. *J.Natcon.15*(2): 537-547.

Dwivedi, S.N., Utpal Bhaumik, T. Paria, S.K. Saha and A. Mitra. 2004. Invasion of Exotic Catfishes Towards Aquaculture. Fishing Chimes, 24 (1): 106-109.

FAO 2003 Year Book of Fisheries Statistics 2001. Food and Agricultural Organization of United Nations Rome 2003.

Galib SM. 2010. Cultured and Ornamental Exotic Fish Diversity of Bangladesh, MS Dissertation, Department of Fisheries, University of Rajshahi, Rajshahi, Bangladesh, 169 pp.

Galib SM and Mohsin ABM. 2010. Exotic Ornamental Fishes of Bangladesh, *Bangladesh J. Prog. Sci. & Tech.* 8(2): 255-258.

Lin, C.K. and J.S. Diana, 1995. Co-culture of catfish (*Clarias macrocephalus* x *C. gariepinus*) and Tilapia (*Oreochromis niloticus*) in Ponds. Aquatic Living Resources, 8: 449-454.

Mathew, P.M., 1989. Role of Exotic Carps in Composite Fish Culture.pp. 85-89. In: M.Mohan Joseph (Ed.) Exotic Aquatic Species in India. Proceedings of Workshop on Exotic Aquatic Species in India, 25-26 April, 1988. Special Publication 1,132 pp. Asian Fisheries Society, Indian Branch, Mangalore, India.

Mohamad-Zaini. S., S.K. Saadon. And A.B. Omar (1991). Study on the Spawning of Bawal Merah (*Colossoma brachypomun*). Paper Presented in the Departmental of Fisheries Research Seminar on P. Pinang on 30th Sept-2nd Oct. 1991.

M.F.A. Mollah, M.R. Amin, M.N. Sarowar and Muhammadullah (2008), Induced Breeding of the Riverine Catfish *Rita rita*. Journal, Bangladesh Agril. Univ. 6(2): 361-366, 2008 ISSN 1810-3030, p. 1.

Pearson M.D., Chinabut S. Karnchanakharn S. & Somsiri T. (1994) Jaundice Disease in the Farmed Catfish Hybrid, Clarias Macrophalus x C. Gariepinus, in Thailand. Journal of Fish Diseases p. 17.

Research & Farming Techniques on "Induced Breeding of Pacu (*Piaractus brachypomus*)" by Chattarjee, N.R. & Mazumdar, B., Department of Aquaculture, Faculty of Fishery Science, West Bengal University of Animal and Fishery Sciences, 5 B.H. Road, P.O. Panchasayar, Kolkata-700 094,West Bengal, India.

Singh, A.K. and Arvind Mishra, 2001. Environmental Issues of Exotic Catfish Culture in Uttar Pradesh. *J. Environmental Biology* 22 (3): 205-208.

Sy, D.Y. and T.D. Vien. 2002. The Role of Aquaculture in Pollution-remediation in Tay Lake and Truc Bach Lake of Ha Noi. Paper Submitted to the RUAF email Conference on Appropriate Methods for Urban Agriculture, 4-16 February 2002.

Technology Information Forecasting & Assessment Council (TIFAC), (2001) Utilization of Slaughter House Wastes for the Preparation of Animal Feed, TLBP.

Teugels G. (1986) A Systematic Revision of the African Species of the Genus Clarias (Pisce).

Thilsted, S.H., N. Roos and N. Hassan. 1997. The Role of Indigenous Fish Species in Food and Nutrition Security in Bangladesh. Naga 20(3-4), 82-84.

Vitule J., Umbria S. & Aranha J. (2006), Introduction of the African Catfish Clarias Gariepinus into Southern Brasil. Biological Invasions, 8, 677-681.

Pages: 184-195

FISH HABITAT AND AQUACULTURE

Edited by: Dr. Sanjay Kumar Gupta; Dr. Pawan Kumar 'Bharti'

ISBN: 978-93-5056-744-9

Edition: 2015

Published by: Discovery Publishing House Pvt. Ltd., New Delhi (India)

10

Coliform Bacterial Populations in Aquatic Environments

Madhumita Das and Biswajit Dash

ABSTRACT

Coliform bacteria including faecal coliforms and *E.coli* get into different aquatic systems through domestic sewage and addition of organic resources. Their abundance is measured by following different enumeration methods. Drinking waters sometimes harbour enteric bacteria through different sources and require regular monitoring and evaluation. Coliform bacterial populations in water and sediments of fish ponds treated with cow manure and biogas slurry were in the ranges of 3-140/ml and 0-1.40 x10^4/g. The abundance of these microbial indicators can be reduced following different physical, chemical and biological microbial bioaugmentation processes. The mean counts of coliform bacterial populations in ponds, open wells, tube wells and streams in the Puri district, Odisha were upto 1100/100ml and faecal coliforms upto 23/100ml water.

Key words: Coliform, Faecal, *E.coli,* Aquatic, Environments.

INTRODUCTION

Municipal sewage contains human wastes and pathogenic bacteria which are perilous to human health. Discharge of municipal waste in aquatic systems is one of the important issues in relation to quality of water. Usually these bacteria are coliform bacteria and are present in clumps in association with particulate organic matter (Souter *et al.*, 1976; Henry *et al.*, 1983; Yers *et al.*, 2005; Guber *et al.*, 2006). These are indicator organisms which assess the microbiological quality of water and other aquatic resources (Mohapatra *et al.*, 1992; Leclerc *et al.*, 2001; Rompré *et al.*, 2002; Derlet *et al.*, 2008). Faecal coliforms are a subset of coliform bacterial group which are widely used to evaluate the quality of waste water effluents, sources of fresh waters, sea water at bathing beaches, raw water for drinking water supply and recreational waters (Heron *et al.*, 1993; Standard Methods, 1998; Geissler *et al.*, 2000). Both of these bacteria belong to a large family known as Enterobacteriaceae or enterics. Most of the enterics belong to total coliform group but very few belong to faecal coliform group.

Total colifroms are large group of gram negative, rod shaped bacteria which include *Citrobacter, Enterobacter, Klabsiella,* Faecal coliforms and *Escherichia* which serve several characteristics (DWAF, 1996). Enumeration of the counts of total coliform bacteria is the standard test for drinking water as their presence indicates contamination of a water supply by an outside source. In laboratory total coliforms are grown in a medium containing lactose and are identified by the production of acid and gas by the fermentation of lactose at a temperature of 35 or 37°C. Lechevalier and McFeters (1985) studied the interaction between heterotrophic bacteria and coliform organisms.

Faecal coliform bacteria are specialized types of bacteria which are dominated by *Escherichia coli* and include genera which originate in feces. The presence of total coliforms may or may not indicate faecal contamination. Faecal coliforms are also called thermotolerant coliform which grows at 44 or 44.5°C and ferment lactose to produce acid and gas. Fecal coliform analysis is an effective tool for evaluating potential public health. Due to their lack of ability to form spores they are more susceptible to destruction by environmental conditions. Although faecal coliforms are principal indicators of faecal pollution in waters enterococci are also included in faecal contamination studies.

Usually 95% of thermotolerant coliforms isolated from water are the *Escherichia coli*, commonly called gut bacteria existing in lower intestine of warm blooded organisms. *E.coli* colonizes the infant gastro-intestinal tract within hours after birth and remains dominant in the human colonic flora. It is a prokaryotic model organism and an important species used in recombinant DNA technology in the fields of biotechnology and microbiology (Brosius *et al.*, 1978; Sabat *et al.*, 2000). *E. coli* is an indicator microorganism for fecal contamination. Most types of *E. coli* are harmless but some cause serious illness or even death. Virulent strains of *E. coli* cause gastroenteritis, urinary tract infections and neonatal meningitis. All types of food get contaminated by *E. coli* without following proper safety measures. It contaminates unpasteurized milk, ground and processed meat. Vegetables get contaminated by the use of manure based fertilizers. Most strains of *E. coli* are present in sewage and other organic waste containing waters (Mulder, 1975; Anderson *et al.*, 1983; Giammanco *et al.*, 1992; Kudva *et al.*, 1998). Nutrient-rich environments encourage the growth or persistence of some species of thermotolerant coliform other than *E. coli* (Barcina *et al.*, 1986). Concentration of *E.coli* or faecal coliforms provides only one part of the picture and it is necessary to combine the information of this indicator with chemical quality parameters and determines the status of water for portable and other uses. Simultaneous detection of faecal coliforms and *E. coli* has practical benefits confirming whether wastes from warm-blooded animals caused pollution of water resources (Chang *et al.*, 1989; Garbow, 1996). *E. coli* is predominantly an indicator but under certain circumstances it can be a pathogen.

Studies on the survival of *E. coli* in different types of water and organic sources are of great interest. McFeters and Stuart (1972) observed that the survival of *E. coli* exposed to river and estuarine waters were inversely proportional to temperature (5 to 15 °C). Several authors have reported that visible light has a negative effect on *E. coli* cells in seawater (Fujijoka *et al.*, 1981). Soracco *et al.* (1975) detected prolonged survival of pure *E. coli* in a warm freshwater pond (> 25°C). Use of chemical disinfectants, rapid sand filtration, UV irradiation and combined UV/Chemical treatments helps in inactivation of enteric bacteria and bacteriophages have been considered as biotic factor affecting removal of coliforms from natural environments and can be used beneficially (Lazarova *et al.*, 1998; Hill *et al.*, 2002; Stampi *et al.*, 2002; Koivunen *et al.*, 2003, 2005; Rajala *et al.*, 2003). Jannasch (1968), McCambridge and McMeckin (1979) and Gonzalez *et al.* (1990) using fluorescent labeled bacteria showed that protists, both flagellates and ciliates, ingested and digested enteric bacteria in both freshwater and marine water samples. Xu *et al.*, (2002) explained waste-water disinfection by ozone.

ENUMERATION METHODS

To detect the presence of coliform bacteria in water and sediment usually two techniques are used. The first method is multiple fermentation tube or Most Probable Number (MPN) method which is brilliant green lactose bile broth (Peptone 10g, Lactose10g, Tryptone 20g, Brilliant green (1% Aq.) 13.3ml, distilled water 1000ml). In this method measured portion of water samples are placed in test-tubes containing a culture medium in triplicates with successive dilutions of the samples. The tubes are incubated for a standard time at a standard temperature. Observations on the number of positive tubes in each dilution are used for computing the bacterial counts from MPN tables values expressed as number per hundred milliliters (Rodina, 1972; Collins and Lyne, 1976).

The second method is called "membrane filter technique" in which a measured volume of sample is passed through a cellulose acetate membrane filter (0.45 ìm) that retains the bacteria. The filter is then placed on MFc Agar culture medium petriplates and incubated at 44°C for 24 hours. Colonies exhibiting shades of blue are counted as faecal coliforms. If the bacterial colonies overlap then serial dilution of the sample can be done for obtaining accurate results. Membrane filter technique is based on the principle that each bacterium or clump of bacteria will give rise to a single visible colony and this method is used to test large number of samples and yields results more rapidly than the multiple fermentation tube method (Van Poucke and Nelis, 2000). *E. coli* are enumerated by culturing on a selective Endo medium (Bio Merieux: peptone 1%, di-potassium hydrogen phosphate 0.25%, lactose 1%, sodium sulfite, anhydrous 0.33%, fuchsine 0.03%, agar 1.25%). Plates were incubated at 37°C for 24 hours, then the number of colony forming units (CFU) with red, greenish, metallic fuchsine sheen are counted.

Sometimes presumptive results may not be adequate and it is required to do confirmatory tests on pure subcultures. To confirm total coliforms, each colony formed is subcultured to tubes of lactose peptone water and incubated at 35 or 37°C for 48 hours. Gas production during this period confirms the presence of total coliforms. To confirm the presence of thermotolerant coliforms and *E. coli* on membrane filters wheather incubated at 35, 37 or 44°C, each colony is subcultured in a tube of lactose peptone water and a tube of peptone water. Both the tubes are incubated at 44°C for 24 hours. Bacterial growth with the production of gas in the lactose peptone water confirms the presence of thermotolerant coliforms. For confirming the presence of *E. coli* requires the addition of 0.2-0.3 ml of Kovac's reagent to each tryptone water culture tube. Production of red colour indicates the synthesis of indole from tryptophan and confirms the presence of *E. coli.*

COLIFORM BACTERIA IN DRINKING WATER

Drinking water does not contain fecal coliform bacteria or *E. coli* and is usually not associated with health risk and is safe from bacteriological contamination. Unless a resample shows that fecal coliform bacteria or *E. coli* is present in the water supply, it is recommended that bottled water can be recommended for drinking and cooking purposes. The presence of these bacteria in drinking water is generally a result of problem with water treatment or the pipes which distribute the water. Coliforms in drinking water can be detected using a tyrosinase composite biosensor (Serra *et al.*, 2005). Bastholm *et al.* (2008) developed a simple bioluminescence procedure for early warning detection of coliform bacteria in drinking water. Jazrawi *et al.* (1988) isolated antibiotic resistant coliform and fecal coliform bacteria in drinking water from tap water and storage tanks. There is a need for regular bacteriological examination of drinking water and restriction on the use of antibiotics.

The results of a survey of over 109 freshwater habitats comprising ponds, open wells, tube wells and streams in the Puri district, Odisha for heterotrophic and coliform bacterial flora in the water medium with reference to chemical conditions and suitability of water fror human consumption are presenred. The ranges of bacterial counts were aerobic heterotrophs 30-22,000/ml, total coliforms upto 1100/100ml and faecal coliforms upto 23/100ml water. The coliform concentration levels beyond the permissible limits were 77% in ponds, 69% in open wells and 50% in tube wells, requiring appropriate treatment before use for drinking purpose (Ayyappan *et al.*, 1993).

Coliform Bacteria in Aquatic Systems

The occurrence of enteric bacteria in water and sediment media has been used to define the microbial ecology as also analyze the sanitary conditions of the aquatic environment by several workers (Kittrell and Furfari, 1963; Srikantaiah *et al.*, 1985). The coliform bacteria are indicative of water quality and sources of pollution in a water body (Rao and Burnison, 1976; Gerba *et al.*, 1978; Want and Doyle, 1998). They usually enter into inland water sources through the discharge of waste by birds, animals, human sewage and plant materials like paper mill effluent (Davenport et *al.*, 1976; Silverman and Munoz, 1979; Berg and Fiksdal, 1988; Apte *et al.*, 1995). In coastal waters these microorganisms get into through domestic sewage and through the dumping of fish wastes generated from fish markets and also putrefied discards at fishing harbours and different landing centres. These bacteria get transferred through water and detritus to fish and other aquatic resources. The microflora of fish in both freshwater and marine waters gets contaminated with these enteric bacteria. Contaminated fish is not suitable for human consumption and cause foodborne diseases (Feldhusen, 2000).

Patterson and Gibbs (1977) found coliform bacteria on frozen broilers. Studies on the removal of faecal bacteria in cattle slurry after different treatments have been carried out by Sorline *et al.* (1987). Rai and Hill (1978) reported positive relations between coliform bacterial densities and nitrate levels. The addition of phosphate to water has been shown to improve the water quality by reducing the occurrence of coliform bacteria and inhibits biofilm growth despite the fact that phosphate serves as an essential nutrient for microorganisms (Appenzeller *et al.*, 2002). Sharma *et al.* (1992) analyzed the effects of different water quality parameters on coliform bacterial populations. Jagger (1975), Kapuscinski and Mitchell (1981) and Curtis *et al.* (1992) showed that sunlight damaged fecal coliforms in waste stabilization ponds and the rate of damage is proportional to oxygen concentration. Seasonal variations of faecal indicator bacteria such as faecal streptococci, total coliforms and thermotolerant coliforms in surface waters were studied by Neimi (1985). Verstraete and Voets (1976) made a comparative study of *E. coli* survival in two aquatic ecosystems. Treatment of sewage with chemicals is common to reduce faecal populations but are expensive and not ecofriendly (Zanetti *et al.*, 1996). Occurrence of antibiotic- resistant strains of coliform bacteria in both water and sediment were recorded by Baldini and Cabezali (1991). Different studies have shown that aquatic plants are capable of reducing the intensity of indicator bacteria from sewage containing aquatic systems (Falabi *et al.*, 2002). Duckweeds are free floating macrophytes are promising for use in sustainable wastewater treatment in the reduction of total coliforms and faecal colifrms by 86% and 92% (Jena *et al.*, 2010).

Microbial bioaugmentation is suitable for addressing high levels of fecal coliform in natural lakes, ponds and rivers. The most common method to reduce pathogenic bacteria in lakes and ponds is to remove the sediment and muck. By adding muck eating bacteria which will feed on the bottom muck and providing acration system to the pond or lake and slowly the muck and the organic sediment at the bottom begin to disappear (Enzinger and Cooper, 1976). The purpose of bioaugmentation is to facilitate gradual shift in the microbiological population of an aquatic system. It is ideally suited for treating areas used for public recreation, swimming and boating. Some microbial accelerators can control *E. coli* in sewage or effluent without using bleaching powder or chlorine and the result is a cleaner pond and lake water.

At many instances waters get contaminated with different heavy metals by various processes and have adverse effect on living organisms. Bioremediation is an environmental friendly and can be used to remove heavy metals from contaminated sites. Microorganisms when encountered with heavy metals produce metal binding peptides such as phytochelatins and mtallthionein. These peptides bind to heavy metals and reduce their toxicity by sequestration. In one such effort, the *Arabidopsis thaliana* phytochelatin synthase (AtPCS) responsible for enzymatic PC synthesis was over expressed in *E. coli* leading to 20-fold higher heavy metal accumulation (Sauge-Merle *et al.*, 2003).

COLIFORM BACTERIA IN FISH PONDS FERTILIZED WITH DIFFERENT ORGANIC MANURES

Das (1996) studied the total coliform bacterial populations involved in the organic decomposition and nutrient cycling in ponds with manure applications of: (i) cow manure at 10t/ha/yr; urea at 100 kg N/ha/yr and single super phosphate at 50 kg P/ha/yr; (ii) biogas slurry at 15t/ha/yr and inorganic fertilizers; (iii) biogas slurry at 30t/ha/yr; and (iv) biogas slurry at 30t/ha/yr with supplementary feed were assessed over a period of 15 months.

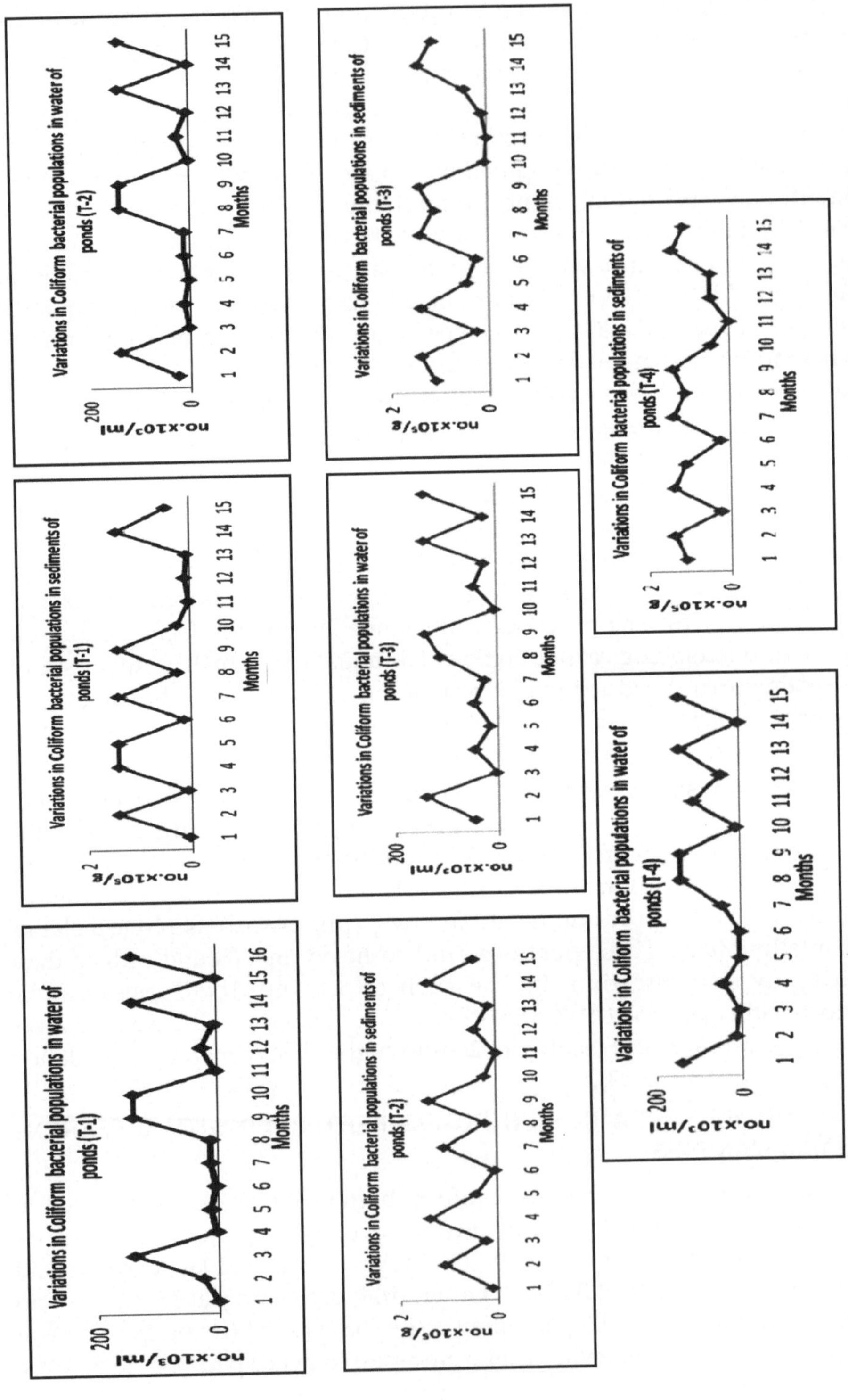

Fig. 10.1: Variations in Coliform Bacterial Populations in Water and Sediments in Ponds Under Different Treatments

The variations in total coliform bacteria in the water media were in the range of 3-140/ml in all the four treatments and those in the sediment were 0.01 - 1.40, 0 - 1.40, 0 - 1.40, 0.01 - 1.40 × 10^4/g with higher values during the months of April- June (Fig. 10.1). The possible effects of treatment of organic wastes on reduction of enterobacterial populations have been studied by Smith and Smith (1985) and Sorline *et al.* (1987). It was clear that coliform bacterial counts in the water medium were low while the sediment counts were comparatively high, attributable to settlement of organic matter on the surface sediment layers. They however did not increase continuously with organic enrichment as the fish ponds act as facultative oxidation ponds (Ogbondeminu and Okoye, 1992).

CONCLUSION

The need for deliberate waste water reuse has stimulated the interest in the ability of wastewater treatment processes to produce an item in which the risk of infection upon reuse is reduced to an acceptable level. Freshwater systems comprise a diverse set of habitats hosting contrasting microbial assemblages with coliform bacteria forming a dominant group. The test methods used for detection of different coliform bacteria are used for assessing water quality. Some of these enteric bacteria cause serious health hazards. By adopting various physical, chemical and biological methods their abundance in an aquatic system can be reduced or eliminated. Future studies include the use of the research tool global positioning system (GPS) for determining the habitat mapping and of different coliform bacteria and management measures to be taken to reduce and eliminate these bacteria form aquatic systems in different cities for obtaining disease free cleaner water bodies.

REFERENCES

Anderson JC, Rhodes MW and Kator KI (1983). Seasonal Variation in Survival of *E. coli* Exposed *'in situ'* Membrane Diffusion Chambers Containing Filtered and Non-filtered Estuarine Water. Appl. Envir. Microbiol., 45: 1877-1883.

Appenzeller BMR, Duval YB, Thomas F and Block JC (2002). Influence of Phosphate on Bacterial Adhesion onto Iron Oxyhydroxide in Drinking Water. Environmental Science & Technology, 2002, 36, (4), 646-652.

Ayyappan S, Dash B, Das Madhumita, Rao PLKM and Tripathi SD (1993). Distribution of Heterotrophic and Coliform Bacterial Flora in Fresh Water Bodies of Puri District, Odisha. VIIIth Annual Conference of National Environmental Science Academy, 16-19 February, 1993, RMRC(ICMR), Bhubaneswar, pp. 22.

Apte SC, Cheryl M, Davies MP and Sharon MP (1995). Rapid Detection of Faecal Coliforms in Sewage Using a Colorimetric Assay of β-D-galactosidase. Water Res., 29: 1803-1806.

Baldini MD and Cabezali CB (1991). Occurrence of Antibiotic-resistant *E. coli* Isolated from Environmental Samples. Mar. Pollut. Bull., 22(10): 500-503.

Bastholm Søren, Wahlstrøm Lasse, Bjergbæk Louise Appel and Roslev Peter (2008). A Simple Bioluminescence Procedure for Early Warning Detection of Coliform Bacteria in Drinking Water. World Journal of Microbiology and Biotechnology, Volume 24, Issue 10, pp. 2323-2330.

Barcina I, Arana I, Iriberri J and Egea L (1986). Factors Affecting the Survival of *E. coli* in a River. Hydrobiologia, 141, Dev. Hydrobiol., 36: 249-253.

Berg JD and Fiksdal L (1988). Rapid Detection of Total and Fecal Coliforms in Water by Enzymatic Hydrolysis of 1202 1119 V 2 4-methylumbelliferone-, β-D-galactosidase. Appl. Environ. Microbiol., 54: 2118-2122.

Brosius J, Palmer ML, Kennedy PJ and Noller HF (1978). Complete Nucleotide Sequence of a 16S Ribosomal RNA Gene from *Escherichia coli*. Proc Natl. Acad. Sci., USA, 75: 4801-4805.

Chang G, Brill WJ and Lum R (1989). Proportion of β-D-Dglucuronidase-Negative *Escherichia coli* in Human Fecal Samples. Appl. Envir. Microbiol., 55: 335–339.

Collins CH and Lyne PM (1976). Microbiological Methods. Butterworth & Co. (Publ.) Ltd., London, 521 pp.

Curtis TP, Mara DD and Silva SA (1992). Influence of pH, Oxygen and Humic Substances on Ability of Sunlight to Damage FC in Waste Stabilization Pond Water. Appl Environ Microbiol., 58: 1335-1343.

Das M (1996). Microbial Ecology and Biological Productivity of Fish Ponds Fertilized with Biogas Slurry. Ph.D. Thesis, Utkal University, 389 pp.

Davenport CV, Sparrow EB and Gordon RC (1976). Fecal Indicator Bacteria Persistence Under Natural Conditions in an Ice-covered River. Appl. Envir. Microbiol., 32: 527-536.

Derlet RW, Ger KA, Richards JR and Carlson JR (2008). Risk Factors for Coliform Bacteria in Backcountry Lakes and Streams in the Sierra Nevada Mountains: A 5-year study. Wilderness Environ Med., 19: 82-90.

DWAF (1996). South African Water Quality Guidelines, Vol. 1, Directorate of Communication Services, Department of Water Affairs and Forestry, Pretoria.

Enzinger RM and Cooper RC (1976). Role of Bacteria and Protozoa in the Removal of *E.coli* from Estuarine Waters. Appl. Envir. Microbiol., 31: 758-763.

Falabi JA, Gerba CP and Karpiscak MM (2002). Giardia and Cryptosporidium removal from waste-water by a duckweed (*Lemna gibba* L.) covered pond. Letters in Applied Microbiology, 34, 384-387.

Feldhusen F (2000). The Role of Seafood in Bacterial Food Borne Diseases. Microbs. Infect., 13: 1651-1660.

Fujijoka RS, Hashimoto HH, Siwak EB and Yorng RHT (1981). Effect of Sunlight on Survival of Indicator Bacteria in Seawater. Appl. Environ. Microbial., 41, 690.

Garbow WAK (1996). Water Borne Diseases: Update on Water Quality Assessment and Control. Water SA, 22(2), 193-202.

Giammanco G, Pignato S and Biondi M (1992). An Enzymatic Procedure for the Confirmation of Total Coliforms and *Escherichia coli* Enumeration from Water. Zbl. Hyg., 193: 99-105.

Gerba CP, Farrah SR, Goyal SM, Wallis C and Melnick JL (1978). Concentration of Enterovirus from Large Volume of Tap Water Treated Sewage and Sea Water. Appl. Env. Microbiol., 35(3): 540-548.

Geissler K, Manafi M, Amoros I and Alonso JL (2000). Quantitative Determination of Total Coliforms and *Escherichia coli* in Marine Waters with Chromogenic and Fluorogenic Media. J Appl. Microbiol., 88: 280-285.

Grigsby P and Calkins J (1979). The Inactivation of a Natural Population of Coliform Bacteria by Sunlight. Photochem. Photobiol., 31: 291-294.

Gonzalez JM, Sherr EB and Sherr BF (1990). Size Selective Grazing on Bacteria by Natural Assemblages of Estuarine Flagellates and Ciliates. Appl. Environ. Microbiol., 56, 1851.

Guber AK, Shelton DR, Pachepsky YA, Sadeghi AM and Sikora LJ (2006). Rainfall-induced Release of Fecal Coliforms and Other Manure Constituents: Comparison and modeling. Appl. Environ. Microbiol., 72: 7531-7539.

Heron SJE, Wilkinson JF and Duffus CM (1993). Enterobacteria Associated with Grass and Silages. J. Appl. Bacteriol., 75: 13-17.

Henry DP, Frost AJ, Samuel JL, O'Boyle DA and Thomson RH (1983). Factors Affecting the Survival of *Salmonella* and *Escherichia coli* in Anaerobically Fermented Pig Waste. J Appl. Bacteriol., 55: 89-95.

Hill VR, Kantardjieff A, Sobsey MD and Westerman PW (2002). Reduction of Enteric Microbes in Flushed Swime Wastewater Treated by a Biological Aerated Filter and UV Irradiation. Water Environ. Res., 74: 91-99.

Jagger J (1975). Inhibition by Sunlight of the Growth of *E. coli* B/r. Photochem. Photobiol., 22: 67-70.

Jannasch HW (1968). Competitive Elimination of Entero-bacteriaceae from Seawater. Appl. Microbiol., 16: 1616-1618.

Jazrawi Sameer F, Al-Doori Zainab A and Haddad Tahreer A (1988). Antibiotic Resistant Coliform and Faecal Coliform Bacteria in Drinking Water. Water, Air, and Soil Pollution, Volume 39, Issue 3-4, pp. 377-382.

Jena JK, Patro B, Patri P, Khuntia CP, Tripathy NK, Sinha S, Sarangi N and Ayyappan S(2010). Biological Treatment of Domestic Sewage Through Duckweed-cum-fish Culture: A Pilot-scale Study. Indian J. Fish., 57(4): 45-51.

Kapuscinski RB and Mitchell R (1981). Solar radiation induces sublethal injury in *E. coli* in sea water. Appl. Microbiol., 41: 670-674.

Kittrell FW and Furfari SA (1963). Observations of Coliform Bacteria in Streams. J. Wat. Pollut. Cont. Fed., 35: 1361-1385.

Koivunen J, Siitonen A and Heinonen-Tanski H (2003). Elimination of Enteric Bacteria in Biological-chemical Wastewater Treatment and Tertiary Filtration Units. Water Res., 37: 690-698.

Koivunen J and Heinonen-Tanski H (2005). Inactivation of Enteric Microorganisms with Chemical Disinfectants, UV Irradiation and Combined Chemical/UV treatments. Water Res., 39: 1519-1526.

Kudva IT, Blanch K and Hovde CJ (1998). Analysis of *Escherichia coli* 0157: H7 Survival in Ovine or Bovine Manure and Manure Slurry. Appl. Environ. Microbiol., 64(9): 3166-3174.

Lazarova V, Janex M, Fiksdal L, Oberg C, Oberg C, Barcina I and Pommepuy M (1998). Advanced Wastewater Disinfection Technologies: Short and Long Term Efficiency. Water Sci. Technol., 38: 109-117.

Lechevalier MW and McFeters GA (1985). Interactions Between Heterotrophic Plate Count Bacteria and Coliform Organisms. Appl. Envir. Microbiol., 49: 1338-1341.

Leclerc H, Mossel DAA, Edberg SC and Struijk CB (2001). Advances in the Bacteriology of the Coliform Group: Their Suitability as Markers of Microbial Water Safety. Ann. Rev. Microbiol., 55: 201-234.

McCambridge J and McMeekin TA (1979). Protozoan Predation of *E. coli* in Estuarine Waters. Wat. Res., 13: 659-663.

McFeters GA and Stuart DG (1972). Survival of Coliform Bacteria in Natural Waters: Field and Laboratory Studies with Membrane-filters Chambers. Appl. Microbiol., 24: 805-811.

Mohapatra SP, Saxena S K and Ali Arif (1992). Occurrence of Coliform Bacteria in Channels Receiving Municipal Sewage. Indian J Environ Prot., 12 (7), 509-511.

Mulder RWAW (1975). Radiation-inactivation of *Salmonella panama* and *Escherichia coli* K 12 Present on Deepfrozen Poultry Carcasses. Quality of Poultry Meat, *Proceedings, Symposium on Poultry Meat Quality*, 2nd, Oosterbeek, The Netherlands, pp. (14) 1-7.

Neimi M (1985). Faecal Indicator Bacteria at Freshwater Rainbow Trout. Vesientutkismuslait. Julk., Helsinki Publ. Water Res. Inst., Helsinki, No. 64, 49 pp.

Ogbondeminu FS and Okoye FC (1992). Microbiological Evaluation of an Untreated Domestic Waste Water Aquaculture System. J. Aqua. Trop., 7: 27-34.

Patterson JT and Gibbs PA (1977). Incidence and Sources of Enterobacteriaceae Found on Frozen Broilers. *Proceedings of the 3rd European Symposium on Poultry Meat Quality*, pp. 69-75.

Rai H and Hill G (1978). Bacteriological Studies in Amazona, Mississippi and Nile Waters. Arch. Hydrobiol., 81(4): 445-461.

Rajala RL, Pulkkanen M, Pessi M and Heinonen-Tanski H (2003). Removal of Microbes from Municipal Wastewater Effluent by Rapid Sand Filtration and Subsequent UV irradiation. Water Sci. Technol., 17: 157-162.

Rao SS and Burnison BK (1976). Bacterial Distribution in Lake Erie (1967, 1970). J. Fish. Res. Bd. Rodina AG (1972). Methods in Aquatic Microbiology. Tr. Rev. R.R. Colwell and M.S. Zambruski, Univ, Park Press, Baltimore and Butterworth Co, Ltd. London, 481 pp.

Rompré A, Servais P, Baudart J, de-Roubin MR and Laurent P (2002). Detection and Enumeration of Coliforms in Drinking Water: Current Methods and Emerging Approaches. J Microbiol. Methods, 49: 31-54.

Sabat G, Rose P, Hickey WJ and Harkin JM (2000). Selective and Sensitive Method for PCR Amplification of *Escherichia coli* 16S rRNA Genes in Soil. Appl. Environ. Microbiol., 66: 844-849.

Sauge-Merle S, Cuine S, Carrier P, Lecomte-Pradines C, Luu DT, Peltier G (2003) Enhanced Toxic Metal Accumulation in Engineered Bacterial Cells Expressing Arabidopsis Thaliana Phytochelatin Synthase. Appl Environ Microbiol, 69: 490-494.

Serra B, Dolores Moralez M, Zhang J, Julio Reviejo A, Hall EH and Pingarron JM (2005). In-a-day Electrochemical Detection of Coliforms in Drinking Water Using a Tyrosinase Composite Biosensor. Anal Chem., 77: 8115-812.

Sharma S, Kulkarni P, Gokhale A, Kulkarni N and Kapadnis BP (1992). Water Analysis with Reference to Coliforms, Residual Chlorine and Carcinogens. Proc. 32nd Ann. Conf. Assoc. Microbiologists of India, Madurai, Jan. 10-12, Abstract EMP 2-31.

Silverman MP and Munoz ES (1979). Automated Electrical Impedance Technique for Rapid Enumeration of Fecal Coliforms in Effluents from Sewage Treatment Plants. — Appl. Environ. Microbiol., 37: 521-526.

Smith WE and Smith WL (1985).The Effects of Advanced Waste Water Treatment on the Coliform Concentration in Hillsbrough Bay. Proc. Sea Grant Programme, Bellwether Press, USA, pp. 563-567.

Stampi S, De Luca G, Onorato M, Ambrogiani E and Zanetti F (2002). Peracetic Acid as an Alternative Wastewater Disinfectant to Chlorine Dioxide. J. Appl. Microbiol., 93: 725-731.

Standard Methods (1998). Standard Methods for the Examination of Water and Waste Water, (20th Edn.) (Eds. A.D.Eaton, L.S.Clesceri,A.E. Greenberg). American Public Health Association, Washington DC, 9-1-9-117.

Sorline C, Allievi L, Ranalli G and Ferrari A (1987). A Note on the Removal of Fecal Bacteria in Cattle Slurry After Different Farm and Lab Treatments. Biological Wastes, 22: 39-47.

Souter BW, Sonstegard RA and McDermott LA (1976). Enteric Bacteria in Carp (*Cyprinus carpio*) and White Suckers (*Catostomus commersoni*). J. Fish. Res. Bd Can., 33: 1401-1403.

Srikantaiah M, Shenoy MG and Mohan Kumar KC (1985). Studies on the Occurrence of Enteric Bacteria in the Estuarine Waters Along the Mangalore Coast. Fish. Technol., 22(1): 74-78.

Van Poucke SO and Nelis HJ (2000). Rapid Detection of Fluorescent and Chemiluminescent Total Coliforms and *Escherichia coli* on Membrane Filters. J. Microbiol. Methods, 42: 233-244.

Verstraete W and Voets JP (1976). Comparative Study of *E. coli* Survival in Two Aquatic Ecosystems. Wat. Res., 10: 129-136.

Want GD and Doyle MP (1998). Survival of Enterohemorrhagic *Escherichia coli* 0157: H7 in water. J. Food Prot., 61: 662-667.

Xu P, Janex ML, Savoye P, Cockx A and Lazarova V (2002). Waste-water Disinfection by Ozone: Main Parameters for Process Design. Water Res., 36: 1043-1055.

Yers HL, Cabrera ML, Matthews MK, Franklin DH, Andrae JG, Radcliffe DE, McCann MA, Kuykendall HA, Hoveland CS and Calvert VH (2005). Phosphorus, Sediment and *Escherichia coli* Loads in Unfenced Streams of the Georgia Piedmont, USA. J. Environ. Qual., 34: 2290-2300.

Zanetti F, Stampi S, De Luca G, Varoli O and Tonelli E (1996). Comparative Disinfection of Secondary-treatment Sewage with Chlorine Dioxide and Bromine Chloride. Zbl. Hyg. Umvelmed, 198: 567-579.

Pages: 196-219

FISH HABITAT AND AQUACULTURE
Edited by: Dr. Sanjay Kumar Gupta; Dr. Pawan Kumar 'Bharti'
ISBN: 978-93-5056-744-9
Edition: 2015
Published by: Discovery Publishing House Pvt. Ltd., New Delhi (India)

11

Organic Aquaculture

H.A. Kaoud

ABSTRACT

Organic aquaculture is an ecological production management system that promotes and enhances biodiversity, biological cycles and soil biological activities. It is based on minimal use of off-farm inputs and on management practices that restore, maintain and enhance ecological harmony. Water pollution as well as all aquaculture operations for drugs, biologics, and other chemicals, collectively referred to as "regulated products" can cause immediate damage to an ecosystem. Organic aquaculture aims to provide fish and other products that are ecologically, economically and socially sound, safe the soil, water and nature, help property reduction in remote areas, improve health for both producers and consumers, value added for export products and avoid to sink our land. Today, organic aquaculture production takes place primarily in Europe, where certified organic salmon, carp and trout are grown and sold. Certified organic mussels, tiger shrimp, white shrimp and tilapia also cultured in such diverse places as Vietnam. Peru, Ecuador, Chile, New Zealand and Israel.

Key words: Water pollution; Organic aquaculture; Food quality and safety; Certification requirements.

INTRODUCTION

Humans have been catching fish for tens of thousands of years, since the age of hunter-gatherers. Fish were farmed as early as around 3500 BC in China, where fish, mainly carp, were held in artificial ponds after river floods. Some species like salmon and trout have been selectively bred specifically for fish-farming. The species raised in fish farms include salmon, trout, cod, carp, catfish, sea bass, tilapia, and others. Today the vast majority of Atlantic salmon and rainbow trout are farmed intensively in fish farms. Fish in fish farms are reared in large numbers in densely stocked tanks or enclosures in rivers, lakes or at sea in sea-cages. Aquaculture, also known as aqua-farming, is the farming of aquatic organisms such as fish, crustaceans, mollusks and aquatic plants. Aquaculture involves cultivating freshwater and saltwater populations under controlled conditions, and can be contrasted with commercial fishing, which is the harvesting of wild fish. Broadly speaking, finfish and shellfish fisheries can be conceptualized as akin to hunting and gathering while aquaculture is akin to agriculture. Mari-culture refers to aquaculture practiced in marine environments and in underwater habitats. According to the FAO, aquaculture "is understood to mean the farming of aquatic organisms including fish, mollusks, crustaceans and aquatic plants. Farming implies some form of intervention in the rearing process to enhance production, such as regular. Aquaculture is an established and growing industry in the some countries, and an increasingly important supplier of foods for consumers. Aquaculture is an important contributor to agriculture and a cornerstone of aquatic natural resources management. All aquaculture operations will have a demand for drugs, biologics, and other chemicals, collectively referred to as "regulated products".

This may include:

1. Disinfectants as part of biosecurity protocols
2. Herbicides and pesticides used in pond maintenance.
3. Spawning aids,
4. Vaccines used in disease prevention
5. Marking agents used in resource management.

Despite the best efforts of fish culturists to avoid pathogen introductions, therapeutic drugs are also occasionally needed to control mortality, infestations, or infections. It is critical that culturists have access to regulated products that are safe and effective and apply them in a manner that is consistent with their intended use, best management practices, and relevant rules and regulations.

Disinfectants are compounds which have antimicrobial properties that are generally applied to equipment and structures and are not intended to have a therapeutic effect on cultured animals. Greater emphasis on biosecurity in aquaculture has led to increased demand for disinfectants and greater need for aquaculturists to understand how to apply these compounds safely and effectively. Although a number of compounds classified as drugs in aquaculture may also be considered disinfectants in other industries, they are described in the section on drugs. The disinfectants section describes the most common uses for disinfectants in aquaculture, as well as appropriate compounds and application rates for aquaculture facilities.

Pesticides are not widely used in aquaculture; however, herbicides can be an important part of aquatic weed management in pond production. Certain algaecides, and fish and invertebrate toxicants may also be used in some situations. The pesticides section of the Guide will focus on the most common pesticides applications in aquaculture.

In common, POCs all have the following characteristics: they are stable and toxic, and share a similar structure. It has emerged that some highly stable organic compounds - chiefly halogenated hydrocarbons - can have serious environmental effects in the sea. Such substances have in common the presence of a halogen in their molecule (chlorine, iodine, fluorine, astatine), have a low polarity and low water solubility. Aromatic compounds are more reactive and susceptible to chemical and biochemical transformation and include pesticides (chlorinated such as DDT – DDE, Polycyclic Aromatic Hydrocarbons, Hexa Cyclo Hexan, and organometallics such as tributyltin). There are 209 congeners of Poly-Chloro-Biphenyls, all with different properties.

The metabolic pathways of polychlorinated biphenyls (PCBs) congeners are complex. Though the use of PCBs has been prohibited for a long time, emissions from unidentified sites still occur. Organometallic compounds such as tributyltin have been used extensively as antifouling agents and are now banned in many countries because of its effect known as imposex. Imposex refers to a change of sexual characteristics in invertebrates, female gastropods growing a penis, for instance. Compounds in alternative antifouling products form a special field of interest, since these compounds are especially applied to display their toxic effects in the marine environment. Their use is expected to increase in the near future due to the total ban on tributyltin-based antifouling chemicals by the International Maritime Organization IMO in 2003.

Persistent Organic Pollutants (POPs) Organochlorine pesticides (OCPs) are capable of persisting in the environment, transporting between phase media and accumulating to high levels, implying that they could pose a risk of causing adverse effects to human health and the environment.

Consequently, most OCPs are designated as persistent organic pollutants (POPs) and even as endocrine disrupting chemicals (EDCs). POPs, including aldrin, chlordane, chlordecone, DDT. (Prein, M., et al., 2010).

Biologics include a range of products of biologic origin used in the diagnosis, prevention, and treatment of diseases. In aquaculture, the most commonly used biologics are vaccines used to immunize animals and prevent infections from occurring. The biologics section of the Guide will go over the vaccines that are currently available for use in aquaculture, as well as provide recommendations for their usage.

Water pollution as well as all aquaculture operations for drugs, biologics, and other chemicals, collectively referred to as "regulated products" can cause immediate damage to an ecosystem. For example, toxic chemicals spilled directly into a river can kill nearly all living things for miles downstream. But the effects of water pollution can be even more far reaching. Many pollutants accumulate in the environment because they do not decompose quickly. As the pollutant levels increase, they can threaten an entire ecosystem. Consider a river ecosystem. Soil tainted with pesticides washes into the river and settles to the river bottom. Some of the pesticides enter the bodies of tiny, bottom-dwelling organisms, such as insect larvae and crustaceans. A hundred of these organisms are eaten by one small fish. A hundred of these small fish are eaten by one big fish. A predatory bird, such as an eagle, eats 10 big fish. Each organism stores the pesticide in its tissues, so at each step along the food chain, the amount of the pesticide passed on to the next organism increases. This accumulation of pollutants at successive levels of the food chain is called Biomagnifications, which is illustrated in Figure 11.1, has alarming consequences for organisms at the top of the food chain. Biomagnifications is one reason why many amount of fish that people can eat from certain bodies of water.

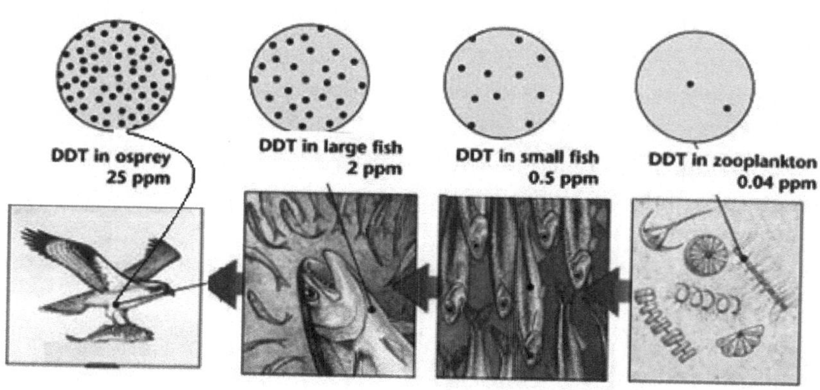

Fig. 11.1: The Accumulation of Pollutants at Successive Levels of the Food Chain is Called Biomagnifications

ORGANIC PRODUCTION SYSTEM

An ecological production management system that promotes and enhances biodiversity, biological cycles and soil biological activities. It is based on minimal use of off-farm inputs and on management practices that restore, maintain and enhance ecological harmony.

Why go to Organic Production

Consumer expectations for food quality and safety and environmental, social and economic benefits for farmers and for society:

- Safe the soil, water and nature
- Help property reduction in remote areas
- Improve health for both producers and consumers
- Value added for export products
- Avoid to sink our land
- Organic aquaculture also aims to provide fish and other products that are ecologically, economically and socially sound.

The Principles of organic production as it applies to organic fish farming (according to: International Federation of Organic Agriculture Movements (IFOAM) and "Organic Aquaculture Meeting Fundamental Organic Certification Requirements):

- The production systems must correspond to the species-specific physiological and behavioral needs of animals.
- Feedstuffs must be either from certified organic agriculture or from suitable fisheries products.
- Use of chemical and synthesis pesticides and similar substances on the farm is prohibited. Net cages may not be treated anti-fouling agents to regulate algal growth.
- Prophylactic use of antibiotics and other conventional treatment is prohibited.
- Absolute prohibition of GMOs (genetically modified organisms), referring not only to feed and other inputs, but to animal stock being cultivated.
- Processing takes place according to organic principles (use of sodium meta-bisulfate in shrimp processing, application of liquid smoke in salmon smokeries is not allowed...)
- Social sustainability is an increasing important aspect of organic aquaculture.

The variety of species produced in aqua cultural systems and vast differences in cultural requirements for finfish, shellfish, mollusks, and aquatic plants add to the complexity of defining "organic" for this sector. Some species and some production systems may prove quite difficult to adapt to a traditional "organic" system.

- Extensive "organic" Carp production in early nineties by Organic farmers and Organic Farming Association in Austria and Germany.
- Establishment of organic salmon project in Ireland, in 1995 based on IFOAM organic farming principles with the involvement of Naturland.
- Successful organic salmon, first in Germany, later in the united kingdom and france, followed by seabass, seabream, freshwater salmonids and carp.
- Organic shrimp started in Ecuador, in 1998, then in Peru and Brazil.
- In china most are carp in polyculture, crab, shrimp, turtle or sea cucumbers.
- Black tiger shrimp in Bangladesh, Thailand and Vietnam.
- Today, organic aquaculture production takes place primarily in Europe, where certified organic salmon, carp and trout are grown and sold. Certified organic mussels, tiger shrimp, white shrimp and tilapia also cultured in such diverse places as Vietnam. Peru, Ecuador, Chile, New Zeland and Israel.

ORGANIC AQUACULTURE

Has become more important as consumers have become more environmentally aware and concerned about sustainability and harmful impacts of aquaculture. Aquaculture has the highest rate of expansion Bergleiter et al., 2009) and Certified organic aquaculture products have increased since the mid-1990s (Willer and Kilcher, 2009) It has become more mainstream, especially in Germany, the United Kingdom and Switzerland (Bergleiterr et al., 2008), but many consumers can be confused or sceptical about organically labelled product due to conflicting or misleading standards around the world (Aarset et al., 2010).

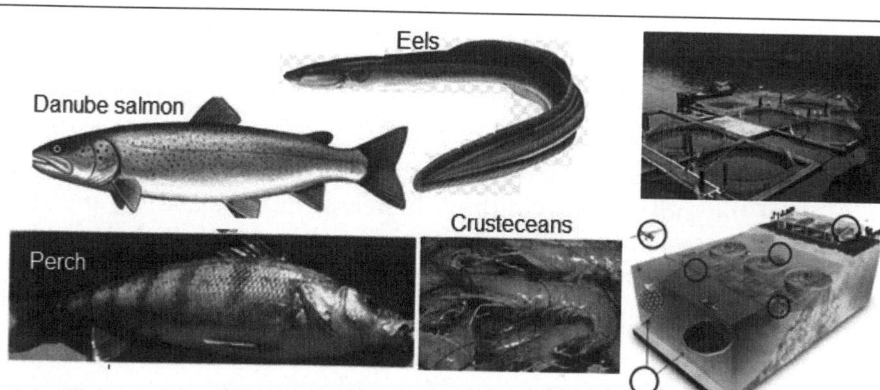

Some of raise species and Integrated Multi-Trophic Aquaculture (IMTA) :Various methods and complementary processes are being investigated for organic aquaculture.

Fig. 11.2: Some of Raised Species in Organic Aquaculture

INTEGRATED MULTI-TROPHIC AQUACULTURE (IMTA)

Various methods and complementary processes are being investigated for organic aquaculture, most notably Integrated Multi-Trophic Aquaculture (IMTA) and aquaponics (Victor, 2007), (a land-based outgrowth of aquaculture in many places). Organic methods of farming various species are also topics of interest, particularly shrimps (Diver, 2006). Salmon Rönnbäck, 2003), and Atlantic Cod (Pelletier and Tyedmers, 2007).

Integrated multi-trophic aquaculture (IMTA) (Figure 11.3) provides the by-products, including waste, from one aquatic species as inputs (fertilizers, food) for another. Farmers combine fed aquaculture (e.g., fish, shrimp) with inorganic extractive (e.g., seaweed) and organic extractive (e.g., shellfish) aquaculture to create balanced systems for environment remediation (biomitigation), economic stability (improved output, lower cost, product diversification and risk reduction) and social acceptability (better management practices) (Birt et al.,2009; Stinner, 2007;Willer et al., 2009).

1. Inorganic fertilizer use has also significantly supported global population growth — it has been estimated that almost half the people on the Earth are currently fed as a result of synthetic nitrogen fertilizer use (Aarset et al., 2014).

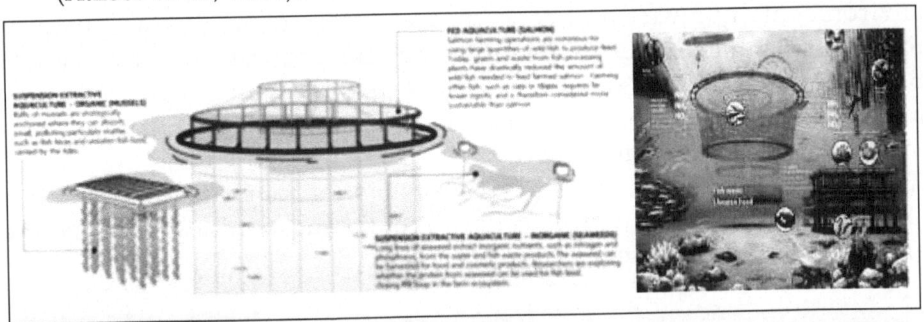

Fig. 11.3: Integrated Multi-trophic Aquaculture (IMTA) Provides the by-products, including Waste, from One Aquatic Species as Inputs (Fertilizers, Food) for Another

Mined inorganic fertilizers have been used for many centuries, whereas chemically synthesized inorganic fertilizers were only widely developed during the industrial revolution. Increased understanding and use of fertilizers were important parts of the pre-industrial British Agricultural Revolution and the industrial Green Revolution of the 20th century.

2. Fertilizers typically provide, in varying proportions:
   - Six macronutrients: nitrogen (N), phosphorus (P), potassium (K), calcium (Ca), magnesium (Mg), and sulfur (S);
   - Eight micronutrients: boron (B), chlorine (Cl), copper (Cu), iron (Fe), manganese (Mn), molybdenum (Mo), zinc (Zn) and nickel (Ni) .

3. The macronutrients are consumed in larger quantities and are present in plant tissue in quantities from 0.15% to 6.0% on a dry matter (0% moisture) basis (DM). Micronutrients are consumed in smaller quantities and are present in plant tissue on the order of parts per million (ppm), ranging from 0.15 to 400 ppm DM, or less than 0.04% DM (Erisman et al., 2008; AESL, 2010).

Fig. 11.4: The Organic Trout farm Skravad Mølle Between Viborg and Hobro, Denmark Produces About 8 Tonnes of Portion Sized Organic Rainbow Trout per Year

Source: http://sokhcn.baria-vungtau.gov.vn/anngai.

HISTORY OF ORGANIC AQUACULTURE

A detailed account of the history of organic aquaculture and its certification standards is given in Bergleiter *et al.* (2009). The earliest standard was established in 1994 in Austria for common carp (*Cyprinus carpio*) (Table 11.1). The first national general standards for organic aquaculture were established by France and the United Kingdom in 2000. The first global organic aquaculture criteria were established by the International Federation of Organic Agriculture Movements (IFOAM) in 2000. In the United States of America, the State of California in 2005 banned the labelling of organic aquaculture products pending the establishment of state regulations for such products. Numerous conferences and workshops enabled practitioners, traders, certifiers and other stakeholders to continually progress the approach.

The market for organic aquaculture shows strong growth in Europe, especially France, Germany and the UK - for example, the market in France grew 220% from 2007 to 2008. There is a preference for organic food, where available (Ribeiro et al., 2010) Organic seafood is now sold in discount supermarket chains throughout the EU (2014) The top five producing countries are UK, Ireland, Hungary, Greece and France (EU, 2014) 123 of the 225 global certified organic aquaculture farms operate in Europe and were responsible for 50,000 tons in 2008 (nearly half global production).

Table 11.1: Organic Production in Asian Countries (Ribeiro et. al., 2010)

Country	Organically Managed Area [ha]
Bangladesh	2'000
Chila	415'000
Ecuador	6'382
Indonesia[1]	1'317
Thiland	33
Total	424'732

[1]Indonesian Shrimp farms are locally certified as organic but a recent study found them to be highly environmentally damaging

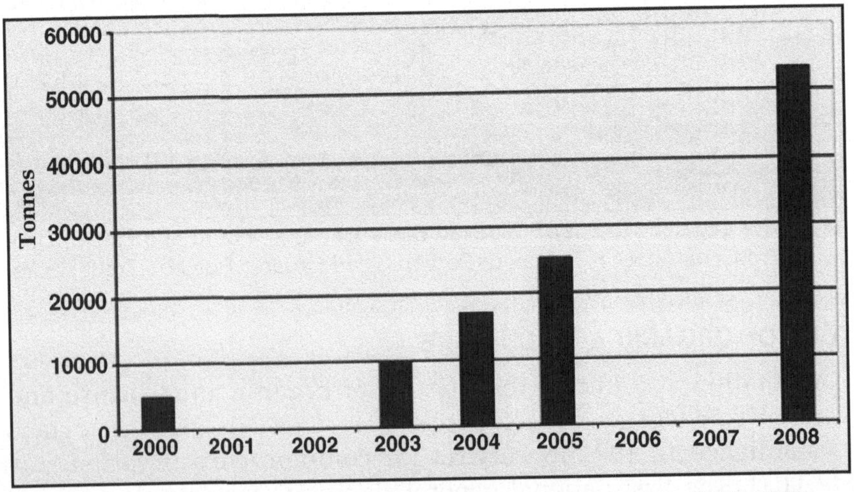

Fig. 11.5: Trend in Global Organic Aquaculture Production, 2000-2008

Source: Adapted from Bergleiter et.al., (2009)

Organic seafood products are a niche market and users currently expect to pay premiums of 30-40% (Ribeiro et al.,2010) Organic salmon is the top species and retails at 50% (EU, 2014) Market demand is drving Danish rainbow trout farmers to switch to organic farming (European Commission Fisheries, 2010).

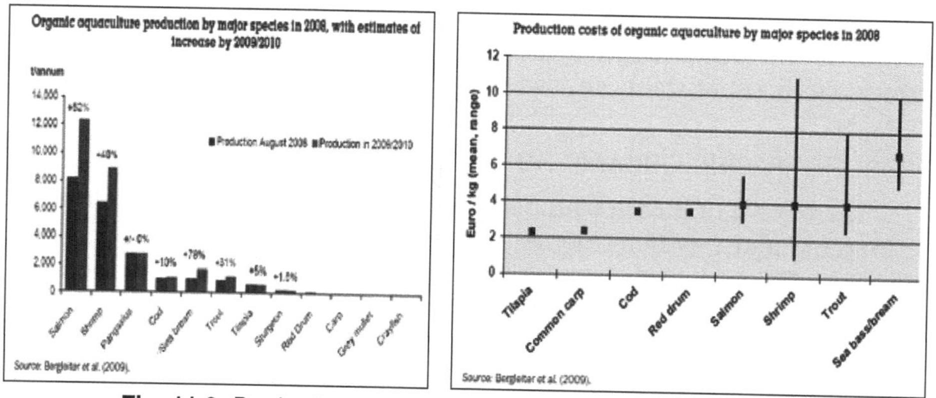

Fig. 11.6: Production Species and Coasts of Organic Production

1. Europe

   Current situation in Norway

   - Denmark: Rainbow Trout. Organic production ~400 tonnes (1% of total trout production)
   - UK:

Cod and carp, Trout, Salmon Rainbow Trout (Denmark) Salmon (80% of organic aquaculture production in 2000 and shrimp (Europe)

- Carp (low volume production, poorly marketed - Europe)
- Organic farming in New Zealand (Aquaculture in New Zealand.
- The first certified organic aquaculture farm in New Zealand was a salmon farm which was the largest producer outside of Europe contributing to the European market
- New Zealand green-lipped mussel
- Salmon 12 tones/year

2. Asia

The International Federation of Organic Agriculture Movements (IFOAM) is the worldwide umbrella organization for the organic agriculture movement, which represents close to 800 affiliates in 117 countries.

In reference to the Codex Alimentarius Commission (2011), organic aquaculture refers to the production processes and practices of ecological production management systems that promote and enhance biodiversity, biological cycles and biological activity (Bergleiter 2003; Bergleiter et al., 2009). It is based on minimal use of off-farm inputs and on holistic management practices that restore, maintain and enhance species diversity and ecological harmony (IFOAM EU Group, 2010; Costa-Pierce, 2010). More generally, the primary goal of organic agriculture is to optimize the health and productivity of interdependent communities of soil life, plants, animals and people. However, details are often unclear to the consumer, e.g. the exclusion of synthetic fertilizers and genetically modified organisms (GMOs) in the production process (Mansfield, 2003, 2004; Hatanaka, 2010). This contribution presents the current status and issues in organic aquaculture production and markets.

PROBLEMS FACING ORGANIC AQUACULTURE

There are a number of problems facing organic aquaculture: difficulty of sourcing and certifying organic juveniles (hatchery or sustainable wild stock); 35-40% higher feed cost; more labour-intensive; time and cost of the certification process; a higher risk of diseases, and uncertain benefits (Ribeiro et al.,2010)

- Sustainable Organic Fish Feed

Fish feed is one of the most important factors in aquaculture production. It is widely anticipated that global aquaculture expansion will encounter an inevitable future shortfall of non-renewable resources such as fishmeal and fish oil, necessitating the exploration of alternative strategies for fish feeds. The principles of organic aquaculture encourage the development of feeds that do not deplete global fish stocks. Fish discard and cut-offs may be potential alternative ingredients. The main focus is on the need for competitive, organically produced vegetables with high protein content. As plant crops generally have lower protein content than fishmeal, this also includes the possibility of concentrating the protein fraction of existing protein sources with a relevant amino acid profile compared to that of fishmeal. The plant crops pea, rape and lupine have been processed and the protein fractions elevated to 72%, 37% and 55%, respectively. In comparison, fishmeal contains 70-72% protein and regula-tions stipulate that the fishmeal used in aquaculture production should come from sustainable stocks.

The aquaculture industries in general are still figuring out how to be sustainable, what best practices are and what ecological considerations is can or should be implemented. Current standards are often quite strict and some people argue they are unattainable (and therefore should be relaxed). Organic regulations designed around soil-based systems don't transfer well into aquaculture (Mansfield, 2006) and tend to conflict with large-scale, intensive (economically viable) practices/goals. There is a definite consumer demand for organic seafood, and organic aquaculture may become a significant management option. Currently integrated aquaculture systems may form the base of approved organic farming practice.

- Certification

There is some controversy over licensing restrictions, as some seafood companies propose that wild caught fish should be classified as organic [(ICROFS), 2007-2010] This is a situation where the flexibility and ambiguity of the term 'organic' is clearly demonstrated. While wild fish may be free of pesticides and unsustainable rearing practices, the industry itself is not necessarily environmentally sustainable nor is it actually farming [(ICROFS), 2007-2010] As a rule, Organic Aquaculture certification follows rather strict requirements and standards. These rules may vary between different countries or certification bodies (Bergleiter, et al., 2009; European Commission Fisheries, 2010) Stefan This leads to confusion when products are imported from other countries which can result in a backlash from consumers (for example, the Pure Salmon Campaign).

A number of countries have created national standards and certifying bodies. A number of 'self-labeling' organizations also exist at local scales in many countries. One of the largest certification organizations is IFOAM which supports and connects organic movements internationally. The variation in standards, as well as the unknown level of actual compliance and the closeness of investigations when certifying are all also variable, and are one of the major problems in consistent organic certification (Downey, 2014; The Fish Site, 2008). In 2010, new rules were brought in on 30/06/2010 in the European Union to consistently define the organic aquaculture industry (European Commission Fisheries, 2010; Martin, 2006) However, aquaculture was only first included in the organic agriculture standards in 2007(EU, 2010).

- Regulations

A harmonizing process of the European regulations for organic aquaculture is under way. The challenge in this harmonization of international regulations is there are many questions and ethical dilemmas. There is major debate in organic circles about whether aquaculture as a whole can be certified organic and, if it can be, what organic aquaculture should involve. Scientific documentation is needed in order to develop good regulations which are necessary to build consumer confidence and for the industry to develop organic aquaculture in the future.

Norway and Sweden lead by example when it comes to regulations for organic food. It is therefore important that Norway, as the world's largest aquaculture nation, leads from the front and increases the level of knowledge about organic aquaculture so that the regulations are the best possible and are adapted for Norwegian production conditions.

For example, the maximum stocking density for salmon is set at 10 kg per cbm (kg/m^3) in net pens in sea water and 20 kg/m^3 in freshwater. For sea bass and sea bream the maximum density is 15 kg/m^3 in the sea and four kg/m^3 in earth ponds and lagoons. The animal welfare standards specify that biodiversity should be respected and prohibits stimulated spawning via artificial hormones. Organic feeds should be used while supplemented by fish feeds obtained from sustainably managed fisheries, with special provisions made for bivalve mollusk production and seaweed.

SPECIES IN ORGANIC AQUACULTURE PRODUCTION

The number of species from organic aquaculture has increased from four species in 2000 to around 30 species in 2009, including at least 15 finfish species, six crustacean species, at least one molluscan species, one holothurians, one turtle, and at least four species of microalgae (IFOAM EU Group, 2010).

1. *Molluscan shellfish*

Molluscan shellfish ("Molluscan shellfish" means an edible species of fresh or frozen oysters, clams, mussels, and scallops or edible portions).

Organic production of crops and livestock in the United States is regulated by the Department of Agriculture's National Organic Programme (NOP). While it does cover aquaponics, it did not properly cover aquaculture until the recent 2008 amendment, hampering the progress of organic aquaculture in the states.

Fig. 11.7: Shellfish: Organic production; Farms and Species

The development of organics standards for molluscan shellfish has been problematic within the context of general aquaculture practices. Several topics which need to be considered differ significantly between these two distinct operating systems. The Aquaculture Working Group was unable, within the allotted time frame, to develop standards that addressed issues specific to shellfish. Shellfish aquaculture could comply with those sections in the Final Report that are relevant, but there are gaps that must be addressed specific to shellfish farming and areas of the report that have no bearing on the industry at all. This White Paper is intended to provide the NOSB with relevant information not contained in the Final Report, in the hope that organics standards for shellfish will be developed.

- Molluscan shellfish farming is very unlike other fisheries operations in that mollusks tend to be stationary creatures. The practices employed by shellfish farmers and harvesters are in many ways more akin to vegetable crop production than to wild or aquaculture fisheries. Farmer's plant or set oyster, clam, mussel, scallop or geoduck seed in a designated area, watch over their crops during grow out (18 months to 5 years, depending on the species, location and environmental variables) and then harvest their crops much as a farmer would harvest corn or soybeans. In some instances, shellfish may be moved at some point during maturation to another carefully demarcated area to optimize growth.

- Shellfish planted for grow-out graze strictly on the microalgae found naturally in the water column. Shellfish differ from both finfish and vegetable crops in that fertilizers and feed are not used and antibiotics, vaccines, biologics and growth hormones are not used. The rare exception to this could occur occasionally in the hatchery (larval) phase when antibiotics may be used.
- *Hatchery Operations*
- Increasingly growers are utilizing hatchery raised seed, rather than relying on wild-caught seed. In this case, antibiotics may, on rare occasion, be used in the earliest stages of larval development. This would be in all cases prior to what has been referred to in the Working Group as "spat," which has been defined as seed that has reached 10 mm. By this time, shellfish seed has been set out for growth, and the recommendations of the Working Group is that this is the point in time when the "organic's clock" would start ticking. In either event, the National Organics Programme (NOP) Final Rule, Section 205.204 (a) (1) provides that "Non-organically produced, untreated seeds and planting stock may be used to produce an organic crop when an equivalent organically produced variety is not commercially available."
- *The Foundation for Organic Management*

The public health regulations governing shellfish farming and harvesting are among the strictest imposed upon any food producer in the U.S., and pose an excellent foundation that aligns well with organics standards. Although the argument has been well presented that Organics Standards is about process, not food safety, the public health safety standards the shellfish industry operates under also lends itself well to developing organic management systems due in part to the boundaries that are required for farming in the open water.

The National Shellfish Sanitation Programme (NSSP), under the auspice of the FDA, is the standard used in every shellfish producing and receiving state in the country. It requires that both farmed and "wild" harvest growing areas be distinctly demarcated. Each growing area must be tested for pathogens for several months or years (depending upon the environmental variables such as nearby shoreline homes and septic systems, industries, etc.) before they are classified.

Growing areas are classified according to water quality as determined by fecal coliforms which are the national indicator species used by the FDA to determine the presence of warm blooded animals, considered to be the most likely vector for potential pathogens. The Approved classification is reserved for areas with the highest level of water quality and allows harvest at all times; Conditionally approved areas include those areas where fecal coliforms levels spike above the maximum level during or after storm events. Harvest is therefore allowed only when there has not been a recent storm event. (Each area has a specific number of required closure days after a specific amount of rainfall which is uniquely developed according to environmental variables for each area); A Restricted classification applies to areas where fecal coliforms counts are routinely higher than the maximum level allowed by the NSSP and requires that product be relayed out to an Approved or Conditional area to purge for several months. Health regulators perform regular shoreline surveys to assure growing areas are not in proximity to sewer outfalls, marinas, industrial effluent discharge areas or other potential sources of contamination. Areas within these zones are disqualified for consideration as growing areas and classified as "Prohibited."

The Principles of organic agriculture as it applies to Shellfish Farming (according to: International Federation of Organic Agriculture Movements (IFOAM) and "Organic Aquaculture - Meeting Fundamental Organic Certification Requirements):

1. To be certified organic, the farmed area must be managed and monitored within clearly marked boundaries.
2. Be designated as to where crops will be gathered or harvested.
3. Have a three year history showing no prohibited substances have been applied.
4. Have a plan for harvesting the crops to guard against environmental destruction and assure sustainability in the growth and production of the wild crop.
5. Improve the physical, chemical and biological conditions of the marine ecosystem.

This guidance document states that: "Organic agriculture is based on holistic production management systems which promote and enhance agro-ecosystem health, including biodiversity, biological cycles and biological activity." Molluscan shellfish aquaculture meets each of these criteria.

1. Molluscan shellfish are not fed so there are no nutrients being added to the marine environment. Molluscan shellfish are biofilters which feed on phytoplankton which occurs naturally in the water. This biofiltering activity has the beneficial secondary effect of taking up nutrients and purifying the water column, thereby "enhancing ecosystem health." Shellfish also create habitat for other marine creatures. As three-dimensional structures, shellfish are host to flora and fauna which make

their homes in shellfish beds. These beds also provide cover and forage for species such as salmonids during their juvenile out-migration stage, enhancing biodiversity, biological cycles and biological activities through the creation of critical habitat.

2. Shellfish growers cannot control currents, winds, storm events, rainfall or other environmental conditions that might cause drift of an unwanted substance into their growing area. The NOP Final Rule addresses this by providing that the organics certifier has the ability to require residue testing.
3. Organic livestock must be fed 100% organic feed their entire lifespan.
4. Shellfish can pose health hazards because of contamination of naturally occurring pathogens in the water.Open water molluscan shellfish aquaculture is akin to "wild" stock issues, therefore we must wait until a decision on the "wild" issue is determined before moving The open water debate does suggest a kinship with "wild" raised fish, but given the stationary nature of mollusks and the fact that growing areas have determined boundaries which are regularly monitored and managed, the similarities with terrestrial agriculture is a closer parallel.. Forward.

2. ***Organic Farmed Salmon***

The organic salmon was raised in an open net cage that directly discharged waste into the marine environment. Or, that it could have been treated with toxic chemicals. Or, that it might have been fed non-organic feed. Or, that it may not be cleaned of harmful contaminants such as PCBs, dioxins and DDT (even though the technology exists).

"Organic" salmon is that it is farmed in an open net cage system, the same system used for conventional farmed salmon. In turn, what we're relatively certain of is that the organic farmed salmon on the market today:

- Ate wild fish for feed (though the makeup of the diet can vary considerably)
- The farm provided no complete barrier between farmed fish and the marine environment
- The farm did not contain wastes - uneaten feed, feces and possibly harmful chemicals
- Farmed did not prevent the transmission of diseases and parasites to/from wild fish

And, depending on where your organic salmon came from and who certified it, it may have been:

Treated with toxic chemicals (some like Cypermethrin and Emamectin benzoate classified as"marine pollutants") used to kill parasites called sea lice.

- Treated with antibiotics at some stage of its life cycle
- Fed wild fish products that did not come from certified sustainable sources

- Fed feed that was not tested for or cleaned of PCBs, dioxins and other contaminants
- From a farm site that experienced escapes of farmed fish into the environment

Global Production

- Around 100 countries offer consumers certified organic products. France, Germany, Switzerland and English-speaking countries are the largest and fastest growing markets for organic salmon.
- Norway, Ireland and Scotland produced organic salmon for the European market in 2008.
- In 2007, the global production from organic aquaculture totaled 60,000 tones.
- From 2008, the anticipated growth in the global production of organic seafood is 15-25%. Organic seafood products account for less than 0.1% of the world's total seafood production (*Source: Organic Monitor 2008*).
- The production of organic fish in Norway is so far modest (two fish farms for salmon and one for cod in 2008). BioMar and Ewos produce Debio-certified feed which can be used to farm organic cod and salmon.
- Murphy's Irish Seafood produces organic salmon, certified under the standards set by Agriculture Biologique (AB) of France and EU Organic. In addition, Murphy's Irish Organic Salmon is raised according to organic guidelines set by the Irish Organic Farmers and Growers Associations (IOFGA).

Table 11.2: Criteria for Organic Aquaculture Farms

Criteria	Organic
Prohibition of toxic pesticides	✓
No GMOs	✓
No antibiotics	✓
No growth hormones	✓
Animal welfare requirements	✓
Lower levels of environmental pollution	✓
Audit trail from farm to table	✓
Maintenance or enhancement of water quality	✓
Healthy use and proper care of water, water resources and all life therein	✓
Low density (<10kg/m^3 in saltwater)	✓
Legal restrictions on allowable materials	✓
Encourages use of local resources/services	✓

Source: The Organic Food Federation, 2012.

Glenarm Organic Salmon is farmed according to standards set by the UK's leading certification body, The Organic Food Federation, which was established in 1986 and oversees all areas of organics. They raise their salmon giving, "priority to the health and welfare of the fish, to the long-term protection of the environment and to deliver an outstanding product to customers. We achieve this and more by ensuring strict adherence to the organic standards allowing us to work in harmony with nature whilst producing salmon that are as close to 'wild nature' as you will find!", said John Russell, Managing Director.

AQUAPONICS

Is the marriage of aquaculture (raising fish) and hydroponics (growing plants in water and without soil) together in one integrated system. The fish waste provides organic food for the growing plants and the plants naturally filter the water in which the fish live. The third and fourth critical, yet invisible actors in the play are the beneficial bacteria and composting red worms.

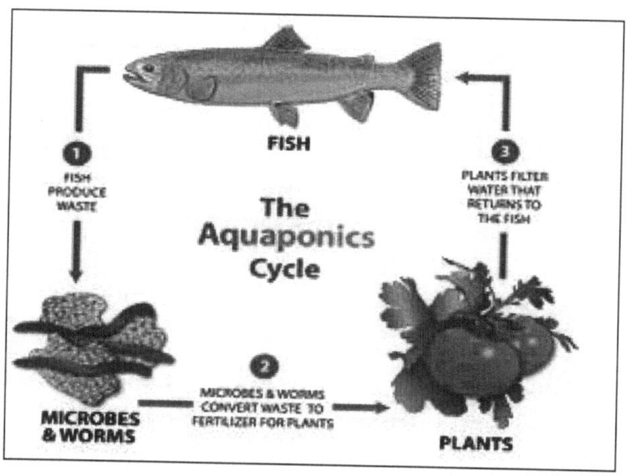

Fig. 11.8: Aquaponics *(http://govdocs.aquake.org/cgi/content/ Abstract/2005/801/ 801017)0.*

Hydroponics is the production of plants in a soilless medium whereby all of the nutrients supplied to the crop are dissolved in water. Liquid hydroponic systems employ the nutrient film technique (NFT), floating rafts, and noncirculating water culture. Aggregate hydroponic systems employ inert, organic, and mixed media contained in bag, trough, trench, pipe, or bench setups. Aggregate media used in these systems include perlite, vermiculite, gravel, sand, expanded clay, peat, and sawdust. Normally, hydroponic plants are fertigated (soluble fertilizers injected into irrigation water) on a periodical cycle to maintain moist roots and provide a constant supply of nutrients.

These hydroponic nutrients are usually derived from synthetic commercial fertilizers, such as calcium nitrate, that are highly soluble in water. However, hydro-organics—based on soluble organic fertilizers such as fish hydrosylate— is an emerging practice. Hydroponic recipes are based on chemical formulations that deliver precise concentrations of mineral elements. The controlled delivery of nutrients, water, and environmental modifications under greenhouse conditions is a major reason why hydroponics is so successful.

In aquaponics, nutrient-rich effluent from fish tanks is used to fertigate hydroponic production beds. This is good for the fish because plant roots and rhizobacteria remove nutrients from the water. These nutrients—generated from fish manure, algae, and decomposing fish feed—are contaminants that would otherwise build up to toxic levels in the fish tanks, but instead serve as liquid fertilizer to hydroponically grown plants. In turn, the hydroponic beds function as a biofilter- stripping off ammonia, nitrates, nitrites, and phosphorus— so the freshly cleansed water can then be recirculated back into the fish tanks. The nitrifying bacteria living in the gravel and in association with the plant roots play a critical role in nutrient cycling; without these microorganisms the whole system would stop functioning.

Fish effluent contains sufficient levels of ammonia, nitrate, nitrite, phosphorus, potassium, and other secondary and micronutrients to produce hydroponic plants. Naturally, some plant species are better adapted to this system than others.

Greenhouse growers and farmers are taking note of aquaponics for several reasons:

- Hydroponic growers view fishmanured irrigation water as a source of organic fertilizer that enables plants to grow well.
- Fish farmers view hydroponics as a biofiltration method to facilitate intensive recirculating aquaculture.
- Greenhouse growers view aquaponics as a way to introduce organic hydroponic produce into the marketplace, since the only fertility input is fish feed and all of the nutrients pass through a biological process.
- Hydroponic produce into the marketplace, since the only fertility input is fish feed and all of the nutrients pass through a biological process.
- Food-producing greenhouses— yielding two products from one production unit—are naturally appealing for niche marketing and green labeling or encirculated back into the fish tanks.
- Aquaponics can enable the production of fresh vegetables and fish protein in arid regions and on water limited farms, since it is a water re-use system.

- Aquaponics is a working model of sustainable food production wherein plant and animal agriculture are integrated and recycling of nutrients and water filtration are linked.
- In addition to commercial application, aquaponics has become a popular training aid on integrated bio-systems with vocational agriculture programmes and high school biology classes.

The technology associated with aquaponics is complex. It requires the ability to simultaneously manage the production and marketing of two different agricultural products. Until the 1980s, most attempts at integrated hydroponics and aquaculture had limited success. However, innovations since the 1980s have transformed aquaponics technology into a viable system of food production. Modern aquaponic systems can be highly successful, but they require intensive management and they have special considerations.

Aquaponics is a hybrid food growing technology that combines aquaculture (growing fish) and hydroponics (growing veggies in non-soil media and nutrient-laden water). This is a relatively new hybrid technology; a survey of readily available professional and hobbyist Internet resources will quickly give one an appreciation of the wide breadth of and passion for this technology.

Aquaponics is intended to be a highly sustainable production system that incorporates principles of water conservation, sustainable vegetable production and perhaps organic plant and animal agriculture. Systems vary in size from small indoor or outdoor home or classroom hobbyist units to immense commercial units. The systems are usually fresh-water based, but salt-water systems are used for some high-value fish or crustacean production. It should be noted that the corrosive effects of salt-water can greatly increase the establishment, maintenance and depreciation costs of the production system.

In traditional tank-type aquaculture systems, the fish are raised within a mostly closed system where water is recirculated. Since it is a closed system, filters are required to remove fish effluent and remove aqueous toxic compounds that result from the effluent or its decomposition. If not removed, the effluent and its toxic nitrogenous bi-products quickly reach levels that are fatal to fish. In aquaponics systems, the effluent is as passively managed as possible within the system using sumps and biofilters. Some solids may be physically separated and removed; however, the majority of the toxic compounds are biologically converted into plant-usable nutrients through bio-conversion by beneficial bacteria within the biofilter. This nutrient-laden water is now the fertilizer component of the plant aspect of the system. The plants then remove the nutrients and the "de-nitrified" clean water is returned back to the fish, crustacean or mollusk aspect of the system as their water input.

Aquaponics is a food production system that combines conventional aquaculture (raising aquatic animals such as snails, fish, crayfish or prawns in tanks) with hydroponics (cultivating plants in water) in a symbiotic environment. In normal aquaculture, excretions from the animals being raised can accumulate in the water, increasing toxicity.

Fig. 11.9: The Australian Red-Claw Crayfish is an example of a crustacean that can be reared alone or with fish in an aquaponic system (Example of "deep-water culture" or "floating-raft" plant-growth technology). An intermediate-scale pre-commercial aquaponic system.(AGMRC http://www.agmrc.org/curriculum).

In an aquaponic system, water from an aquaculture system is fed to a hydroponic system where the by-products are broken down by nitrogen-fixing bacteria into nitrates and nitrites, which are utilized by the plants as nutrients. The water is then recirculated back to the aquaculture system.

TYPES OF SYSTEMS

Aquaponic systems can be created using a variety of hydroponic techniques, although systems that run-to-waste are not considered true aquaponics because they don't close the loop by returning filtered water back to the fish tank. The most prevalent aquaponic growing methods are Deep Water Culture¥ or raft-based, and Flood and Drain, or media-based. NFT and aeroponic techniques have also been used, but less widely and with limited success because solids from the fish waste – no matter how filtered – will eventually clog up the smaller tubing used by these system types. The Speraneo System. In the early 1990s, Tom and Paula Speraneo—owners of S & S Aqua Farm near West Plains, Missouri—modified the North Carolina State method by raising tilapia in a 500-gallon tank, with fish effluent linked to gravel-cultured hydroponic vegetable beds inside an attached solar greenhouse. Later, they expanded to a full-size commercial greenhouse.

FISH SPECIES

Several warm-water and cold-water fish species are adapted to recirculating aquaculture systems, including tilapia, trout, perch, Arctic char, and bass. However, most commercial fleshed meat suitable to local and wholesale markets. The literature on tilapia contains extensive technical documentation and cultural procedures. Barramundi and Murray cod fish species are raised in recirculating aquaponic systems in Australia.

¥: http://en.wikipedia.org/wiki/Aquaponics

WATER QUALITY CHARACTERISTICS

Fish raised in recalculating tank culture require good water quality conditions. Water quality testing kits from aquacultural supply companies are fundamental. Critical water quality parameters include dissolved oxygen, carbon dioxide, ammonia, nitrate, nitrite, pH, chlorine, and other characteristics. The stocking density of fish, growth rate of fish, feeding rate and volume, and related environmental fluctuations can elicit rapid changes in water quality; constant and vigilant water quality monitoring is essential.

BIOFILTRATION AND SUSPENDED SOLIDS

Aquaculture effluent contains nutrients, dissolved solids, and waste byproducts. Some aquaponic systems are designed with intermediate filters and cartridges to collect suspended solids in fish effluent, and to facilitate conversion of ammonia and other waste products to forms more available to plants prior to delivery to hydroponic vegetable beds. Other systems deliver fish effluent directly to gravel-cultured hydroponic vegetable beds. The gravel functions as a "fluidized bed bioreactor," removing dissolved solids and providing habitat for nitrifying bacteria involved in nutrient conversions.

CONCLUSION

Water pollution as well as all aquaculture operations for drugs, biologics, and other chemicals, collectively can cause immediate damage to aquatic food and to humans.

Organic aquaculture aims to provide fish and other products that are ecologically, economically and socially sound. It has become more important as consumers have become more environmentally aware and concerned about sustainability and harmful impacts of aquaculture.

REFERENCES

Aarset, B; Suzanna B, Enrique B, Malcolm B, Trond B, Jane, Pierre M, Catherine M, James M, Andrea P, Lucia R, Andrew S, Ragnar T and James Y(2010). "The European Consumers' Understanding and Perceptions of the "Organic" Food Regime: The Case of Aquaculture". British Food Journal (Emerald Group Publishing Limited) 103 (2): 93-105. doi:10.1108/00070700410516784.

"AESL Plant Analysis Handbook – Nutrient Content of Plant". Aesl.ces.uga.edu. Retrieved 25 August 2010.

Birt, B; Rodwell, Lynda D.; Richards, Jonathan P. (2009), "Investigation into the Sustainability of Organic Aquaculture of Atlantic Cod (Gadus Morhua)", SSPP 5 (2)

Bergleiter, S; Berner, N; Censkowsky, Udo; Julià-Camprodon, G. (2009), "Organic Aquaculture 2009 : Production and Markets", in Naturland e.V.; Organic Services GmbH, Gräfelfing/Munich.

Bergleiter, S; Willer et al. (2008), "Organic Aquaculture", The World of Organic Agriculture., Frick; ITC, Geneva: IFOAM, Bonn and FiBL.

Bergleiter, S. 2003. Organic Aquaculture: Completing the First Decade. The Organic Standard, 30(October): 14-16.

Bergleiter, S., Berner, N., Censkowsky, U. & Julia-Camprodon, G. 2009. Organic Aquaculture 2009 – Production and Markets. Munich, Organic Services GmbH and Graefelfing, Naturland e.V. 120 pp.

Ceresana, Market Study Fertilizers - World, May 2013, http://www.ceresana.com/en/market-studies/agriculture/fertilizers-world/

Codex Alimentarius Commission. Rome, FAO. 3 pp. (available at: ftp://ftp.fao. org/codex/ccfl39/fl39_10e.pdf).

Costa-Pierce, B.A. 2010. Sustainable Ecological Aquaculture Systems: The Need for a New Social Contract for Aquaculture Development. Marine Technology Society Journal, 44(3): 88-1

Codex Alimentarius Commission. 2011. Proposed Draft Revision of the Guidelines for the Production, Processing, Labelling and Marketing of Organically Produced Foods (GL 32-1999) (to Include Aquaculture Animals and Seaweed) at Step 3. Joint FAO/ WHO Food Standards Programme Codex Committee on Food Labelling, Thirtyninth Session, Quebec City, Quebec, Canada, 9-13 May 2011. Secretariat.

Diver, S. (2006). "Aquaponics—Integration of Hydroponics with Aquaculture". ATTRA.

Downey, R.(2014). Developing Organic Standards for Molluscan Shellfish.

Erisman, Jan Willem; MA Sutton, J Galloway, Z Klimont, W Winiwarter (October 2008). "How a Century of Ammonia Synthesis Changed the World". Nature Geoscience 1 (10): 636. Bibcode: 2008NatGe...1..636E. doi:10.1038/ngeo325. Retrieved 22 October 2010.

European Commission Fisheries "New Organic Aquaculture Rules a Route to a more Sustainable and Profitable Future for Aquaculture". European Commission Fisheries. 30 June 2010.

Hatanaka, M. 2010. Certification, Partnership, and Morality in an Organic Shrimp Network: Rethinking Transnational Alternative Agrifood Networks. World Development, 38: 706-716.

FOAM EU Group. 2010. Organic Aquaculture EU Regulations (EC) 834/2007, (EC) 889/2008, (EC) 710/2009. Background, Assessment, Interpretation. (A. Szeremeta, L. Winkler, F, Blake & P. Lembo, eds.) Brussels, International Federation of Organic Agriculture Movements EU Group and Valenzno, Bari, CIHEAM/IAMB. 34 pp. IFOAM EU Group, 2010.

International Centre for Research in Organic Food Systems (ICROFS) "Organic Aquaculture", The International Centre for Research in Organic Food Systems (ICROFS), 2007-2010 http://www.icrofs.org |url= missing title (help)

Mansfield, B. (2006), "Organic Views of Nature: The Debate Over Organic Certification for Aquatic Animals", Sociologia Ruralis 44 (2): 216-232.

Martin, A. (2006). "Free or Farmed, When is a Fish Really Organic?". The New York Times.

Mansfield, B. 2003. From Catfish to Organic Fish: Making Distinctions About Nature as a Cultural Economic Practice. Geoforum, 34: 329-342.

Mansfield, B. 2004. Organic Views of Nature: The Debate Over Organic Certification for Aquatic Animals. Sociologia Ruralis, 44(2): 216-232.

Pelletier, N; Tyedmers, P (2007), "Feeding Farmed Salmon: Is Organic Better?", Aquaculture 272 (2): 399-416.

Paull, J.(2006) The Farm as Organism: The Foundational Idea of Organic Agriculture Elementals ~ Journal of Bio-Dynamics Tasmania 83: 14-18.

Paull, J. (2011). "Attending the First Organic Agriculture Course: Rudolf Steiner's Agriculture Course at Koberwitz, 1924". European Journal of Social Sciences 21 (1): 64-70.

Ribeiro, L; Soares, F; Cunha, Maria E; Pousão-Ferreira, P. (2010), "Organic Aquaculture: A Strategy for Valorisation of Semi-intensive Aquaculture?", International Workshop on Sustainable Extensive and Semi-intensive Aquaculture Production in Southern Europe, Tavira, Portugal: Stiftung Ökologie & Landbau (SÖL)

Real, N. (2010), "Organic Aquaculture Laws go into Effect", Fish Info & Services Co.Ltd. (FIS), Archived from the Original on 2010-07-09.

Real, N. (2010), "Proposed Organic Aquaculture Standards Opposed", Fish Info & Services Co. Ltd. (FIS), Archived from the Original on 2010-01-09.

Rönnbäck, P.(2003), "Critical Analysis of Certified Organic Shrimp Aquaculture in Sidoarjo, Indonesia.", Swedish Society for Nature Conservation (SSNC).

Stewart, W.M.; Dibb, D.W.; Johnston, A.E.; Smyth, T.J. (2005). "The Contribution of Commercial Fertilizer Nutrients to Food Production". Agronomy Journal 97: 1-6. doi:10.2134/agronj2005.0001.

Stinner, D.H (2007). "The Science of Organic Farming". In William Lockeretz. Organic Farming: An International History. Oxfordshire, UK & Cambridge, Massachusetts: CAB International (CABI). ISBN 978-0-85199-833-6. Retrieved 30 April 2013 ebook ISBN 978-1-84593-289-3

The Fish Site, 2008 "Organic Aquaculture: What's in a Label?", The Fish Site, 2008, archived from the original on December 2008

Victor, Gonzálvez (2007), "Organic Farming in Spain 2007", FiBL http://www.organic-europe.net)

Willer, H; Kilcher, L, eds. (2009). "The World of Organic Agriculture. Statistics and Emerging Trends 2009. FIBL-IFOAM Report.", Frick; ITC, Geneva: IFOAM, Bonn; FiBL,

http://www.seacase.org/PDF/WP7/SEACASE%20International%20Workshop%20TAVIRA%20PT/PDF%20Comunica%C3%A7%C3%B5es%20Orais/VII/VII_Oral_Ribeiro.pdf |url= missing title

-www.steenbergs.co.uk

Index

* * * * * * *